BETWEEN THE STIRRUP AND THE GROUND

ANDREW SIMPSON

BETWEEN THE STIRRUP AND THE GROUND

It is arguable that the equestrian world is one of the few cultures that haven't been spoilt by "progress." This is because horses, apart from being gorgeous, are the same as they always have been: creatures of the wilds in spite of centuries of domestication, and therefore more or less complicated, more or less explosive, more or less predictable, more or less charming or unpleasant, more or less intelligent or dumb.

As for the people who live with horses and thrive in their company, they have to be bright, brave, strong, optimistic, patient and resourceful. The bar is set high, and those who are comfortable at that level are second to none in the human pecking order.

This is a story of two such equestrian communities – I hope it does justice to the characters involved, equine and human, and that the reader enjoys it.

THANKS

Without the help and guidance of

Stephen and Sallie Keen

This sparrow would never have left the nest

CONTENTS

BETWEEN THE STIRRUP AND THE GROUND

ANDREW SIMPSON

Part One

CHAPTER ONE

John Dunne lived with his widowed grandmother (a retired teacher with a passion for archaeology) in the village of Monxton, just outside Andover in Hampshire. This temporary arrangement had started when he was three years old - when his parents went to Chile, in South America. His father was an engineer involved in an irrigation project designed to turn a desert into a Garden of Eden.

It became permanent a year later. His parents boarded a plane in Argentina, heading home to Chile after a holiday. A combination of poor visibility and miscalculation drove the plane straight into one of the higher peaks of the Andes. The tragedy was less traumatic for John than for others, because he had almost no recollection of his parents, he loved his grandmother, she loved him even more than before, and life went on as usual.

At the age of eight John began writing to racehorse trainers and asking for photos of their more famous horses. The origin of this addiction is uncertain, but there is evidence that Granny might well have been partly responsible.

She had taken him to spend a fortnight in Cheshire, staying with a farming family whose main sporting interest was horses. There Sally, the fair-haired girl-groom who ran the stables like a sergeant-major in the Coldstream Guards, let him ride a pony, off which he fell, and back on top of which he clambered.

Human frailty only affected Sally when there was a race meeting in the area. A horsebox might well come trundling up from the south, on an expedition which usually involved an overnight stop. On such occasions, Sally would go pink, stay out late and have her leg pulled the next morning. She was being courted by the Travelling-Head-Lad of the racing stable which owned the horsebox.

This glance into the world of adult behaviour puzzled John, but much else was clear and exciting: he had ridden a pony, had fallen off and remounted, had been to a race meeting, had seen the inside of a horsebox and had learnt what a Travelling-Head-Lad was. He returned to Monxton clutching a one-pound coin that Sally had given him, the foundation of a fund with which one day he intended to buy a pony of his own. He was aflame with a burning desire concerning horses in general and racing in particular.

*

At twelve John wagered fifty pence on the winner of the Ascot Stakes at 100 – 8, which added a rounded-down £6 to his fund and helped to keep the flame alive. Indeed it fanned it into an increased intensity. One afternoon at the beginning of the summer holidays of the following year, he bicycled two miles to the home of a racehorse trainer called Richard Fearnley, which lay half a mile beyond the village of Weyhill, standing in its own extensive grounds. At the impressive stone gateway he paused with one foot on the ground, considered retreating, then cycled on up the drive.

At sixty years of age, Mr Fearnley was a big man with an extra chin just beginning to add itself to the contours of his face, which was plum-coloured, a shade that worried his doctor a little bit. His other features were a head of curly dark brown hair with traces of grey round the edges, an easy smile and brown eyes for which the word "piercing" was surely invented.

Seriously wealthy, he was a bachelor who lived in some style at Weyhill House, a handsome red brick edifice dominating a cluster of offices, garages and accommodation for single lads, a settlement that had developed over time beside and behind the trainer's house – for the place had been devoted to the training of horses for more than a hundred years. Married staff lived in cottages in the nearby village.

Fifty yards from the trainer's front door, beyond a gravel forecourt and a wide strip of tidy grass, there was more red brick: a high wall pierced by an archway surmounted by a clock tower. This was the entrance to two stable yards, which accommodated up to eighty high-class horses (flatracers outnumbering jumpers by about three to one). The Front Yard was square, red and tall (two stories: loose boxes below, lofts, store rooms and some accommodation above). Protected by the red brick was a large gravelled yard, in the middle of which was a circular patch of lawn. In the worst winter weather, snow could be cleared by a tractor pulling a chain harrow and a string of horses could comfortably trot round and round on the exposed gravel for as long as was necessary to keep them sensible.

A lesser archway led to the Back Yard, which was smaller, ground-floor only and timber built. The Back Yard was mainly for horses that were off games for one reason or another.

Mr Fearnley was crossing the gravel from his office to his front door when John arrived. He invited John in and gave him a cup of tea and a bun, served up by his butler. He then lit a cheroot and questioned him closely, but in a friendly fashion. As a result, John was offered a month's trial as a "dogsbody" whose job description was simply to make himself useful during school holidays. This offer was dependent on parental permission. When John explained his situation in that regard, Mr Fearnley sent him away with a message to his grandmother. A few days later he drove over to Monxton and had tea with her. The result was a meeting of the minds and agreement on all points discussed.

Thus began a period in John's life dedicated to mucking-out, squaring-up the muckheap, filling and spilling water-buckets, setting boxes fair, filling haynets, learning how to groom a horse and clean a set of tack – and riding a pony, without a saddle, under instruction from one of the senior lads (most stables have a pony or two for the apprentices). Soon John was allowed a saddle and was riding a pony with the string of racehorses which went out for "first lot" at eight o'clock each morning; sometimes with "second lot" after breakfast as well.

Later in the morning he would also take his turn sorting out the Loose School. This imposing structure stood on an area of grass at the back of the establishment. A loose-school is an enclosed mini-arena. The outer wall is wooden panelling, seven foot high. Inside is a sand track, shaped like a miniature running track (two bends and two straights), about fifty yards in total length. The sand track, eight foot wide, is railed on both sides. In the centre, inside the inner rail, a grassy space is big enough to accommodate a horse trotting round on the end of a lunge rein. The loose school is so designed that jumps can be positioned practically anywhere around the track. Its primary purpose is teaching horses to jump, at first riderless, which they enjoy, and which teaches them to use their judgement. They have to make up their own minds as to where to take off at the jumps, and how to negotiate the bends which are quite sharp.

The central patch of grass is also useful for breaking-in the yearlings.

Hanging on the wooden wall outside the double doors was a very large rake with steel tines, and next to it stood a garden roller. After horses had been using the school, John was often one of the two lads who would rake and roll until the surface of the track was restored to a state of perfection. In the afternoon there would always be other chores to keep him busy before he was released in time to cycle home for tea. To begin with, he did not do "evening stables." His was still a pretty good day's work, however, and he couldn't help but thrive on such a regime.

His trial period was a success, and his welcome was extended "until further notice". The return to school didn't please John at all, but he made the best of it by spending most of every weekend at the stables. Granny told him that the harder he studied the quicker the time would pass. He suspected that she had made that up, but took her advice, and it seemed to work. The time did pass, and he had no difficulty passing his exams.

That was the way of things for the next two years, during which a certain amount of pocket money began to find its way from Mr Fearnley's pocket to John's pony fund. His wardrobe was also enriched. By the time he was fifteen, he found himself the proud owner of jodhpurs, jodhpur boots, a crash-helmet, and a dark blue waistcoat (a canvas item, lightweight, padded, reinforced and adjustable). It was called a back-protector. He was required to wear it whenever he rode the pony.

On work mornings, Mr Fearnley, riding one of his heavyweight hunters, would lead a string of about twenty horses down to the Weyhill gallops, a mile to the east of the yard, with John bringing up the rear. Their destination was a vast expanse of green, across which rivers of darker green, punctuated by pairs of white markers, identified the various gallops. The string would "take a turn" round the trainer, while he sorted out the work, and John kept just behind him and prayed that the pony wouldn't start messing about.

"Give us three minutes," Mr Fearnley would say when everybody knew what they had to do. "Come on, John!"

He would set off at a steady canter, a majestic figure on a majestic horse, and the pony would scuttle along behind. At first John had no idea where they were going, but he soon learnt the lie of the land. In this instance they were taking a short cut to the place from which Mr Fearnley could watch his gallopers. When they passed him, they would be doing their best work, before pulling up at the end of (in this case) a seven-furlong spin.

When the trainer and his young companion passed the end of a wild and overgrown length of hedge (free-standing, no gates, a relic from the days before farming made way for the sport of kings), they would take up a position and wait. Larksong was the only sound to be heard.

Soon, off to the right, just visible to the watchers, things were moving. Close up against the tall hedge that defined the western boundary of the gallops horses in twos and threes threaded their way swiftly between pairs of white markers: uphill to start with (one furlong), over a brow (a second), down a slope (two more furlongs), a gradual left-hand bend (the fifth) and then accelerating straight up a stiff slope towards the watchers (two more furlongs). Seven furlongs in all (220 yards per furlong, eight furlongs to a mile).

When each group reached the free-standing hedge the twittering of the lark had no chance against the thud of hooves, the creak of leather, the occasional crack of a whip and the steam-engine beat of massive lungs responding to considerable pressure.

John thought he was in heaven.

During those first two years he became competent in all the basics of stable work. Perhaps that was how he developed muscles where muscles had never been before. He stood five foot seven, skinny and still growing; his hair and eyes were brown and his usual expression was one of mild confusion. It went with his tendency to ask questions all the time.

After the first year he began to ride the quieter racehorses. Nothing special, just roadwork and slow cantering. There followed the awful wait that every young lad experiences, until one morning he looks at "the list" and finds himself down to ride a horse that is going to "do a bit of work." A proper gallop - and the need to make no mistakes, plus the certainty that if no mistakes were made there would be more of the same in the future – so this was a major event. John's turn came, and he passed the test – and was ecstatic for a week. Gradually, a step at a time, he moved up the pecking order of the workforce until he reached the "almost useful" level.

The next rung of the ladder found him riding an old 'chaser over the schooling hurdles, giving a lead to a number of young jumpers learning their trade. He made mistakes, but he learnt from them. Horses seemed to go well for him and Mr Fearnley was satisfied with his progress.

For most boys the riding was the priority: it was the bottom rung of a ladder that might lead to a career as a jockey. But for John the riding was only part of his addiction. He was really besotted by every aspect of the racing world. Wherever he looked, there seemed to be an infinite variety of attractions. And when he wasn't working, he was reading old books full of great horses, brilliant trainers, wonderful jockeys and extraordinary owners – all the heroes who had enriched the sport ever since England "created" the thoroughbred in the 18th century.

John wrote regularly to Sally and told her how he was getting on. By this time she had married her Travelling-Head-Lad and had moved to Childrey, near Wantage, where he worked for one of the top flat trainers. Her replies were always encouraging and at Christmas she sent him a fiver for the "pony fund."

Granny was also a regular contributor. So the total rose, but the prospect of spending the money was consigned to the distant future. John had now discovered "horses".

*

When John left school at sixteen, further academic education was of no interest to him. Granny's good advice fell on deaf ears, and he immediately became a junior member of staff at the Fearnley stables.

His adult life began in a flatlet in the warren of buildings behind the trainer's house. This consisted of a minute bedsitting room featuring a small television and an electric kettle (he ate in the Mess just across the way) and a tiny bathroom. Outside his door lived his bicycle and, a year later, a Volkswagen Beetle, which had done sterling service for his grandmother, before she treated herself to something younger. The car, along with a mobile phone, was John's reward for passing his driving test first time. His flight from the nest actually suited Granny pretty well: she could go off for weeks at a time to dig up ancient history without feeling guilty.

For John independence meant more lessons to be learnt. He had to come to terms with The Spread Eagle, the pub that was reached by walking down the drive to the road, turning left and proceeding one hundred yards in the direction of the village, which began two hundred yards further on. The pub was where "racing" kept in touch with the rest of the world - an amicable association that was mutually beneficial.

Racing added an extra interest, and a bit of excitement, to the lives of the locals, and the locals provided the racing folk with the opportunity to spend time in company beyond the confines of their own profession. Harmony prevailed, under the ever-vigilant eye of landlady Meg, who was tiny, but stood no nonsense.

John discovered that he loathed alcohol. It took him a fortnight to say hello and goodbye to wine and spirits (along with the contents of his stomach on two occasions). Then "half of lemonade shandy" came to his rescue. His colleagues sneered and jeered, but he had no choice. When all the consequences of rash experimentation were long gone he would shudder at the very thought of what he had been through.

Girls provided a further factor with which he was not familiar. Since he first began to frequent the Fearnley establishment he had noticed that in spring and early summer warm weather inspired a stream of young women (some very young) to leave the village on foot and head towards the setting sun. They would take up positions around the gateway that led to the stables. This migration would coincide with the time when, up at the yard, evening stables had finished, the staff had had their supper and the younger lads had had time to comb hair and sluice face with various deodorants of dubious quality.

In due course the lads would make their way down to the road. The two groups would merge and chatter. After a ritual that was overt and covert in about equal proportions the participants would sub-divide into pairs and head for the shadows.

All this John was aware of, but.... but he hadn't the time.... but he wasn't at all sure.... but he was halfway through a very interesting book.... and so on. Further investigation must wait. With no regrets, he dedicated himself to the pursuit of wisdom.

CHAPTER TWO

"How's the fund going, young man?" Sally asked.

"Pretty good, really. It got stuck on £36 pounds for almost a year. Then Harry made me have the £6 on a horse he fancied. Not one of ours. It won at ten to one. Last count - £96. Did I thank you for your Christmas present?"

"You did – your Gran would have seen to that! Who's Harry?"

"One of Mr Fearnley's jockeys. He knows everything."

It was a mild October afternoon and they had bumped into each other at Newbury racecourse, by the gate that allows the horses to access the track. John carried a lead rein. Now seventeen and five foot nine, he had just released the horse he had brought to the races and was watching it canter down to the start.

"£96," he repeated. "Did you have something in mind?"

"A pony, a yearling," she said. "It's turned out with a yearling of mine. The girl who owns it has lost interest. You should buy it."

Sally's smart dark green coat was unbuttoned to reveal a silk dress of many colours, bright orange and deep purple predominant. Her eyes were as blue as ever, and her manner had lost none of its briskness.

"What would I do with it?"John asked.

"Nothing. There's nothing to be done for a year at least, perhaps two, and I want it to stay with me as long as possible, as company for mine."

This pony, she revealed, was a bit Connemara, a bit Welsh, perhaps a bit Arab - and very nice. She would keep it for him for nothing. If any money needed spending, she would see that the costs were kept to the minimum. John believed her. He knew that her husband's position entitled her to all the fringe-benefits that the horse world has to offer.

"How much?"

"£80."

"I shouldn't have told you how much I had in ..."

"That had nothing to do with it!"

*

John was particularly attracted by the gap - one (possibly two) years - during which he wouldn't have to do anything. Maybe by then he would be ready for the extra workload. In which case experimenting with a pony might be just what he needed.

Soon after the conversation with Sally, he requested an interview with Mr Fearnley and told him about the proposition. The trainer considered it for a week and then gave his blessing, provided that it did not interfere with the work for which he now paid John a wage. Having received assurances, he added that John needn't pay anything for the keep of the animal. There were a few empty loose-boxes, some of them behind the warren of buildings, and it would no doubt spend most of its time turned out in one of the paddocks in that area. John could look upon this as a perk, which he could rely on as long as he kept up the good work. John gave further assurances, and said "Yessir" and "Thank you, sir" in a sort of litany of gratitude and best intentions.

"Here's something for you to read," said Mr Fearnley.

"Thank you, sir."

It was the biography of Noel Murless, champion trainer in the middle of the twentieth century. That evening John phoned Sally. The yearling pony was still available, and the deal was done without him even seeing it. Thus it was that the pony fund did the job for which it was created and was wound up.

CHAPTER THREE

John's reason for not even inspecting his investment was that he was busier than ever. After riding out two lots in the morning he was assigned to the office for six months, assisting Rosemary, the trainer's Number 2 secretary. Rosemary lived in Hurstbourne Tarrant, four miles away. She drove a neat red Mini Cooper. Her mother was a vivacious divorcee who had show-jumped for England in her prime - or rather in her youth; she considered that her prime was only just beginning. Rosemary was well-made, bright and cheerful: she soon taught John quite a lot about entries, forfeits and withdrawals, about wages and owners' bills, and about most of the many other basic processes that kept the show on the road.

In moments of relaxation he could not help but notice the genius of Mrs Stuart, the Number 1 secretary. Mrs Stuart (short, plump and never flustered) was another person who "knew everything", and was capable of digesting every innovation that the technological revolution threw at her without batting an eyelid. She steered the ship with effortless skill between 7.30 a.m. and half past noon, then returned to nearby Appleshaw to provide lunch for her farmer-husband, leaving her juniors to cruise through the rest of the day, comfortable in the knowledge that if they followed Mrs Stuart's instructions to the letter no harm would befall them or the business.

John had been suitably impressed by this extraordinary woman, and by Rosemary, and indeed by this introduction to office work, but was very happy to be returned to the great outdoors. He was promoted to "dogsbody" for Mr Fearnley's assistant-trainer (riding out first lot, and all over the place thereafter). He found himself in constant demand, and the amazing variety of his duties meant that in a very short time he had become familiar with every aspect of what was going on in every nook and cranny of the extensive establishment that he belonged to.

Assistant trainers are constantly on the move. Not all – but a fair number. They are climbing a ladder and looking for advancement. When they come across any suggestion of an opportunity to better themselves they move like lightning. Their idea of Heaven, at the end of quite a long and winding road, features a very rich patron who will set them up with a yard full of well-bred horses and a fat salary.

John's taskmaster proved to be of this type. After a further six months he announced that he had a pressing engagement in America, and a fortnight later John had inherited his workload and his title – conditionally.

"You're on probation, John," said Mr Fearnley. "If you do well, you can have the job. If it's too much for you, I'll get someone with more experience – and no harm done. Understood?"

An error-free six months followed and John's promotion was confirmed. This surprised nobody, because it had by now become common knowledge that he was slightly mad. He loved work more than anything in the world.

He was also becoming a useful rider. Nowadays on schooling mornings he was on one of the "babies" rather than the lead horse and that he found fascinating. Sometimes he could persuade a novice horse to approach an obstacle in the manner most likely to lead to a happy landing on the other side. Not bad for a beginner.

It was now the middle of a mild November and he had just stopped itching, and combing what looked like garden detritus out of his hair, because he was completing the refurbishment of the all-weather gallop.

One mile plus one furlong in length, it was to be found at Appleton Farm, about a mile to the west of the stables along the Shipley road. Appleton Farm was the location of Mr Fearnley's best grass gallops, only used in the summer and only occasionally then. The all-weather ran along a boundary fence-line on ground that had previously belonged to thistles and nettles. It was in use all the time.

The detritus decorating John's head wasn't detritus at all. It was a man-made combination of substances. The main ingredient was silica sand. Rubber particles were another vital element. Mixed with shredded synthetic fibrous materials, these elements were designed to give the surface of the all-weather track the resilience, elasticity and bounce that would appeal to the galloping horse and provide a safe and reliable footing. Silicon and wax granules were also in the mix, to ensure that the surface would only freeze solid in the very worst winter weather.

This mixture filled a trench twelve foot wide and one foot deep. Underneath was a sheet of tough fibrous man-made carpeting which allowed moisture to drain downwards and prevented flints from working their way up. Below that was a drainage channel to help excess water to get lost.

One of its attractions was the fact that, after a string of horses had "worked" along it, the surface could be restored to a perfect state in twenty minutes, by a tractor pulling a heavy roller. A rake was mounted in front of the roller to flatten all trace of recent traffic, and the result was then compacted by the roller.

When it was dry, the all-weather was light brown, with a touch of slate grey in there somewhere. When wet, it was a deep dark chocolate. When freshly raked and rolled, it was a thing of beauty.

Refurbishment (ensuring that the depth of the surface remained adequate and dealing with any soggy patches that might develop) was an on-going process. It had kept John busy and itching for a month, and he was very happy that it was over for the time being.

CHAPTER FOUR

"Ride it!"

"I don't think I can, sir."

Behind his magnificent desk, Richard Fearnley's brow creased, and he puffed at his cigarillo with unusual vigour. Beyond the window, the February weather also looked pretty grim.

"Something the matter?"

"No, sir. But Saturday week.... Morgan told me I might have to go racing. You look like having runners at two meetings, sir, and Warner, your second travelling lad...."

"Thank you, John, but I do know the name of my second travelling lad, and I do know that he's crocked."

"Sorry, sir. Sorry, sir..."

"This is a decent point-to-point ride I've found for you. In an Open race – good stuff. Would you really prefer to go racing?"

"Yes, sir. It would be the first time, being in charge.... not really in charge.... an extra pair of hands...... Ken Hardy would be in charge if his good horse runs.... but an opportunity for me to.... you know, learn a bit. Some horses behave completely different at the races, don't they, sir?"

"They do, it's a fact of life. Are you sure you want to go racing?"

"Yessir."

"All right. Go away!"

"Yessir. Thank you, sir."

The door had hardly closed before it opened again. John thrust a timid head back into the lion's den.

"Well?"

"Besides, sir... I haven't got a licence or a medical certificate and they take weeks to get..."

"I had no idea," said Mr Fearnley. "In my day all you needed was a horse. I won the only race I rode in – the Bellcastle Hunt Race – quite a long time ago."

"Well done, sir."

"How do you know all this about licences and certificates?"

"Rosemary, sir."

"Rosemary? Rosemary in the office?"

"Yessir. She's done everything else: pony club, hunting, eventing. She told me that this year she wants to ride in point-to-points."

"Indeed? Maybe she should be riding out for us?"

"I asked her. She said no. Early in the morning, she told me, is when you have to make all sorts of decisions, and she has to be on the ball and in the office."

"Good girl! Quite right!"

"But she's got all the paperwork and licences for point-to-pointing."

"Thank you, John. I will look into this possibility. You're a bit of a fool, but not entirely barmy!"

*

Thus it was that, a fortnight later, John was grabbed from behind, rotated like a top, and kissed on the mouth, to the delight of the Saturday night gathering at the Spread Eagle. When good order had been restored, he led Rosemary to a quiet corner seat and said, "Good news?"

"I won!" she whispered."We won! The horse won, and I made no mistakes! I may have to kiss you again." Rosemary was an inch shorter than John and a year younger, but not half as skinny. Her eyes were brown and elegantly framed by dark lashes and graceful eyebrows.

"What was it like?"

"Unbelievable. It turns out that the horse, Certain Sparkle, before he retired from racing under Rules was a really good three-mile chaser."

"Was it a hot race?"

"I think so. Fifteen runners, plenty of winners and several very good riders of both sexes."

"Got to the start all right?"

"Didn't pull at all. Just like a good child's pony. What a relief!"

"Go on."

"He did everything for me. Set off, settled, third or fourth all the way, jumped for fun, never a moment's doubt, never the semblance of a mistake. After fence three I was in heaven. I mean really in heaven. Three fences from the finish he sauntered into the lead and won with his head in his chest. They want me to ride him next time."

"Well perhaps you *should* kiss me again."

"And how did you get on?" she asked when John had freed himself from her clutches. "I haven't heard the results."

"Boy done good. The guv'nor got held up in the traffic. He rang me (I had the mobile) and told me he wouldn't be there for our first runner, so I was to do everything. Saddling, owners, jockey, the lot! Luckily Ken Hardy kept me straight. No cock-ups.... horse won the novice hurdle. When he arrived, the guv'nor patted me on the back. Then Ken's horse won the big 'chase. Both horses came back sound: no cuts or bruises. Perfect day!"

"Two winners! Well done! But why on earth did you not want to ride in the point-to-point?"

"Me? Ride your winner? That would have been very greedy."

"Seriously...."

John eyed the merry throng. The old boy from the Andover undertakers had taken his seat at the piano in the far corner. He was flexing his fingers. The crowded bar was told to be quiet. The rousing introduction to "The Holy Ground" was irresistible, and the massed ranks filled the void with sound and fury.

"The fact is....." said John, leaning close and whispering in her ear. "I might have got a taste for it. If you take up jockeying seriously, you're never at home."

"So?"

"So you miss a lot."

"Well, as far as I'm concerned it was a wonderful decision on your part."

They continued discussing the delights of the day, in a sort of private world, while the music played and the songs were sung, somewhere above their heads. But all good things come to an end sooner or later.

"Come on, you two!"

Morgan, the travelling head lad, was a man of pale complexion, black hair, a brutal laugh and the cruel sense of humour that often goes with it. Pressure, traffic and motorways do that to a person. Underneath he was all right – most of the time. As a Welshman, he was also an authority on matters musical. The patrons of the Spread Eagle hooted and cheered as he led them to a space in the centre of affairs. He raised a hand to create a hush, and gave the order.

"Sing!"

John fluttered his hands beside his ears and gazed intently into Rosemary's eyes. Her hands were also fluttering, her gaze was equally intense. The rhythm beaten out by those sixteen fingers and four thumbs can only have originated in the jungle.

The first verse of "Tea for two" was the basis for their contribution.

John had picked it up from his grandmother. Different from the normal run of Hampshire lyrics, but the regulars had taken a liking to it, and at some stage Rosemary had consented to add an extra dimension to the performance.

Three times they repeated the only words they knew. Then a benevolent audience let them return to the shadows. They took on board one for the road, and crept into the night. As Rosemary drove away and John walked back towards the yard, the stars shone down, the night air was crisp, and more words of wisdom followed him from the pub.

"Where do yon blackbird be? I know where 'ee be.
'Ee be up yon sycamore tree and I be after 'ee.
'Ee sees I, I sees 'ee, buggered if I don't 'ave 'ee,
Wi' a girt big stick I'll knock 'ee down,
Blackbird, I'll 'ave 'ee!"

CHAPTER FIVE

By the end of April, Rosemary had ridden five more winners, two of them on Certain Sparkle, and the other three riding for other owners who had been duly impressed by her performances. She was almost certainly the happiest teenager in the South of England. Mrs Stuart had to be quite severe to stop her singing in the office.

The bigger picture was also looking good. Mr Fearnley had trained twenty-seven winners in the jump season just ended, all ridden by Harry Bridger, the stable's jump jockey, including one at the Cheltenham Festival, so master and jockey had every reason to be content.

General satisfaction was increased by the form of the stable's first runners of the flat season: fifteen winners on the board already, and Mr Fearnley's only "early" two-year-old had cantered home in the prestigious and valuable Brocklesby Stakes at Doncaster, well clear of the hottest field of that age-group to appear in public so far.

Meanwhile the assistant trainer had "done good", as they say. By keeping his nose to the grindstone and double-checking every move he made, John had become to a certain extent the master of all he surveyed. He had also discovered that he was blessed in one particular aspect of his nature: he actually enjoyed getting up earlier than anyone else apart from Mr Cribb, the Head Lad, who was quietly moving from box to box very soon after the sun had put in an appearance, checking the mangers to see which horses hadn't eaten up overnight, and doling out breakfast to those which had.

Thus it was a happy John who answered his phone one evening in the month of May.

"I'm planning to make a start with my three-year-old," Sally announced. "Could you collect yours?"

John was shocked to discover that so much time had flown so quickly, but in the end she convinced him that eighteen months had passed since they had done the deal, and that a three-year-old was what his investment had turned into.

"I'll get myself organised," he promised, "and get back to you."

"Don't be too long. I'd like to have mine broken-in and going well before the summer's over."

"Of course," said John.

What he knew about three-year-olds was that, if they were flat-race thoroughbreds, they had been broken in when they were yearlings, and had quite probably raced as two-year-olds. If they were steeplechasers they were unlikely to be broken in till they were three or four. He wasn't sure where ponies featured in the scheme of things.

Mr Boddy said, "If he's weak and soft, leave him turned out for another year. But if he's mature and strong, break him in, get him going nicely. Then turn him out for another year." He spoke in the uncompromising tones which betrayed his Yorkshire roots.

"Bod" spoke with authority. It was the result of a lifetime spent among horses, plus the wisdom inherited from a multitude of Boddys. Since time immemorial the family's bread and butter had depended on the production of a steady stream of well-trained pit-ponies, cab-horses and horses for working the land; and the jam to spread on the butter depended on hacks, hunters, polo-ponies, show-jumpers, eventers and racehorses. In due course working-horses became largely a thing of the past, but in the other areas the demand increased.

Bod was short, bull-necked and bow-legged; his hair was steel-grey and wiry. Drunk or sober, he commanded respect. In virtually any situation he could take it, and he could dish it out. For a number of years he had been Head Lad for Mr Fearnley, before setting up a livery yard of his own at Amport, quite close by. He took in horses of all sorts, and specialised in Arab show-horses. He was a regular visitor to the Spread Eagle, where John had become one of his disciples, and where the present conversation was taking place.

John heard what he said, didn't understand a word of it, and asked him to explain.

"If an animal is old enough to break, the sooner you break him in the better. If you put it off, he gets stronger and more cunning, which makes breaking more difficult when you do get round to it. But if he's too young to break, you want to leave him alone for another year."

John scratched his head. "Again, please."

Eventually he understood that a horse may be ready to be broken-in quite a long time before it is ready to do a day's work. In which case, one should break it in, and then turn it out to grass until it has matured a bit. When one eventually wants to carry on with the beast, one has a broken-in animal to deal with, and all should go smoothly thereafter. Whereas if one had waited till it was more mature before starting, one would be dealing with a stronger animal, whose potential for resistance has probably increased and whose aptitude for learning has probably diminished. However, starting the process on an animal which is not ready could be a mistake.

"How does one tell?"

"Tell what?"

"Whether he's ready or not."

"He'll tell you himself soon enough."

John was more confused than ever. He decided to defer any major decision until he had had a look at the subject of all this controversy. In the meantime he made preparations.

First, he spoke to Harry Bridger, who had helped him turn £6 into £60. Built like a miniature Mr Boddy, he had blue eyes and a ready smile. Born and bred in Dorset, one of four boys in a farming family, he had arrived in the yard as a minute apprentice, and had shown immense talent from the beginning. Not surprising; since he was eight he had been following the local drag hounds on ponies various and over obstacles equally various. Champion apprentice in his second season, he had ridden plenty of winners on the flat, and had travelled the world during the next decade. Then increased weight caused him to go steeplechasing. The weight range for jumpers is between ten and twelve stone, roughly; on the flat it is more like seven to nine. Harry liked his food, so the transition was inevitable.

At this stage the gifts Harry Bridger had inherited and developed as a small boy following hounds re-emerged: approaching a fence or hurdle, more often than not he could put a horse on the exact spot from which a perfect take-off could be achieved. In a nutshell he "could see a stride", the gift that all jump jockeys need and few are blessed with.

Harry and his wife Annette, plus two young boys, lived in a smart little cottage at the near end of the village. Marriage and fatherhood had reminded him that he was a country boy at heart, with a talent for growing roses. He had put away some money during his years on the flat, which gave him considerable independence. So he simply stopped looking for "outside rides" and was quite happy to confine his race-riding to Mr Fearnley's jumpers, unless something very special was offered him by another trainer. Thus he only rode horses on the racecourse that he knew had been well educated, and he no longer spent hours per week hurtling up and down the motorways from racecourse to racecourse riding for other people.

In addition to being a top class jockey, his opinion on matters equestrian was second to none, and the work he put in, in the yard and on the gallops, was crucial to the success of the stable. Mr Fearnley thought the world of him.

Harry was also a very good driver. When Mr Fearnley became aware of this, he was delighted to let him take the wheel of his middle-aged black Bentley when they were both going racing. They enjoyed each other's company.

When John had started at the yard, Mr Fearnley asked Harry to show him the ropes. This arrangement had created a bond, and it grew stronger with the passage of time. "Harry knows everything," was how John had described him to Sally, and that was still the basis of their relationship. As a mentor, he was even more important to John than Mr Boddy.

"Will you break him in for me?"

"Do it yourself."

"I wouldn't know where to start. Will you?"

"Why not," replied Harry. "Something to do on summer evenings – after the pruning, hoeing, and mowing. A chance to get away from the wife." In fact nobody in the world enjoyed the company of his wife as much as did Harry.

They were standing in the Back Yard; John, Harry, and Jeffery. Jeffery was sixteen, small, slim and agile; an apprentice with a sallow, monkey-like face from out of which poured an endless stream of inconsequential and disrespectful chatter. He was also vice-less and obliging, and horses liked him.

"If I get lucky and make a profit out of the pony," John resumed, "you shall have a nice present."

"That's what I like to hear!" said Harry.

"I'll help," announced Jeffery.

"Help?" Harry exclaimed. "You? We're trying to educate the beast, not ruin it!"

"Yes," Jeffery agreed, untroubled. "And I'll help you."

"All right then," said Harry. "You can ride him – if he turns out to be a real bastard!"

"I don't mind," said Jeffery.

Next, John reserved a loose-box, one of the pair which stood on their own at the back of the buildings, facing towards the loose school and three small paddocks, with the outskirts of the village visible beyond. Then he checked the tack-room and located certain bits of pony-sized equipment. He also asked several people several questions, until he was pretty certain that he knew the whereabouts of other items that he might need to beg, borrow or steal.

He then booked the loan of a Land Rover and trailer, and enlisted the services of Rosemary as his travelling-head-lad for the big move.

CHAPTER SIX

They went on foot down the lane that led from Sally's cottage to the main street of Childrey; Sally and Rosemary side by side, with John bringing up the rear, carrying a length of rope.

They passed a church on their left, then rounded a bend and climbed a hill to the right, with red brick cottages on both sides, and the grey-green dome of the downs up ahead. It was half past five and the sun was shining out of a clear blue sky. Sally turned onto a narrow track off to the left, with the backs of cottages on the low side, and a parcel of allotments on the other, stretching some way along the hillside. It was a patchwork of vegetables except for the furthest section. There, about four tiny allotments had been incorporated into one tiny grass paddock. In it were two ponies.

"Yours is the bay," said Sally.

A dark bay, with a black mane and tail. He had a chunky body and sturdy limbs, and he moved with a long stride and an easy action as he walked down the slope towards them. His eye was bright and inquisitive and his head was finely shaped, as if there really was a bit of Arab in him. John guessed he was about 14 hands high (four foot, eight inches, at the shoulder), maybe a little less.

They went in by way of a barbed-wire Wiltshire gate. John patted his investment's neck and attached the rope to its head-collar; Sally did the same to the other one - a chestnut, smaller and slimmer than the bay. Then Rosemary held open the gate and John led the way back to the road. As the pony reached it, he kicked up his heels, darted across, and bounced up the bank on the other side. Then he swung round on the rope, clattered back across the road, up the other bank and down again.

"Stop it!" said Sally, from behind.

"Stop it!" agreed Rosemary, who had caught them up.

"Stop it!" said John.

Normal service was resumed. The procession wended its way back to Sally's, where she took the chestnut into her yard, and the bay voiced his disapproval of this separation in ringing tones. He had had no warning, he seemed to be saying, that civilisation as he knew it was about to come to an end; no warning at all; it wasn't fair.

When Sally returned, John said, "Is he ready to be broken in?"

"Very much so," she replied. "You can see what a well made specimen he is, and he is already quite full of himself, as you may have noticed!"

John smiled. There was the answer to the question which had bothered him since his conference with Mr Boddy.

Sally helped put the bay pony into the trailer. He got good marks for needing very little persuasion before walking up the low ramp and into the empty stall. Rosemary volunteered to travel with him for a bit of the way, in case he took against this strange environment. They said goodbye to Sally. Rosemary climbed into the trailer through the side door at the front. John got behind the wheel. He let in the clutch with admirable tenderness, and forward momentum developed almost imperceptibly. The vehicle moved out of the village, over a hill and into the next village, where a halt was made on a convenient corner.

Rosemary reported that the pony hadn't turned a hair, so that was all right. As the convenient corner happened to be right outside the house of a friend of hers, they decided not to hurry on but to call in for a drink.

Having drunk, and having admired a litter of busy lurcher pups, they resumed their journey and got home without incident. By this time it was getting dark. The pony was unloaded and put into the loose box John had prepared for him round the back of the buildings. He appeared to have no misgivings about his new surroundings, and attacked his haynet with enthusiasm.

CHAPTER SEVEN

"Any ideas for a name?" John asked.

"How about Weaver?" suggested Harry dryly.

"Yes, how about Weaver?" agreed Jeffery. "He weaves like a bastard."

"A kid shouldn't use that kind of language," said Harry.

"Well, he does."

It was true. A weaver is a horse that stands with its head over the half-door of its box, apparently in a permanent state of nervous tension: its head swings from side to side, its shoulders shift from side to side, its weight moves from one front hoof to the other. From the tip of its nose to the tip of its tail it is in a state of endless and unnecessary activity for as long as it is subject to the circumstances to which this form of behaviour is a reaction.

The cause seems to be some sort of distress brought on by confinement, in this case confinement in a loose-box; its effect is a considerable waste of energy. It is quite common among racehorses, which are frequently in-bred and high-strung; much less common among ponies, which are generally more sensible all round. Waste of energy is worrying in the racing world, but even at pony level it is undesirable.

Consequently it had been a shock to John (the morning after the pony's arrival) to see the signs. And it happened at dawn, when morale is at its most fragile. He had stood rooted to the spot for a little while, and had then got on with mucking out the box and giving the pony hay and water. This interaction revealed that the pony's other personal habits were beyond reproach: he didn't mind being tied up, he knew how to move across the box when told to, he didn't kick or bite, and he didn't weave while he was tied up. After John had catered for his basic bodily needs, pony was left to his own devices for the rest of the day. Those devices had consisted of nothing but weaving. Now it was evening: the team had foregathered, and business commenced.

He stood there, looking rather small amid the throng of humans. And, as is normally the way, once he had something to occupy him the weaving stopped. He was very good-natured about having the dirt knocked off him, and having his feet picked out, and having a large Cavesson bridle draped over his rather small but very elegant head. A Cavesson is a bit-less breaking bridle, designed so that there is no pressure on the animal's mouth. When reins are added, they are attached to a ring on the top of the noseband.

Then Harry attached a lunge rein to the Cavesson and led him out of the box. He scuttled through the doorway rather fast (John imagined that he wasn't used to doorways), then walked across the tarmac track onto a spacious rectangle of turf, roughly two hundred yards long by fifty yards wide. Beyond, working from left to right, there was the loose-school, then a paddock which contained two ponies and a broodmare, all of whom wandered over to the fence to watch what was going on. Next door was another paddock about the same size, containing two stoutly-bred yearlings belonging to Mr Fearnley and destined to be steeplechasers in the fullness of time, and beyond that a very small enclosure, with taller, solider fencing and extra protection at the corners, which was sometimes used to turn out horses after they had run and needed somewhere to relax in the days immediately afterwards.

Once the pony found himself on the grass, his first move was to lower his head and start eating. So Harry explained to him that he was there to work, not to feast, and he trotted round on the lunge-rein as though he had been doing it all his life. He was just as good when they turned him round and asked him to go clockwise, which is usually a bit of a problem at first, because young horses are accustomed to being controlled from their left-hand side, but not from their right. Harry worked the rein and gave the orders, Jeffery maintained a position just behind him as he revolved, and trotted forward waving his hands and making encouraging noises if that was what the situation required. John looked on from a position outside the circle.

When Harry had got him going to his satisfaction, he let Jeffery lunge him (education is often on more than one level in the horse world). To begin with communication between man and beast was limited, so Jeffery was roundly abused; but in a very few minutes he got the hang of it and did well. So they called a halt, congratulated the pony, and gave him his supper.

As regards the weaving, John decided to give him the benefit of the doubt, for the time being. His box looked out on paddocks, with ponies in the nearest one, which might have upset him. They are free and I am not! Help! In addition, he had no immediate company, because his box was one of two, and the other was empty.

Three days later and still he weaved, so John moved him to a box in the Back Yard, where a handful of friendly horses, all models of complete relaxation, were there to keep him company and demonstrate the advantages of taking things easy. He weaved as much as before, if not more so.

Weaving can be contagious, and John didn't want to be accused of sabotaging the racehorses. So after another three days he turned the pony out in the paddock at the back. The two ponies in occupation were called Smokie (a grey) and Golly (very dark brown); the broodmare's name was Parameter. She was a bright chestnut.

The new boy was delighted. First he had a gallop, punctuated by bouts of bucking and kicking, while the other three watched from a distance. Then he trotted over and introduced himself. Then he dropped to the ground and had a most relaxing roll before he set about eating himself into a stupor.

John heaved a sigh of relief. The weaving had knocked the wind out of his sails in no uncertain fashion. Now, however, it could be discussed and researched and dealt with slowly and sensibly. In all other respects, he reflected, the pony was doing well, and it was quite simple to go on with the breaking-in process in the paddock. So far he could walk, trot and canter on the lunge, clockwise and anti-clockwise, and he would change pace when he was told. He had also accepted the insertion of a breaking-bit into his mouth as part of a headcollar. It had stayed there for several hours each day, and he had accepted it without any fuss. All was not lost.

CHAPTER EIGHT

Two days after Pone…. (Pone was as far as they had got in the choice of a name)….. Two days after he had been turned out, John found a small cut on the outside of his off-side hock (the main joint of the right hind leg), so he sprayed it with blue disinfectant spray, which made Pone jump. It wasn't much of a cut, so John thought no more about it.

The next afternoon he was watching Pone in the paddock, when Smokie, the burly grey gelding, rushed up to him and kicked him hard, twice, on that same hock, and as Pone cantered away it was clear that he was quite lame.

John felt sick as a dog. He had in fact harboured misgivings about tensions between the two of them, and had been working overtime to complete the fencing of another paddock, across the road from the big gates at the bottom of the drive, so as to split up the parties concerned. The fencing had been finished at lunchtime that day.

Before matters got any worse, he took Pone and Jeffery took Golly (a perfect gentleman), and they were loosed off together in the new paddock. Pone was sound enough at the walk, so John decided to give him two days' rest, to allow the bruising to wear off.

Seventy-two hours later he was hobbling, which suggested that there was more to it than bruising. John knew that this was no time to be messing around. He explained the situation to the Head Lad. Irishman Tom Cribb was 40 and looked 28, except for a grey border to his curly fair hair. He was quiet as a mouse, strong as an ox, brave as a lion, and he knew everything a Head Lad needs to know, which is a very great deal. When he was informed of the situation, he was not surprised.

"If you'd asked me, I'd have told you not to turn him out where you did. That grey yoke has a jealous streak. He thinks the mare is his property."

"I see," said John, looking stupid, feeling dreadful.

They put Pone in an empty box in the Front Yard, and Mr Cribb came and looked.

"That cut's infected!" he said immediately. "He needs a poultice."

Suddenly the box was full of people, buckets, hot water and steam – a fair bit of scuffling, too, because Pone, though small and outnumbered, did not take kindly to medication.

"Let's give him something to think about," said Mr Cribb. He applied a twitch to Pone's nose, and John found himself holding it in place, with Pone staring at him at close range with red-rimmed angry eyes. Not surprising, really: a twitch is a loop of cord attached to the end of a stout wooden handle about a foot long. The loop goes round the animal's nose, and is tightened by twisting the handle. So long as he stays still, his nose doesn't suffer; if he moves ... Ouch!

Pone stood like a statue while the poultice was applied to his hock and securely bandaged. To give him his due, he didn't seem to harbour a grudge once it was all over. When the twitch was taken off he just snorted and shook his head, the red rim of his eyes disappeared, and he tucked into a square of hay. His carers withdrew. A few minutes later John saw him, with a beard of hay dangling from his mouth, weaving energetically over the box-door.

*

Pone stayed in that box for three days. Then he was trotted out and pronounced cured.

"Walking exercise for a few days?" John suggested.

"He's cured," said Tom Cribb. "Get on with him. He should have the Roller on by now."

"Oh, bloody hell!" said John, because putting on the Roller can be traumatic. However, nobody else seemed to be in a twit about it, so….

So that evening Pone was lunged by Harry, in the paddock across the road and he moved beautifully, perfectly sound again and obviously delighted to be out and about. Golly looked on from a respectful distance for a few minutes, then put his head down and continued to graze.

After ten minutes each way on the lunge Pone had a rest. Then Jeffery held the lunge rein, while Harry put a broad, padded, buff-coloured canvas roller over Pone's back, buckled the breast-girth round the front of his chest (to prevent the roller from slipping backwards), then gently tightened and buckled the roller round his belly. Harry took the lunge-rein from Jeffery, and told the pony to "Walk on!" He stepped out - and immediately felt this strange, restrictive pressure round his midriff. So he flew into the air, bucked, reared, squealed, and dragged Harry halfway across the paddock as he tried to get rid of whatever this diabolical entanglement was.

After about ninety seconds of this performance, which got rid of nothing, he came back down to earth again, shook himself, and sighed. Harry told him he was a good little man, and he responded by lunging properly, without giving the roller another thought. And he was none the worse for the experience: no cuts, bruises, or recurrence of lameness. The roller stayed on him for twenty-four hours, to give him a chance to get used to it. The Roller is of course the pre-cursor to a saddle.

After that he wore it for his lunging sessions for a couple of evenings, and on the third evening a saddle was substituted and he didn't notice the difference. The stirrup irons were left up at the top of the leathers, so that they didn't flap against his sides, and he lunged round in circles like an old hand. Now that he was living in the paddock, the weaving had stopped, and could for the present be put on a back burner, so to speak. This was a great relief for all concerned.

CHAPTER NINE

The week after the Roller was introduced, a snaffle bridle (reins detached) replaced the Cavesson on Pone's head. This was done in the box at the back of the yard which had been his home until he was granted the outdoor life which he so much preferred. Two long lunge-reins were attached to the rings of the bridle, one on either side of his mouth. The lunge-reins went from the bridle to Harry's hands as he stood behind the pony; one rein on either side of the pony; rather like the shafts of a carriage, but flexible. The process about to begin is called "long-reining".

When Harry was ready, he gave the word to Jeffery, who led the pony out of his box and across the track onto the grass. Harry paid out the reins until almost their full length stretched between his hands and the pony's mouth, and he followed the pony out of the box, about four yards behind it. At a word of command Jeffery then let go of Pone's head, and Harry proceeded to drive him from behind, at the walk, making his wishes known through pressure on the reins, accompanied by words of command, like "Whoa!" and "Walk On!" and "Left Turn!" and "Right Turn!" and even "Come Back! Come Back!" (which meant "Walk backwards"), plus a lot of "Good little man!" when he deserved it – which was most of the time. His dark ears flickered back and forth as he listened to what Harry was saying, and he was clearly doing his best to please.

John leant up against the nearest fence and watched, and it was a delight. Except for the "gnashing". Right from the beginning Pone started making the most awful faces, opening his mouth, baring his teeth, and masticating away as though he was chewing gum. It was a phenomenon for which no good reason was immediately apparent, but it wasn't pretty.

The next step was lunging in a circle with the two reins in place. Going anti-clockwise, one rein went direct from the bit to Harry's left hand, the other passed along Pone's far side and round his hindquarters on its way to Harry's right hand. Clockwise, the opposite was the arrangement. Some horses object to a canvas rein slapping against the hocks and under the tail, but Pone took no notice, and circled as if he had been doing it all his life. Clockwise or anticlockwise, no problem.

A lot of horsemen find two lunge reins, each with varying amounts of slack which has to be managed, quite a demanding double handful, but Harry made it look easy. By the end of the week Pone and Harry had aspired to the most difficult trick of all in this discipline. That's when the horse is trotting round anticlockwise, and the man says: "Right Turn! Right Turn!" and, without breaking his trotting gait, the horse turns away from him, and the man has to run forward a few paces to make this possible, taking in one rein as he lets out the other, which takes a bit of doing!

Round goes the horse, a full 180 degrees, and there he is, trotting in the opposite direction, cool as a cucumber, as if nothing had happened. Done properly the manoeuvre is a work of art. Harry did it beautifully, and so did Pone – apart from those awful grimaces.

They tried changing his bit. They tried leaving the bit in his mouth after work, to see if it impeded his eating - not in the slightest. John got the vet to look at his mouth; he reported that the mouth was perfect and the teeth in good condition. So they were none the wiser. Concerned, but not very concerned, as there seemed to be no actual discomfort. Still, John wished he wouldn't do it.

*

"Gerronimtonite!" announced Harry, when he chanced upon John during evening stables. Evening stables (preparing horses and their boxes for night time) last from four to six and this encounter took place at a quarter to five. On June 6th, a day of bright sunshine.

"Really?" said John.

"Why not?" said Harry over his shoulder, going off to do whatever it was he was about to do. In a good yard, people don't hang about chatting during stables. Tom Cribb would not approve.

"Gerronimtonite!" meant that Pone was going to be sat upon for the first time that very evening. The first time a horse is "backed" is another milestone with dramatic implications. John braced himself.

After evening stables, and after a long-reining session that was full of grimaces but otherwise faultless, Pone was led into the box behind the buildings. In addition to his regular team, his entourage now included another lad, Ken Hardy, who watched from the doorway. He had agreed to take charge of operations when Harry took his family to Spain for a fortnight in the third week of June.

The long reins were removed and John fastened a short lead-rein to the rings of the bridle. Jeffery gave Harry a gentle leg-up so that he could just quietly lie across the saddle, with his head over the far side, and words of reassurance on his lips, while his right hand stroked and patted Pone's neck. Pone's ears flickered as he registered what was going on, but he didn't object.

"Lead him round the box," came Harry's voice from the shadows, so John said, "Come on, little fellow", and started to walk, and Pone stepped forward, and hesitated as he felt the weight on his back shift, and then completed the pace and went on, and nothing awful happened, and voices kept saying "Good boy!", including one voice which seemed to come from.... well, somewhere just behind his right shoulder. Two, three circuits of the box, then "Whoa!" said Harry, so they whoa-ed, and he slid gently back to the floor, and everybody congratulated Pone for being so good.

"Now it's your turn", said Harry to Jeffery, and gave him a leg up. Unfortunately the foolish boy thought he was meant to sit on properly (as opposed to just lying across) and he started to put his right leg over the far side. Pone's reaction was, "Hey! What's going on up there? " and there was quite a lot of trampling about, and puffing and banging up against the wooden wall - before they got the young hooligan (Jeffery) in the right position (lying across) and Pone (the victim of aggression) in the right frame of mind to have another gentle walkabout. As they walked, Ken Hardy slanged Jeffery (in tranquil tones, in case Pone thought the criticism was aimed at him) for his stupidity in doing what he hadn't been told to do. Jeffery's muffled voice responded plaintively from Pone's far side: "But I never knew ... Nobody told me ... I thought you wanted me to sit on him!"

When the session was over, friendships were re-established. Lots of pats for the pony, who didn't seem to bear a grudge. Lots of insults for Jeffery - and he didn't seem to bear a grudge either.

Ken Hardy (slim, fair, blue-eyed and West-Country-speaking) had been brought up among ponies and horses. From the moment he arrived in the yard as a sixteen-year-old apprentice, he was different class from the average kid. He rode well, he worked well. He also belied his rather boyish looks by proving as hard as nails and frightened of nothing and nobody - not even Mr Fearnley. Very early on he met up with Bod and they took to each other immediately. Soon Ken was spending all his free time at Bod's livery yard, helping and learning. With horses of all sorts coming and going, this was like an equestrian Oxbridge education and Ken made the most of it. "Will you run me over to Bod's?" was his catch-phrase for a year, until he acquired a yellow Mini, which provided the independence he needed.

*

The next evening Jeffery got it right. He lay across the saddle for the first walkabout round the box, and all went well. As he lay there, on his stomach, Harry told him to put his right leg over, and he did so, slowly and gently, and Pone didn't mind at all, and Harry said, "Keep your bloody head down!" and Jeffery said, "I know, I know!" and crouched on top with his face against the far side of Pone's neck - and the second walkabout was as peaceful as the first. When Harry thought that the novelty of a leg each side had been assimilated, digested and accepted by the pony, he said, "Now sit up slowly", and Jeffery straightened up in the saddle. Two little ears flickered like antennae, one little head cocked to the right as Pone peered over his shoulder. No problem.

Two nights later, Harry led Pone, with Jeffery on top, out of the box and on to the track, and walked him up and down for a bit. Then John took over and led him back in. On his return he scuttled through the door, for which John blamed himself. He was anticipating something of the sort, and had ducked out of the way as soon as he got inside the box, which may have startled the pony. Apart from that, everything had gone nicely.

Another two nights went by, and then Harry rode him out of the box, with Ken on the end of a single lunge-rein. They walked about for a few minutes on the open grass, and then prepared to trot Pone round in a circle. After two paces, Pone decided that trotting with a moving weight on his back was weird, and exciting and scary, so he leapt in the air and set off southwards at speed. Ken stumbled and dropped the rein. John and Jeffery held their breath.

The flying rein pursued the flying pony (with Harry sitting as solid as a rock) across the open grass towards the tarmac of the track. One stride from the tarmac, Pone applied the brakes and stopped dead. Quietly the troops formed up and Ken gathered up the rein. Sighs of relief from the ground-staff - but not from Harry or from Pone, neither of whom had turned a hair.

The circus withdrew from the edge of the track, and education resumed. No more fireworks.

CHAPTER TEN

As Harry's holiday approached, the team discussed how his absence would affect the scheme of things. They decided that riding the pony would be suspended until he got back, but that the driving and lunging should continue, because it would be a mistake to declare a fortnight's complete idleness at this early stage in his education. So that is what happened: each evening the tack went on and Pone was to be seen pottering about the yard, or in the paddock, or up the village street, saddled and bridled, with either Ken or John in charge of the long reins, and Jeffery in constant attendance. In fact, most of the time it was John and Jeffery who did the business, because Mr Boddy had just been sent three horses to break, and Ken was spending much more of his free time over at his yard than he had anticipated.

Jeffery was the one person who hadn't been consulted when the plans were made, which is perhaps why he didn't feel committed to them. He never said as much, but one evening, after he and John had been lunging the pony and driving it around the open grass area next to the loose-school, he suddenly announced, "I ought to get on him tonight!"

There must have been some strange narcotic wafting in the breeze that evening, because John, instead of vetoing the suggestion, said, "Why not?" and added, "In the loose school – it'll be safer!"

They opened the wooden gates, took Pone inside, closed the gates behind them, and stood there on the sand track. Rails on both sides and wooden walls beyond the exterior rails. No jumps were set up, the track was clear. When they had taken off the long-reins and checked the rest of the tack, John gave Jeffery a leg-up. Pone started to scuttle away as he felt the weight on his back, and then relaxed; as if to say, "No cause for alarm. I've done this before".

34

John led him round the track and then Jeffery said, "It's all right. Let him go," and John let him go. Pone walked round the track with every sign of contentment, and then trotted round as though he had been doing it all his life. This was far from being the case. As a ridden pony, he had had four sessions under Harry (the first rather traumatic) followed by no rider for a week. So his composure was laudable. As was Jeffery's.

As he trotted past the spot where John was standing, Jeffery declared himself. "When you start riding a horse," he announced loftily, as befitted a sixteen-year-old with about nine months' experience of horses, "you don't ride him for four days and then give him a week off. That's stupid! You start riding him, and you keep on. It's obvious!" John was momentarily speechless.

After that, the evening sessions were great fun. They started with lunging and driving and ended with Jeffery riding. Pone still tried to scuttle away when first mounted, but that wasn't a problem as long as they were in the loose school. The only half-serious moment was when John tried to put Jeffery on him outside the school, before he had had his warm-up exercise on the lunge. On that occasion there was a lot of indignation and Jeffery landed on his bottom. Half an hour later, after the proper preparation, Pone registered no objection to being ridden.

Strangely enough, it was during this spell that he stopped making those hideous faces. The phenomenon had appeared with no explanation, and its disappearance was equally mysterious.

*

Harry returned on July 6th.

"I've been riding him for a week," Jeffery announced.

"What?"

"Riding Pone. Every night. It's been really good!"

Harry kept his feelings to himself.

Not so Jeffery. "I think it was really silly to stop riding him after four days ... really silly. So I rode him. And it was really good, wasn't it, John?"

John had intended to reveal the change in plan rather more diplomatically. However, Harry had not got where he was by worrying about the antics of a teenage assistant-trainer and an apprentice who was a cheeky monkey of the best sort. Besides, they hadn't managed to do any harm.

*

In general John was satisfied with the way things were going. Doorways were still a problem, and more recently scuttling about on the spot whenever Jeffery tried to mount seemed to have become a habit, so Pone had to have a strong presence at his head, keeping him in one place. But neither idiosyncrasy seemed worth making a fuss about. In racing circles, plenty of horses have their little foibles, and nobody bothers much. Provided everybody knows what to expect, these situations are manageable, and don't affect the animal's effectiveness as a racehorse. The principle surely applied equally to a pony, John assured himself. And in all the more important aspects of his education Pone was doing really well. Really, really well!

Two days after Harry's return, all John's complacency had been blown apart. It was a glorious evening. Rooks grunted placidly and almost melodiously from high up in the nearby trees. Harry was riding Pone, trotting him round in large easy left-handed circles on the grass. Suddenly, at a certain point in the circuit, the pony started pulling away to the right, resisting the gentle left-handed pressure on the rein, with his mouth open and his ears back. Each time he got to that certain spot the same thing happened and it was a battle to get him back on course.

The next evening he was even worse. Harry reported that "he keeps looking back at me." John, who was sitting gloomily on the fence, could see what he meant. Pone trotted round holding his neck at an unnatural angle, with his head slightly turned to the left the whole time. John could see that he was squinting over his shoulder out of the corner of his left eye. His tail revolved ominously whenever Harry pressured him to keep on course, which he did by steadily squeezing with his legs, and by the proper use of the reins - nothing that Pone could possibly resent, and yet resentment is what his body-language was conveying. Why?

The next day was Wednesday, and John gave him the day off, so that he could think about things (so that they could all think about things). On Thursday Pone was perfect. Congratulations all round, because he had obviously got over the problem, whatever it had been. From now on – a piece of cake, surely?

On Friday the cake turned to ashes in John's mouth – Pone was worse than ever. On Saturday John rode Pone's friend, the gentle Golly, to give him a bit of company, in the hope that this would make him enjoy life a bit more. Golly was happy, the rooks were melodious, the evening sunshine had happiness written all over it, and Harry reported that Pone was bloody-minded, sulky and miserable... and hanging to the right as much as ever.

On the Sunday he had a day of rest. The following day John had his first ride on him - a historic occasion. He found that Pone, although he wasn't very tall, felt like a real horse to sit on. There was plenty underneath him, John found, and plenty in front, which is always reassuring. Sitting on a horse with a stunted shoulder, weedy neck and small head can be a bit like sitting on the edge of a moving cliff, which is nobody's idea of fun. Most important of all, Pone behaved beautifully, and showed no negative signs at all (apart from a quick scoot when Jeffery first legged John up).

John rode him up the village street. He met Rachel O'Malley and another girl, riding their ponies.

"Good evening, Rachel," John said,. "Can I come with you?"

The girls giggled. Rachel said, "Yes, course you can," and asked John what he was riding, and he told her. Pone listened to every word, and made friends with the two ponies, and a good time was had by all.

Rachel was thirteen, fair, freckled, blue-eyed. She had just started Pony Club eventing. John wasn't at all sure what that entailed, but he wasn't surprised that she was good at it, because her father was one of about eight O'Malley boys who rode like angels from birth.

Her father, Patrick O'Malley, had now retired, but in his youth had been the stable's first choice jump jockey. His reputation lived on in legend and song. When he rode them, notorious runaways had become tractable and "nutters" had instantly developed a sense of responsibility. It was also said that he could walk into an equine psychopath's box and be received with every courtesy, when all others were violently ejected. It was a gift - inexplicable, but perhaps something to do with being Irish.

Rachel's mother Judy was where the fair complexion and the blue eyes came from. She was extremely pretty. She was also a very energetic, positive, practical person. Since Patrick retired from race-riding, they had taken over a horse-transport business, with Judy in the office and Patrick filling in as a driver when the need arose. All the local trainers knew and respected him and the business chugged along very nicely indeed.

*

Rachel and her friend certainly provided very good company for Pone. He behaved perfectly throughout, and when it was time for the parting of the ways he walked home with a spring in his step. The whole thing had gone so well that John even allowed himself to think that his riding might perhaps be part of the key to success. I'll ride him again tomorrow, he decided.

Luckily for him, the next day Harry wasn't on hand to see this performance, because it was awful. Pone moved like a crab, and he became worse when they met the other ponies in the village, which was meant to be another treat for him. When they came back to the paddock to do some schooling and figures-of-eight, he was back to his old trick of hanging to the right, resisting his rider's wishes and sulking worse than ever. He gave the impression of being a sad little man, rather than a bad little man, but what lay behind it John could not fathom. Later on that evening he went down to the pub for a reviver, and found Harry in conversation with Mr Boddy. He confessed what had happened, and a joint-decision was taken to give Pone a few days off while all concerned scratched their heads.

*

On the following Monday Harry rode him and he was perfect. On Tuesday he rode him again and he was awful. The session took place in the paddock across the road. Harry and John ended up at the roadside, deep in gloomy conversation as they took off the tack.

A red sports-car drew up, and out of it hopped Rosemary's mother. This evening she was chauffeuring her daughter to the garage to pick up her car.

She listened to John's lamentations, then stepped over to Pone and pressed him lightly on the withers. Pone leapt in the air and had a good stab at kicking her with an acrobatic extension of the nearer of his two hind legs.

"It's obvious," said Rosemary's mum, sidestepping nimbly. "This poor animal has sore withers!"

Then she hopped back into her car, signalled left and disappeared up the drive to the office, leaving the experts looking and feeling rather foolish, apart from Jeffery, who said, "I told you so. I've been telling you for weeks that that saddle doesn't fit!"

To give him his due, John reflected, frowning biliously at the annoying monkey, he *had* been saying something along those lines, and John had failed to pay attention.

John's expression grew more bilious the more he thought about it, because the more he thought about it the more obvious his own stupidity became. He began to notice (at last) that Pone had withers which weren't very prominent, but which were extremely broad (a horse's withers form the bump where the neck ends and the back begins). He remembered that he, John, had made a habit of placing the saddle just where it was most likely to pinch those withers. No one else could be blamed, because recently no one else had put the saddle on.

Pone's inconsistency was now understandable. Riding him made him sore, which made him behave badly. The more one rode him, the sorer he got, and the worse he behaved. But when he was given a day off, his withers recovered a bit, which accounted for the fact that he was always at his best after a day off; but it didn't last, because he soon got sore again! Talk about more sinned against than sinning!

Thoroughly deflated, John decreed that Pone should have two days off. Then Mr Cribb came and looked at his withers and said they were all right again, and that he could be ridden, provided that they put the saddle "*just there!*"

The saddle was put on under the Great Man's eye, and to his satisfaction. When he had gone, Pone scuttled through the box door, and scuttled again when Harry arrived and was legged up; but after that he was perfect. No hanging, no ears laid back, no propeller action from his tail. Just interested, willing, eager to please. It wasn't a long session. At the end of it he was suitably rewarded before being turned out for the night. He galloped off to report on events to Golly, and his team dispersed in a better frame of mind than they had enjoyed for about three weeks.

CHAPTER ELEVEN

For John the relief did not last long. The bottom line of the "account to date" made uncomfortable reading. Sore withers were no fault of the pony's. The fault lay with him. The same was true about the "scuttling through doorways" and the histrionics when being mounted. Those were also difficulties arising from arrangements which he had made. It could be (horrible thought) that he was also responsible for the "weaving". Sticking a pony which had probably lived out of doors all its life in a loose box in a strange environment might well have started it off. And then responding by moving the animal from one box to another on an almost daily basis could well have turned the phenomenon into a problem. John was worried. He arranged an audience with Bod in the pub, and told him the whole story.

"So I've decided," he concluded, "to turn him out now, while things are fairly all right, and to forget about him until next year. That's the sensible thing to do, don't you think?"

Mr Boddy's expression suggested that "sensible" was not in fact the first word that had occurred to him.

"Don't you think?" John repeated anxiously.

Bod had a rugged face, shaped as much by failure to concentrate when practising the noble art of self-defence as by troublesome horses. A scarred cheek-bone and a thickening of the nose bore witness to his fight for survival in a world that was full of challenges. However, when the occasion required, he could raise his eyebrows and look reproachful in a way that was almost religious.

"I think you're bloody barmy!"

"Oh!" said John. "Go on."

Bod pointed an accusing finger. "He charges through doors, and he won't stand to be mounted. That's bad drill!"

A hush had descended upon the bar. The regulars understood that Mr Boddy was indignant; which called for respectful silence.

"You have let him develop bad habits, which is the same as teaching him bad habits! This is a pony we're talking about, not a bloody racehorse! What sort of a pony is it that charges through doors and won't stand to be mounted? Who's going to want a yoke like that? What kid would you be wanting to sell it to - in its present state?"

He supped thirstily, his brown eyes steadily conveying, over the tankard's rim, inexorable reproach. John sipped, and waited for the rest of the charge sheet, which was not slow in coming.

"If you turn him out now, without doing anything about anything, he's going to come in next year bigger and stronger, and he'll be convinced that the way he behaves now is the proper way to behave, because *you have let him get away with it!"*

"What should I do?" John bleated.

"Simple! You straighten him out, that's all. You have confused him; now you must straighten him out. Then you can turn him out for a year, and that's that."

"How?"

"Well, just use your bloody head. For example, when you're breaking a pony in, and you're teaching it to stand while it's being mounted, it makes sense to start off in a corner…"

"A corner? What sort of…"

"A corner, you bloody fool! In a yard, in a barn, up against a wall, there's plenty of places with corners. Use your eyes. Just somewhere where he's got a wall on his off-side, and a wall in front of him. So, when he's going to be mounted, there's nowhere for him to dash off to, except straight into a wall! He'll soon get the message, I promise you."

"I *see!"* said John. "What about the doorway?"

"Nothing to it," Bod assured him. "I'll have a word with young Ken. He'll see to it, tomorrow evening."

*

"Steady!" said Ken. He was standing in the doorway of the box, and in his right hand he held a formidable stick about half the size of a cricket stump. He shook it ever so slightly, ever so menacingly. Standing just inside the doorway, Pone looked at it, looked at him, then looked at John (John was at his head, holding the lunge-rein attached to his bridle, preparing to lead him out of the box). Jeffery stood watching from across the track.

41

"Just bring him out nice and steady," said Ken. As John and Pone took their first pace forward, Ken took a pace backwards with an imperious "Steady!" and an ominous flicker of the stick. Then another pace - and another "Steady!" Then another... and so they proceeded until the whole *ensemble* was well clear of the box, with no sign of panic or impatience on the part of any of them. No charging!

Then they went back in again, and out again, and in again. Then out without the stick, and in without the stick. Then out without Ken playing any part in the proceedings except with his voice; then in again under the same conditions.

The entourage stood on the tarmac outside the box.

"What if he'd rushed?" John asked.

"I'd have tapped him on the nose," said Ken. "Just a tap. More him running into the stick than the stick running into him. And I'd have repeated the treatment - until he got fed up with it. You want to keep a stick handy, these next few days, just so he doesn't forget." He gave it a bit of a brandish when they took Pone out of the box for the next stage of the proceedings. Pone treated it with the greatest respect.

The next stage, of course, was the mounting problem. This started with a search for a corner, as Bod had directed. John was immediately covered in embarrassment because the back of the yard was a mass of corners, so were the garages and the barns. Every wall, every building seemed to offer just what was required, if only he had used his brain.

Ken took one look at the possibilities and said, "Here!"

Within seconds John found himself standing at Pone's head with the side of his box in front of them, about a foot away. The side of the box formed one side of a right-angle corner! A stone wall (which the box backed on to) formed the other side. So a foot in front of Pone's nose was a wooden wall, black with creosote; on his right, two foot away from his side, was a grey stone wall, six-foot high. On his left there was space, occupied by John, at his head. Beside him Ken prepared to give Jeffery a leg-up onto his back.

Ken said, "Stand Still!" very firmly, and then started to lift Jeffery by means of a hand under his left shin, raising him off the ground. As he felt Jeffery's weight, Pone began to scuttle. As there was no place to go, he scuttled on the spot, scrabbling away frantically with his hind legs, with a look of panic in the eye nearest to John.

Without hurrying, Ken lowered Jeffery down to the ground. He then took John's place at Pone's head, taking the long lunge-rein from him. He paid out six foot of doubled canvas rein, and slashed Pone round the backside twice. Not particularly hard, but hard enough to make a noise and an impression. Pone bounced sideways into the stone wall, bounced nose-first into the wooden one in front of him, tried to back away from both, got another reminder, and ended up just where he had started, standing still, shivering, ears flickering, eyes full of consternation.

"Stand Still!" ordered Ken in exactly the same tone of voice as before. He gave John back his place at Pone's head, and legged Jeffery up, and Pone stood like a rock. After that Jeffery went up and down like a yo-yo, and "Stand Still!" rang out at regular intervals, and there was no more trouble. In fact, the operation went so smoothly that quite soon there was no need to have anybody at Pone's head.

Once the initial shock was over, Pone seemed to enjoy the new order; as though he realised that it made life an awful lot easier. The same certainly applied to John, who was seriously mortified at the knowledge that this "crime and punishment" situation was all his own fault. But at least he had learnt his lesson and had done something to undo the damage, and to ensure that in future there would be no return to the bad old days.

"Thank you," he said to Ken, after they had congratulated Pone and turned him out for the night.

"That's all right."

"I say," John went on, "you wouldn't ride him around for the next couple of evenings, before I finish with him for the time being? I think it would help to have just a couple of good performances under his belt, so that he can go into his year off feeling proud of himself."

"Sure," said Ken.

*

The next evening Pone only needed the raising of an admonitory finger to remind him how to negotiate a doorway in a civilised manner, and he stood calmly in the corner outside his box to be mounted without any sign of a tantrum.

To start with Ken walked and trotted him on the grass, carving out big circles in both directions, and then small circles in both directions, and then doing figures of eight. At every stage Pone had his ears pricked. He did as he was told beautifully, elegantly, obediently, and cheerfully. And there was no suggestion of resentment in his attitude towards a society with which he had so often been at loggerheads – usually through no fault of his own.

Then Ken remarked that the ground was softer and more suitable in the loose-school (the turf outside was baked hard and quite slippery), so John opened the gates and Ken rode Pone in.

He trotted him round a couple of times and John could see how much better Pone moved on the sand surface, compared with on the grass outside. Then Ken complained that he wasn't too happy with the way Pone went round the bends, "leading with his shoulder". From what he was saying John gathered that the proper way was to bend the head and neck in the required direction, and this, Ken complained, Pone was not doing. As a result, a certain amount of disagreement between horse and rider became apparent.

Just as that thought crossed John's mind, Pone stopped dead and reared straight up in the air. He all but lost his balance, twisted to save himself from going over backwards, and clattered down to earth. Ken straightened him up, gave him a kick and told him to go on - and up he went again, as high as before; then down he came, and stood there shaking.

John advanced from where he was standing at the bottom end of the enclosure. He saw the sweat pouring off the pony, and his eyes glowing like embers. Somehow, in a few seconds, a complete transformation had taken place. Where there had previously been a comparatively happy creature, albeit involved in a difference of opinion, now there was a seething mass of resentment.

"Shall I shoo him?" he asked. On being given the nod, he cracked Pone round the rear with the lunge-rein. The response was a double barrel of hind hooves, aimed at his head, which only just missed. To Ken's kick in the ribs Pone reacted by rearing straight up again. He wasn't very big, but when he reared he seemed almost as tall as the outside timber wall.

"Shall I give him a lead?" John asked.

"You can try."

John went up to Pone's head, and put a hand on his bridle.

"Come on, old man."

He consented to walk, but it felt like pulling at something damp, soggy, listless, dejected, pathetic, miserable. Apart from his eyes, which remained hot, red, angry, unyielding.

After they had walked together for a circuit, John let go the bridle and told him to go on by himself. Then Ken gave him a nudge in the ribs with his heels and he came to life again with a vengeance. Straight up in the air he went - once, twice, three times, and the third time he was only a whisker away from coming over backwards.

John made a decision.

"OK, Ken," he said. "We're packing it in. That's it. Finish. No argument, please."

He held Pone's head while Ken got off. Ken said nothing. A slight flush across his forehead was the only sign of his anger. Not so much

44

with Pone, probably more with John, for capitulating so quickly. Bod's disciple did not believe in letting bad drill prevail.

John led Pone back to his paddock, took off the tack, and turned him loose. Pone walked slowly away. He looked really miserable. Golly came over to say hello. Pone didn't seem to want company. He didn't seem to have much appetite either and hardly seemed to notice the grass. John watched him. "Bet he doesn't feel as bad as I do," he reflected.

Having done what he was told to do about the "bad drill" – and it had worked a treat - why on earth had he ruined everything with his own little brainwave about "a couple of good performances"?

The next day he told Harry Bridger that he was turning Pone out for the winter. This coincided with the new jump season getting into its stride, so the decision suited them both and no harm had been done to their friendship.

CHAPTER TWELVE

August, September, October. The leaves on the trees had had their month of glory, and submitted uncomplaining to their decline and fall. Out in the paddock, Pone and Golly began to grow hairy. Whenever Golly was taken out of the paddock to be ridden (as a first mount for an apprentice, or to provide a sensible lead for a string of newly-broken yearlings - it was that time of year), Pone would just get on with his grazing, with little evidence that he missed his companion, and no great welcome-back when Golly returned. Idleness seemed to suit him pretty well. At least the simple life in a paddock with plenty of grass and generous amounts of fresh air and sunshine wouldn't do him any further harm.

John had plenty of work to keep him from brooding over the sorry state of his pony enterprise. Just outside the village, not more than two hundred yards from the stables, were two adjoining fields, each about five acres. One was on the side of a hill, the other on its crown. The top one, which was level and surrounded by tall thick hedges, was the Jumping Field, where poles and hurdles and two rows of three fences were available for the higher education of the jumpers. Previous to that year, the bottom one had been largely surplus to requirements, apart from three hurdles along the hedge line that bordered the Shipley road, on a strip which was regularly mown. The next door farmer took a cut of hay off the rest of it.

In this field John had been instructed by Mr Fearnley to mark out a track for a small all-weather. Like the loose-school, but on a much larger scale, it was to be shaped like a running track (two straights and two bends). Horses could not go fast on it, because it was on a slope, which meant a bit of uphill at the far end and a bit of downhill at the end nearest the stables. The idea was to produce a track for slow cantering, an activity which ploughs up green turf just as savagely as galloping, if not more so. With two all-weathers, the grass gallops could be used even more sparingly and their quality would improve as a result.

So John spent time pacing, estimating and sticking pegs into the ground, then driving the Land Rover slowly round the curves which those pegs defined, to see how sharp they were and to adjust accordingly. This kept him busy, so that he didn't go mad every time he set eyes on Pone, which was often, since Pone was in the paddock across the road from the yard, the road along which John rode twice a morning, and drove several times an afternoon.

He was on the horns of a dilemma, and finding it extremely uncomfortable – as is often the case. He liked Pone, but Pone had a kink – this was how John viewed the situation. This kink was potentially very dangerous, because full-on rearing must eventually lead to animal landing on top of rider, unless rider is very lucky. What made that prospect even more unpleasant was the fact that the victim would most likely be a child, or teenager, because Pone, now nearly fifteen hands, would probably never be big enough for an adult.

He thought of Rachel O'Malley, for example, who was continuing to win prizes in Pony Club events and was just beginning to outgrow her 14-hand pony. In fact the hunt for a larger model was already under way. Pone would have been just right for her, if only.... John groaned – and groaned again, knowing that he himself must take responsibility for the way things had turned out.

*

Autumn, winter, spring, and the new track ceased to be a sequence of pegs and became a trench, a foot deep, nine foot wide, and four furlongs in length. Give or take some levelling and some basic drainage, all that was missing was several container loads of the mysterious "mixture". In due course those containers arrived and tipped. Raking and rolling followed, and thundering hooves proclaimed the successful completion of the project.

Meanwhile, out in the paddock, the ponies shucked off their winter coats, and John found he was no nearer a solution to his problem. His problem, incidentally, was now a four-year-old.

CHAPTER THIRTEEN

John was repairing a broken rail in the fence-line of the paddock across the road when he saw the boys loitering at the bottom of the driveway leading up to the stables. He finished what he was doing, gathered up his tools and set off for home. This took him along to where they were standing. He reckoned they were fifteen-ish, one stocky, ginger-haired and freckled, the other brown-haired, leaner, paler.

Ginger said, "Got any work for us?"

John stopped. "What sort of work?"

The thin one said, "We heard you was looking for people to work on the gallops." He had a friendly face with a mildly idiotic expression. "Work on the gallops?" he repeated. He giggled nervously.

"And we want to lcarn to ride," said Ginger. "Work on the gallops and learn to ride. Any chance?"

They lived in the village, next door to each other. They were at school, but on holiday just then, and looking ahead to the long light evenings of summer. Did they want to become jockeys? For the moment, the ginger one said, they just wanted to try it and see. His name was David Sayers. His pal Wayne Smith endorsed this cautious approach with several nods.

With Mr Fearnley's blessing John established that the exchequer would finance cash payments for a few hours work per week on the grass gallops. He then had a word with the boys' parents about the riding, to make sure that they approved of an activity which might end in tears, concussion, broken bones, and so on. They raised no objection.

The final subtlety was to make the boys work three evenings running before the first riding session, to establish their integrity. They were issued with garden forks and driven to the field in which the second all-weather had just been completed. There they were introduced to the strip of turf beside the hedge, which had been cut to pieces by the hooves of horses jumping the three practice hurdles. They were shown how to replace divots, if these had survived in one piece, and how to manufacture replacement divots if they hadn't. It was a slow, dull, laborious, and thankless task. They stuck it; they even stuck it when it rained on them. John was impressed. It's lucky there are two of them, he reflected. One on his own might well have jacked it in when it rained. In recognition of their moral fibre the stable invested in a couple of lightweight waterproof capes.

*

The fourth evening was dry and sunny. At the appointed hour John walked down the drive carrying a bridle and a lunge rein. In his pocket was a hoofpick. The boys were already at the roadside rendez-vous. They had caught Golly, as instructed. Pone had wandered off, grazing assiduously; watching what was going on out of the corner of one eye.

. "This is a bridle," said John. "You undo this buckle, and then you have bridle in one hand, reins in the other. Put reins over horse's head - so. Now horse can't run away. Safe to take off head-collar - so. Put bit into mouth - so... and bridle over horse's ears - so. Buckle the throat lash." Then he removed the bridle and replaced the head-collar.

"Now you do it," he said to David. "Slowly, no rush."

The boy stepped up, took the bridle, worked out how to set about it, and got it done pretty well. Wayne was slower. Golly was very patient. Ever the gentleman.

John told them what the different parts of the bridle are called, identified various parts of a horse, and explained a few things, like how to get a horse to open its mouth (to insert the bit), and how to pick up its feet to check its shoes, and to clean out any mud and stones that might have accumulated in the hooves.

"Now, you first," he said to Wayne.

"What?"

"Ride him."

"There's no saddle."

"True," said John. "You start without a saddle."

"Without?"

"Trust me," said John, remembering his own initiation. "Without a saddle you will learn twice as much, twice as quick."

He showed Wayne how a leg-up worked, and then legged him up onto Golly's broad back. Then he attached the lunge-rein to the bridle,

49

and walked the pony round in a circle. He talked about how to sit, how to balance, how to hold the reins. This was followed by a short lecture on where Wayne should keep his hands, bottom, knees, and heels. Finally he explained which muscles would be required to do the work of keeping him on board. Then he said, "Forget all that."

"Forget?"

"Forget," John repeated. "It will all come back to you gradually, as you progress. Now we're going to trot. Your job is to relax, bounce a bit, try to stay on the middle of his back, look between his ears, don't lean forward or back. OK? OK. Here we go. Trot on, Golly! Trot on!"

Golly trotted on, and Wayne began to bounce in various directions, one after the other and in no predictable order, but without ever looking as though he was going to fall off.

"Not bad, not bad, not bad! Trot, trot, trot, trot! Get the rhythm, just relax, just relax. Not bad, not bad!"

Steadily the dark pony circled in the evening sunshine. Unsteadily his rider grappled with the problems of a brand-new relationship. All credit to him, it was still intact when John called out, "Walk! Walk!"

Golly walked, Wayne hitched himself back into a central position, and the uncertain look which had taken possession of his face turned into a grin.

"What can you feel now?" John asked.

"My knees. They're - like - shivering."

"Trembling?" John suggested.

Wayne nodded.

"Whoa, Golly!" John said.

When the pony had halted, he went up to its head.

"Give him a pat on the neck. It's sort of 'thank you and well done.'"

Wayne did so, liberally, as if he meant it.

"Now the dismount. You lean forward and swing your right leg backwards and over. OK?"

As Wayne returned to terra firma, he staggered.

"What's up?" John asked.

"My legs – they've gone!"

"When you ride, you use muscles that you don't use for anything else. When you begin, they're weak. The sooner you strengthen those muscles, the sooner you will start to ride better. That's why we don't use a saddle. Bareback, you work those muscles three times as hard; so you'll improve three times as quick. Understand?"

The boys nodded.

"OK, David," said John. "Your turn."

David seemed to be better balanced, more at home on the pony's back. Most of the time his seat stayed just above the pony's spine. Maybe because he was shorter and stockier.

Dusk was falling when they loosed Golly off and prepared to call it a day.

"Forgot to tell you one thing," John said. The boys turned back.

"Bareback also makes you three times as sore. Let me know if it gets unbearable"

"See you tomorrow," they said.

The boys set off up the village. Golly trotted over to where Pone was grazing. Pone had watched the performance from a distance for a while, then lowered his head and returned to the serious business of a green grass supper.

John picked up the tack and headed for home. He was pleased with the boys and felt a sense of relief. He had taken control of another pony and so far nothing awful had happened.

*

Each evening the sessions grew longer and more complicated. By the end of the first week, the boys could walk, trot and canter, and the lunge rein was unnecessary. They could also touch the left toe with the right hand (and vice versa) while trotting. They fell off regularly (Wayne rather more often than David), but they never let Golly escape – not that he would have charged off; he was too polite. And when John asked if they were suffering, they grinned, but didn't complain - maybe the money they were earning helped to ease the pain.

The second week, it occurred to John that Golly was in danger of being overworked. Another pony would be a good idea. He thought about the brutal grey Smokie, who was still lurking in the back paddock. The broodmare Parameter had gone (sold in foal), but Smokie had retained his grazing rights by acting as companion to a chestnut yearling, which needed more time before it started its education. Smokie actually belonged to a girl who lived in the village. She had lost interest in riding, and hadn't made up her mind what to do with him.

With her permission, Smokie joined the team, and the two boys rode together, which made it more fun for them, and John devised more and more complicated exercises. Jumping up onto the ponies' backs (with no leg-up), cantering in tight circles, figures of eight, reining back (walking backwards), sidesteps, diagonals, all sorts of figures that call for flexibility and require a certain amount of sympathy between horse and rider; all without saddle or stirrups. The result was that, in a very short time, they were sitting on those ponies like Red Indians and Irishmen, as though they belonged there; using their legs to some effect, and falling off less and less often. At the end of each session, Smokie returned to the back paddock, and Golly rejoined Pone.

When school started again, they had no time to do much gallop-work, except at the weekends; but most evenings they would appear for a riding lesson. In due course John let them go off together on their own, having threatened dire retribution if he caught them galloping the heads off the ponies. However, they were allowed to canter round the nearer of the two all-weathers. Still no saddles.

One May evening he sent them off to do a canter round the all-weather, and told them to meet him back at the loose-school. Halfway along each side of the track were the fixtures and fittings which allowed one to put up jumps of a variety of shapes and sizes – mainly using wooden poles. While the boys were gone John put up two low poles, about a foot off the ground, one halfway along each side of the track (the two straight bits).

When they got back, he pulled out a slip-rail from the rail on the inner side of the track and told them to ride into the grass space in the middle. He closed the outside gate and told the boys to dismount. Next he had David bring Golly back through the gap on to the track.

"Take off his bridle," he said. David complied.

Golly, tackless, looked about him. John replaced the slip-rail.

"Now get behind him and tell him to GO! Swing the bridle, if you need to! "

Golly needed the minimum of encouragement. He cantered off, popped over the first pole, cantered round the bend, popped the second, and David had to scramble under the rail to avoid being run over.

When Golly had been round twice, he was stopped and caught and the bridle was put back on.

"Concentrate," said John to David. "Did you see how he did it?"

David nodded.

"How?"

"He was brilliant."

"That's right. He knows everything. He can put himself right, whatever the difficulty. So you don't have to do anything. Just sit and grip. Do you think you can do that?"

"Me?"

"Certainly."

"I'll try."

"Don't pull on his mouth. Don't interfere. Enjoy it, and get the feel of lift-off and landing. Concentrate on balance."

John gave David a leg-up, and as the pony turned away he clicked and clapped his hands. Canter, canter, pop! Round the bend at the top, then canter, canter, pop! And round they went again. Hooves almost silent. Just the breathing of the pony and the faint clatter of sand bouncing off the wooden walls. By the fifth and sixth "pops", David had stopped leaning forward at take-off; he was sitting nicely and looking good. Except that his face was getting redder and redder. As Golly headed round the top bend, John ducked onto the track ahead of him, watched him pop over the pole, and then said "Whoa!" Golly changed down to a trot, and David nearly fell off sideways – but recovered.

"How was it?" John asked.

"Brilliant!"

"What do you think of jumping?"

"It was easy, once I got the hang of just… going with him. The bends were harder work than the jumps; you have to keep changing your balance." He grinned. "My legs are knackered. I nearly fell off when he changed down to a trot."

He took Golly into the in-field, and Wayne brought Smokie on to the track. Smokie was just a little bit bigger than Golly, with a longer stride. Balancing was more difficult on him, and Wayne did well to do a clear round, and then another, and then a few more.

At the end of the session, John watched the boys lead the ponies away to turn them out in their different paddocks. The ponies looked all right, but there was something a bit odd about the boys: with each pace they seemed to sag at the knees! Am I imagining things, he wondered. He had another look. No, they really were sagging at the knees!

CHAPTER FOURTEEN

The vagaries of human nature were designed to confound man's best-laid plans. John had just begun to congratulate himself on his newly created gallop-maintenance team when the boy Wayne started missing riding-lessons. He even started missing the gallop-work on which his pocket money depended. Explain yourself, John suggested, and the boy complied. He was a footballer (a centre-half, to be precise). The village had a thriving football club, and he looked like making a first-team spot his own, provided that he stayed sound and trained four nights a week. Pre-season training had now started, and he did love his football.

John sympathized. If a chap gives the impression of being mildly goofy, it must make life a great deal more fun to have one activity in which he shines. He thanked Wayne for the work he had done, and wished him well. Then he eyed David Sayers speculatively and wondered whether the latter's enthusiasm would survive without the company of his friend. It did. He didn't say much - simply carried on as before. John was pleased: David's riding was beginning to look interesting.

When the bareback torture had done its work and it was time for the uncomplaining David to be allowed a saddle on Golly, John put tack on Smokie for himself, and rode out with him, so that he could introduce him to the odds and ends that are involved with a saddle and stirrups (like the proper place to put the saddle on a horse's back, which John had only recently discovered himself!) and the need to check one's girths more than once, if one wishes to avoid the calamity that lies in wait for those who don't.

The age-gap wasn't that large and didn't seem to cast a blight on proceedings, so they began to ride together in the evenings on a regular basis.

It was then that fate intervened. Just like that. One minute he was there; the next, gone! So sudden was it that John was standing at the gate to the paddock round the back, with his tack in his arms, when he discovered that Smokie had disappeared.

Later it transpired that he had been sold. But at the time John stood rooted to the spot in a state of shock. He then turned about, put away his tack, walked down the drive and crossed the road to the gate, on the other side of which David was tacking up Golly. John opened his mouth to break the news that he himself was horse-less, and then his eye lit upon Pone who was standing a few yards away, with his head up, watching. Without a second thought, John retrieved his tack and returned. He dropped the tack and rummaged in his pocket for the Polo-mints.

Ten minutes later Pone had been brushed a bit, and bridled and saddled for the first time in about nine months, and he didn't seem to mind; just crunched on his second Polo. Then David jumped up onto Golly, so what was John to do? He said a prayer and jumped up on Pone - and Pone stood like a statue. No scrabbling, no flailing hooves, no sudden dash. He just stood, and then walked on, when asked, as if being ridden was something he did on a daily basis.

They walked along the road (Pone had no shoes on, so trotting on the road was not an option) towards the field where the small all-weather was. John wasn't sure if he was doing the right thing, so he said a prayer and hoped for the best.

"You're the lead horse," he said to David. "When we get into the field, trot off along the all-weather, and I'll follow. We'll see what happens."

Pone was pacing along the road briskly and with gusto. Head at a nice angle, ears pricked. He's grown, John noticed. More neck in front of him, more substance underneath.

Through the open gate and into the field, and Golly trotted on, and Pone followed: light, easy, athletic. Onto the all-weather and away they went. Trot ... trot ... trot.

"Canter on!" John called, and Golly strode away. John clicked twice, and Pone broke into a canter, bucked and squealed, then cantered happily in Golly's wake. Along the bottom, round the bend to the left, up the hill and along the straight at the top.

"Pull up at the end!" John called.

"Wasn't that something?" he said as they pulled up.

David looked at him and said nothing. John reminded himself that David was unaware of the disagreement between Pone and Ken Hardy which had brought the pony's education to a sudden end the previous year. He probably thinks, John reflected, that this is just a fairly ordinary evening. But it's much more than that. Much, much more than that.

Might it not be the beginning of a new and vastly improved relationship between Pone and his owner?

*

On the basis that the best way to learn how to approach obstacles is to get as much practice as possible, John used to steer David towards the loose-school as often as he could, and Golly seemed to enjoy popping round over various combinations of poles. The theory was that Golly was too clever to get into trouble, and if David concentrated on the various stride patterns on the run-up to each leap, he would in time learn what the pony was doing in order to get it right every time. Somewhere in the hazy future there might even be a day when he, David, could help an inexperienced horse to correct itself, by making it either shorten its stride, or lengthen it.

John waxed eloquent as he tried to explain the value of this skill, a skill which could be honed into something magical if the rider kept working at it. Not that John considered himself an expert, but he had read all the best literature on the subject. David listened, nodded and kept his thoughts to himself.

Meanwhile, miracle of miracles, Pone hadn't put a foot wrong since his rehabilitation, and seemed to be enjoying every second of his new life. John was having a glimpse of how things could have been if he hadn't been quite so ignorant in practically everything he had done previously. He kicked himself continually.

*

One evening, Golly had just finished his stint of circuits of the loose school, with John in the central enclosure, watching, and holding Pone, who was grazing.

"Bring him in here a minute," John said. When David had ridden Golly through the gap into the middle, John left him in charge of both ponies while he reduced the two obstacles; each became a rustic pole a foot off the ground, with a second pole on the track about a foot in front of the first, to provide a ground line.

He then led Pone out on to the track, and replaced the rail. He ran the irons up the leathers, and double-looped the reins round the pony's neck, to keep flapping leather to the minimum. Then he let Pone have a good look (and sniff) at the nearest of the obstacles. Finally he led him about

56

ten yards back, turned him round, got behind him and made noises indicating "Go!"

Pone trotted away, hesitated in front of the obstacle, heard a wealth of encouragement from behind, and popped over. Roars of applause! He trotted round the top bend and did the same on the other side. Fun, he decided, and broke into a canter. When he got round to the first pole again, he met it all wrong, and changed his stride as quick as a cat.

After four or five circuits, John ducked through the rails, spread his arms and told the advancing Pone to "Whoa!" Then he patted him on the neck and that was the end of the session. Pone seemed happy enough, but no more than that. Calm-eyed, relaxed, enigmatic. A bit like David.

John was in thoughtful mood that evening: Pone had shown a touch of natural talent in the way he went about the jumping business. Talent is grand in normal circumstances; but when it is found in a pony that has shown signs of being dangerous to ride, it might encourage one to go further along a path that could end in tears. After mulling it over for some time, John decided that a problem of such complexity was at present beyond him.

CHAPTER FIFTEEN

So John just carried on riding Pone, simply to provide a lead-horse and companion for Golly and David. There was actually another dimension to that particular policy, in that David was a worker, and reliable, and probably honest, as well as showing signs of becoming a good rider. Such people are to be encouraged, especially if, as was the case, the person concerned also showed signs of wanting to become an apprentice jockey when he left school.

Sometimes David would ride Pone and John Golly. The change worked well. John enjoyed the pushbutton ride that Golly gave him, and he could see how Pone reacted to David's handling. They got on really well together.

Over a period of time Pone's sessions in the loose-school grew more ambitious. The original pair of two-pole jumps became a pair of three-pole jumps (about two foot high, with an eighteen-inch spread). No problem. Round he went, rider-less. Round he went with David on board. He went clear over the jumps, his balance was perfect round the two tight bends and he seemed to be enjoying it just as much as his rider and his owner.

When John rode him in the school, the wonderful thing was the feeling of power and athleticism that Pone gave him. He was like a racehorse - only slightly nearer the ground, and with a mouth like silk instead of something rather less responsive.

All John had to do was to sit still, go with the flow, and keep from jabbing him in the mouth. He managed all three most of the time, but had a sneaking suspicion that if Pone was choosing his jockey he would go for David every time.

*

One night John bumped into Patrick O'Malley down at the pub. At 46 the ex-jockey hadn't put on an ounce of weight since he retired from the saddle. His auburn thatch was unravaged by the passage of time and his grey eyes had lost none of their brightness. Add a healthy complexion and a friendly smile and he was a fine advertisement for the horse-transport business.

Patrick offered to buy, John was pleased to accept, and they took their refreshments to a table.

"How's Rachel doing?" John asked.

"She's won twice just recently."

"What sort of competitions?"

"Pony Club One-Day Events. Bits of this and bits of that."

"Sounds good!"

"Better, anyway," agreed the Irishman. "In the spring she was riding really badly and her pony was going badly as a result. So I gave her a rollocking. It made things worse. Her mother was not pleased with me. Maybe Rachel's simply losing interest, she said. It happens at that age, and you can't fight it. Fair enough, I agreed. No more rollocking. Then we sent her pony to be schooled by a woman called Joan Ferris. Someone had recommended her to Judy, and Rachel went over there for a few lessons. It was amazing. The pony's improved two stone, and the girl... she's a different person. She's enjoying herself, and her riding is better than ever it was."

"A riding coach, then – this Joan Ferris?"

"She teaches. She competes. She's got an old horse called Dalesman, a useful eventer in his younger days, so she tells me. Her husband James - as Irish as I am – is in business of some sort - spends a lot of time in London. The daughter, Kate, the same age as Rachel, is a really good young rider. They live the other side of Hungerford, outside Wickham. And she doesn't know a thing about racing. Half the time she thinks I'm speaking a foreign language. It's very interesting."

"What's eventing all about?" said John.

"I'm the last person you should ask," said Patrick. "But I know a little bit more than I pretend. It's the modern version of the cavalry training of long ago. The cavalryman and his horse had to be smart on parade and cool under fire; the man handy with sword, lance or carbine (which I think was a gun), and the horse capable of taking messages from one general to another across miles of open country at great speed. When horses were replaced by tanks and suchlike, soldiers took that training into the sporting world when they retired. There was a natural place for it, alongside racing and hunting. It caught on, became an Olympic sport, and Bob's your uncle! Everybody's doing it. It is now a three-part test:

dressage, cross-country and show-jumping. And it's good stuff!"

"I learn something every day," said John. "Thank you. Doing anything tomorrow evening?"

"Why?"

"You could have a look at my pony."

"From what I've heard," said Patrick, "he's a bit of a beast."

"He's not the main attraction," said John. "It's my young gallop-man I really want you to see."

*

In a well-worn brown suede windcheater, Patrick O'Malley stood in the middle of the loose-school and watched as David cantered round on Golly. Beside him stood John, holding Pone, who was waiting his turn, saddled and bridled. The reins were doubled round his neck.

John had constructed a comparatively demanding course for the occasion. Three-foot-high poles on the right hand side; a low single pole on the crown of the top bend; on the left-hand side more poles; three foot, six inches high, with a spread of about three foot.

Soft crunch of hooves on the sand as David rode the dark pony round. Pop over the three-footer. Hop over the little one. Stretch and soar over the bigger one. As they landed, David muttered, "Steady, steady!" and the pony's head tucked in and his stride shortened, as he went into the bottom bend.

As they set off on another circuit, John said quietly, "What do you think?"

"Sits nice and still. How long's he been riding?"

"A couple of months."

"Not bad."

"I'm a good teacher, don't you think?"

Patrick snorted.

Golly was immaculate as usual, and in due course John stopped him. David rode him into the central area and dismounted.

"Well done," said Patrick. "Very well done, young man. But you want to pull your jerk up."

David looked nonplussed.

"Shorter stirrup leathers," John explained. "But not yet," he added, sounding, he suspected, a bit like a mother hen.

"He won't ride racehorses riding that length,"

"I know," agreed John. "But all in good time. First build up the muscles...."

"That's true," said Patrick with a smile. "You may even be right for once."

He glanced at Pone. "Let's see this little fellow."

John led Pone onto the track and loosed him off. All he needed was a click of the tongue and he was away. Relaxed and balanced, he cantered round, and there was an easy competence about the way he adjusted his feet, cleared the obstacles and handled the bends. Even when his approach was wrong, he seemed to have plenty of time - a quick double shuffle, and over he went.

After half a dozen circuits John climbed between the rails and called him to a halt.

"Good little man!" he said giving him a pat. He turned to Patrick. "What do you think?"

"Very good," Patrick replied. "A natural. Knows his job. The way he moves, he'd be ideal for the dressage. Eventers are always going on about elegance, and this fellow looks elegant all the time."

"There you are, then," said John. He unlooped the reins from around Pone's neck and pulled the stirrups down to the bottom of the leathers. "Like I keep saying - if only one could trust him! Would you just hold Golly for a moment?" he added.

Patrick took hold of Golly and David joined John on the track with Pone. John tightened Pone's girths and gave David a leg up.

"Be good," he said, and joined Patrick in the middle.

Pone continued to make it look so easy, and David sat as quiet as a mouse. Half a dozen circuits and never the semblance of a wrong move by either of them. Mr O'Malley was duly impressed.

*

As the weeks passed, the two ponies did a bit more, and then a bit more again. Popping over logs became an entertainment whenever suitable logs were discovered. There were instances when John would drive the Landrover to a recumbent tree trunk and shift it a few yards in order to make it jumpable. The gallops at Appleton were a regular destination and jumping the hurdles beside the small all-weather was often a bit of fun on the way home. There were plenty of opportunities for Pone to get involved in arguments with his rider, but no arguments materialised. John couldn't help wondering whether perhaps increasing maturity had ironed out the problem that had previously lurked somewhere beneath and between those two pointed ears.

CHAPTER SIXTEEN

"Am I good enough to ride the racehorses?" David asked.

A Sunday morning in July, and they were on their way back from a ride up to Appleton. There they had cantered the full length of the all-weather from finish to start, and then back again.

"Definitely," John replied after a moment's reflection.

"Will you tell Mr Cribb?"

John looked at him. "Let me guess. School finishes on Tuesday. You're starting full-time in the yard Wednesday morning. On trial for a month."

"You know?"

"The Boss put me in the picture yesterday. I gave you a good reference. Have you been negotiating behind my back?"

"I thought I ought to ... you know, make my own arrangements."

John nodded. "Take responsibility?"

"Sort of... I spoke to my Dad, and he spoke to Mr Fearnley..." A sideways glance at John, and he fell silent.

"But you don't want to spend all day mucking out," John speculated, "so it would help if I spoke to Tom Cribb and assured him that you ride quite well enough to ride two lots a morning, if not three! Is that it?"

A smile on David's face suggested that John had fully understood the position. John felt better: it's nice to know that one is needed, even if one isn't needed as much as one might like to be.

On Wednesday morning, about the time when second lot pulled out, John happened to be in the office. He peered through the window and watched David Sayers being legged-up on a three-year-old thoroughbred colt. Riding out for the first time, David seemed quite unmoved by the significance of the occasion. When the horse gave a little buck and kick, he gave it a pat down the neck. The partnership disappeared down the drive with the rest of the string, and when the string came back an hour and a half later the partnership was still intact.

Later in the day John had a chat with Harry Bridger and with Tom Cribb himself. Their verdict? David was "all right", and the proof was in the riding-out list for the next day: David was down for both lots.

John sighed. It was the parting of the ways. Sad, and yet not sad at all. David was launched. He was on the bottom rung of a ladder that might lead.... who knows where? On a practical level, however, this development had consequences. When David wasn't riding racehorses (two, sometimes three lots a morning), he was part of a team that worked from dawn to dusk on the demanding routine involved in providing the care and attention which a large number of horses require. By and large, stablemen enjoy their work, but that does nothing to reduce the weight of the workload. Consequently David no longer had the time to ride Golly. So John rode Pone by himself.

*

One fine Sunday morning, a few weeks later, the partnership trotted up the road to the Appleton gallops. As usual Pone squealed with delight and humped his back as he set off along the all-weather. Up and over the rise, round the bend, and along the six furlong straight. Smooth green turf and a stretch of woodland on the right; on the left, in shadow, a steep green hillside mottled with grazing sheep and punctuated by thorn bushes.

On their way home, John rode Pone through the narrow gap into the field which contained the hurdles. He headed towards them.

"On we go!" he announced joyfully, and Pone responded with enthusiasm. Canter, canter, bounce, stretch, land. Canter, canter, adjust with a shuffle, bounce, stretch, land. Canter, canter, lengthen, ping!

"Brilliant!" John chortled, patting him down the neck as they pulled up. "Let's do it again!"

He turned Pone round, and instantly felt all the machinery go dead on him. Pone seemed to have been turned to stone. Just like that.

"Come on, lad, let's do it! We're having fun! Aren't we?" John pleaded, patting and squeezing, and clicking; but the response was a rigid neck, ears flat-back, and the corner of Pone's nearside eye glaring back at him. Hostile, uncompromising. Just like that. "Doing it again", as far as Pone was concerned, was apparently not an option.

"I can't bear it!" John shouted. Why should a good mood turn sour for no apparent reason? "I can't bear it!" He raised his right hand, and cracked Pone round the backside with his stick.

Pone reared as high as he could, and his forefeet punched the sky. He went backwards two paces towards the all-weather to keep his balance, as John clung on and prayed. Then down to the ground he came with a thump. Up again, even higher; no way could he avoid falling, but... Two more paces backward and a twist to the right as he overbalanced, and down he came again - still on his feet.

"Calm down! Calm down! Steady!" John cried, but the lines of communication were dead. Up Pone went again; higher and higher, and further over... beyond the vertical. Then John felt a jolt, and he was falling with Pone's thick black mane pressed against his face, and then something smashed into his back.

*

When awareness returned, he found himself lying on his back in a trench. A grassy ridge hung above him. The sun was shining, birds were singing. Gingerly he pushed himself up into a sitting position. He was lying on the all-weather track. He was alone.

He had a nose-bleed. In addition there was something wrong with his pelvis: no pain, but no strength either and very little response if he tried to put his legs together.

The side of the all-weather track was broken by a jagged vertical gulley - it looked new; and the surface to the right of where John was lying had been disturbed by small hooves. He reckoned that Pone, as he reared, had backed towards the edge of the track and then, the last time he went up, the bank had given way, and down had come 'baby, cradle and all!' John first, Pone on top. Hence sore pelvis, hence bleeding nose.

The deep indentation in the shavings suggested that John had perhaps been very lucky. If it had happened on the grass and the landing had been on very firm turf, he hated to imagine which bits of him would have been dented. Then Pone must have scrambled up, and made himself scarce.

A yellow mini edged through the gateway at the far end of the field and approached along the grass. The passenger's window wound down.

"You all right?" It was Ken Hardy.

"I think so," said John. He tried to get to his feet. That was all right. Straightening up was a different matter: forty-five degrees was possible; vertical was not. However he found he was able to walk provided he kept his feet wide apart. He crept towards the car and lowered himself gently on to the passenger seat.

"Did Pone come home?"

"Yes."

"Is he all right?"

"Not a scratch. We took his tack off and turned him out."

*

No broken bones, no damage to his back, but enough strained and stretched muscles, ligaments and sinews in the pelvic area to keep John bent and hobbling for three weeks.

Mr Fearnley complained.

"If you're going to crock yourself up, John, you must do it on one of my horses. That's acceptable; it's part of the unwritten agreement between a trainer and those who ride out for him."

"Very sorry, sir."

"If you damage yourself by being injudicious in relation to a pony that has nothing to do with me, and you accept wages from me while you are incapable of doing a full day's work, well that's fraud."

"I don't know what to say, sir."

Fearnley began to laugh. "Say nothing. It could have been very much worse. Get well soon. Be more careful next time. Wear your back protector."

*

His new configuration made standing quite uncomfortable. The answer was to perch on the common or garden bar-stool. This gave him ample opportunity for listening to what the world had to tell him.

Even the most charitable among the experts were of the opinion that persevering with Pone was madness. The beast had a kink; he had hurt one person, he would certainly hurt another. It wasn't his fault, it was something over which he seemed to have no control, but it made him a considerable liability.

"So what should I do?"

Approximately a third of the experts shrugged and found something more cheerful to talk about. Two thirds said, "Shoot him" – or words to that effect - and saw no reason to apologize for the suggestion.

"You know something?" said John to Patrick O'Malley one evening. "I can't see any alternative to having that bloody pony put down."

"That's the first sensible thing you've said in about two years."

"In that case," said John, "all he's worth is carcass-money."

Patrick nodded.

"So I might just as well give him away, if there was any reason to think that somebody else might straighten him out."

65

Patrick held up a hand. "Don't look at me. I wouldn't have anything to do with him. Not even as a gift! Let's not forget that he tried to put you in hospital!"

They sat and sipped in silence. It was a pity things had turned out the way they had. Patrick hadn't forgotten the performance in the loose-school: the pony had real talent, and a bit of class. And elegance.

"I'll tell you what," he said. "Why don't you get Joan Ferris to come and have a look at him?"

"Joan Ferris?"

"Rachel's coach."

"Ah, yes. You think she might...?"

"She'll probably listen to the history, then take one look at the beast and walk away - in which case you would have had the benefit of some good advice, and no harm done. She knows more about ponies than you and I ever will. She might spot something that you can't see. You've got nothing to lose."

"I don't want her to get hurt."

"Nor do I," said Patrick. "But this is her territory - her business as well."

The first chill of autumn was in the air as John hobbled back to the yard. As he reached the drive, he saw Pone out in the paddock, grazing beside Golly. They looked thoroughly satisfied with life. John emitted a mixture between a grunt, a growl and a groan – his pelvis was giving him some gyp, and his soul was in torment.

CHAPTER SEVENTEEN

It was dark when the headlights drove up the back drive and the car stopped beside John, now fully fit again. Lights dowsed, engine silenced. Out climbed Judy and Patrick O'Malley, and their passenger.

"Joan," said Patrick, "this is John Dunne. John, this is Joan Ferris."

John shook hands, but he couldn't really see who he was meeting. They all moved over to the light streaming out over the half-door of the loose-box. John pushed back the bolt and held the door open.

She walked into the box. The others stayed by the door. A tall woman, dressed in a green weatherproof coat and brown corduroy trousers. Brown hair, pale skin, broad forehead, big brown eyes - an attractive, intelligent face. Late thirties, John guessed. He was hopeless about ages, particularly women's.

Joan looked long and quizzically at Pone, and Pone looked long and quizzically back.

"What's his name?"

"Pone."

"Surely you could do better than that!"

"It could be short for Al Capone," said John. He shrugged. "He's turned out to be a bit of a gangster, as I imagine you've heard, Mrs Ferris."

She smiled. "Yes, my spies have told me quite a lot about him!"

Pone was wearing the beginnings of his winter coat and a layer of mud. In spite of the mud it was apparent that he now stood just above fifteen hands at the withers, deep-chested and handsome.

She went up to him, talking quietly. She patted his neck, ran her hand down his spine, had a good feel of the tendons of his legs. Next she stood back and just looked at him. Then she told him to get over, and

Pone moved across the box. She went round the far side of him, and continued to prod, pat and feel – still talking quietly.

She came back to the near side, and asked John to remind her of Pone's history. While he did so, she leaned up against the wooden wall and gazed at Pone in an abstracted sort of manner, as though only half of her mind was on what John was saying.

*

During supper, down at the O'Malleys, she was full of banter and fun, and every argument seemed to end in a laugh. She made it clear that she thought racing people were rather odd, because their use of horses was so limited (true, John suspected), and their attitude to them was so unimaginative (this he wasn't so keen to accept, but just now he was in no position to argue).

Hardly had she established her perspective, when she said, "You probably think I'm odd. Perhaps you think I'm mad... It's just a matter of living in different worlds, and trying to do different jobs. When two cultures overlap, there is bound to be a certain amount of misunderstanding."

The O'Malleys were divided. Mother Judy and daughter Rachel considered Joan to be the fount of all equestrian wisdom. Patrick, on the other hand, was clearly a fan, but pretended to treat her with the very polite disdain which is the jump jockey's traditional attitude towards all branches of the horse world other than steeplechasing.

At coffee time John said, "What do you think, Mrs Ferris?"

She looked at him with her very bright brown eyes. After a pause she said, "He's extremely well put together. Very alert. And he's got a rather worried expression in his eyes."

"Could there be a future....?"

"It must be very doubtful. I mean, the weaving one can live with; likewise the napping –"

"Napping?"

"That business of hanging away from the direction his rider wants him to go."

"Eventing people call that napping," Patrick translated, raising his eyes to heaven. ""And I notice that when she is asked to explain the word she calls it hanging. No wonder we don't understand each other."

He was verbally chastised by wife and daughter.

"Whatever we call it," said Joan with a smile, "it's forgivable because the saddle was pinching him. The rearing is the obstacle. A rearing pony is the worst thing in the world. No child should be exposed to such an animal."

John nodded gloomily.

"On the other hand, I like the look of him, and they tell me he jumps and moves well, so…."

She thought for a bit, frowning.

"I could have a closer look, I suppose."

"I'd be grateful if you would," said John.

"Why don't you leave him out in the field till after Christmas? Then start riding him, and get him fit. I just want him muscled up and clean-winded, so that if I try to do something with him he won't fall apart because he's too fat and too soft."

She looked deep into John's eyes. "Don't – have - fights, young man," she said – quietly, but with great emphasis. John suddenly felt about eight years old.

"Avoid situations which are likely to cause arguments. Just get him fit, keep it simple, no battles. Try to deliver him to me with a clean slate in his head. Not with fresh memories of some ghastly confrontation. Do you understand what I mean?"

"I do, Mrs Ferris," John said earnestly. "I do. I'll certainly try. I will try my very best."

"Then, towards springtime, when the evenings are getting a bit longer, send him over to me for a month. I'll certainly be able to tell you whether he'll ever be any real use, and I'll probably know if he's absolutely hopeless."

She shrugged. "Rearing is not at all nice!"

CHAPTER EIGHTEEN

John looked into the office the following afternoon. Rosemary was alone, her desk heavily laden with the bits and pieces that are essential if the wages are to be paid to the workforce on Friday, two days hence.

"Go away!" she said. "Come back at teatime."

At teatime he told her all about Mrs Ferris. It turned out that Rosemary knew of a Ferris daughter (an only child), who was a few years younger than her and doing well in Pony Club competitions. Rosemary thought Mrs Ferris's suggestion was a good idea, especially the "No fights" bit. Together they made a plan. It was decided that springtime should begin on the 1st of March of the following year, and that it would take two months to get Pone fit; so John should start the process on the 1st of January.

In the meantime Pone stayed in his paddock with Golly, and John applied himself to his job. This seemed to embrace more and more aspects of life at the Weyhill establishment with each passing week. The key was the fact that he was conscientious and got things done. The more he got done, the more problems found their way into his "in-tray" – not that he had an in-tray. For a chap with a passion for horses, it was amazing the amount of hours he spent on drains, thatch, tarmac, vehicle maintenance, catering facilities for the lads' hostel and clothing for the apprentices. It helped that he loved his work and that he enjoyed learning new things. The other factor that kept him happy was the riding out each morning – always one lot and some days two. It was that which kept him healthy and fit, and delighted to get up in the morning.

*

A cold spell struck early in the winter. As a result racing was cancelled everywhere for several weeks, and every sort of regular surface became too hard to use. "All-weather" turned out to be less all-weather than it claimed to be. The trainer retaliated by taking convoys of horse-boxes down to Brean Sands, where he could gallop his string on the edge of the Atlantic. When the tide is at a certain level on its way out, there is a strip of sand of a certain quality, moist but not soggy, which delights galloping horses.

John had read all about the immortal Red Rum. This horse had suspect feet all through his career. His trainer Ginger McCain used to work him on Southport Sands near Liverpool and walk him in the surf. Therapeutic? It enabled him to win three Grand Nationals. John was thrilled to find himself taking part in a process that had played a vital part in so much racing history.

These outings made a nice change for the horses and for the lads - everybody gets bored and disheartened by a prolonged freeze-up. Pone and Golly, however, benefited: they got a feed of oats every day, to help keep them warm.

Then the weather improved and things got back to normal, but John went on feeding the ponies, as an insurance policy. The next intervention was Christmas. There is no racing on Christmas Day or on the two days just before it, but the needs of horses have to be attended to, all day and every day, and racing on Boxing Day is a major feature in the racing calendar. Consequently the suffering of those who would insist on overdoing festive consumption, both solid and liquid, was painful to experience and awful to behold.

During this perilous period, half pints of shandy and the occasional glass of wine saved John from the worst of the seasonal malaises, and he prevailed upon the blacksmith to trim Pone's feet and shoe him all round.

So it was that on a drizzly January 1st, before lunch, John put Pone in the loose-box round the back, and left him to weave himself dry. It was his fifth birthday. An hour later John returned, wearing his back protector under his windcheater. He tacked Pone up, took him outside (no scuttling), stood him in the corner while he was legged-up (no scuffling) and rode him down the back drive. It was a moist, mild, grey afternoon and Pone never put a foot wrong. He was pleasant, biddable, responsive, cooperative, and, it seemed, delighted to be back in work.

They went round the block (a circuit of the roads running round the field in which were the schooling obstacles and the adjacent one which contained the new all-weather track), trotting the hills and walking the rest. Pone blew a bit on the uphill stretches, but not too much, and John reckoned that two months of ever-increasing exercise (and no fights) would find him as fit as a flea by the beginning of March. One down, fifty-nine to go, he calculated as he rode back to base. Fingers crossed.

*

In the worst of the frosts it wasn't possible to exercise, and in the worst of the rain it was too unpleasant to be countenanced. But when the elements were reasonable a steady progression developed. Round the block became twice round the block, and then it became twice round the block with a canter round the small all-weather for afters, followed by a gentle walk up the village and back to cool off.

Once Pone was completing this routine without showing signs of fatigue, John committed him to a more demanding schedule. Some days they would trot up the road towards the Appleton gallops and ignore the lane to the gallops. Instead they would continue along the road towards Shipley. Half a mile further on the road dipped down into a valley, and another lane on the right led to an old barn, a row of six loose boxes and two paddocks. Behind the evidence of human occupation, open downland stretched up to a ridge, at the east end of which the Appleton Clump looked down on the Shipley road on the near side, and the grass gallops on the far side. All this land belonged to Mr Fearnley, and the boxes were occasionally used as an isolation unit, if ever a contagious infection visited the yard.

Beyond the buildings and between the paddocks a track led to a gate. Beyond the gate two tracks climbed the hillside. One ran straight up the steepest part and down the other side to the grass gallops. It reached the valley floor a couple of hundred yards beyond the end of the big all-weather. The other was a much more substantial byway. Over many hundreds of years a drovers' road had carved its way diagonally upwards across the slope to the top of the ridge, along the ridge and down the other side to the hamlet of Appleton, which no longer existed. The ascent and the stretch along the ridge provided three quarters of a mile of good firm turf, originally compacted and levelled by agricultural traffic of all sorts, and subsequently maintained in pretty good order by the appetite of many sheep. Thereafter a further three-quarters of a mile of good turf brought the traveller down to the valley floor.

John would trot Pone steadily up that track to the top of the ridge. The higher they got, the more they could see, and Pone seemed to enjoy the view as much as his rider.

At the top they could look down on the far side. A hundred feet below, the slate-grey of the all-weather strip stretched along the valley bottom. Beyond it was the brighter green of the summer gallops. In winter it didn't look like much – just a large open expanse of grass in the shape of a T. The only clue to its purpose in life was down the middle of the main drag – the six furlongs that ran parallel to the straight bit of the all-weather. Along the middle of that stretch there was a line of neatly-trimmed berberis bushes, one every half furlong (jockeys, for the use of). They had been there for more than a hundred years. In winter, when there was no galloping going on, the casual observer might well look down on them and scratch his head.

John and Pone would walk along the ridge at the top of the hill for a level hundred yards or so, and then downwards, ending up just exactly at the corner where the all-weather curved to the left and started along the straight.

On a reconnaissance some weeks before, John had identified a very old gate beneath a forest of brambles and nettles. Probably it had been closed for the last time when the gallops were laid out, many years ago. Returning to the site in the Land Rover, John went to work with a machete. When he had finished, the gate opened, creaked, groaned and swung. It even latched.

Some days he and Pone would start their long trot down by the isolation boxes and end at this gate; or they might travel the route in the opposite direction.

It was good exercise. The only disadvantage was the fact that, on the way home the road surface was very smooth, just a bit slippery and slightly downhill all the way. Not the best combination in the world. An alternative route would have provided a better surface, but it added a bit of time to the outing. Besides, Pone was well-balanced and agile as a cat, if ever his feet began to slide.

As Pone's workload increased, so did the amount of grub that John dished out. After exercise, Pone would be left in his box with a bowl of oats. An hour later the manger would be empty, and Pone would be turned out. So he was getting fitter by the day, and he seemed to love every moment of it - which was just what Mrs Ferris had ordered!

No intense drilling, no jumping, no fights; just easy, relaxed, enjoyable stuff. That was the plan, and it seemed to be working. Barring accidents, John reflected after a month, they might just do a clear round. Fingers crossed.

An accident happened the next day. They were walking homewards along the Shipley road; it had been raining, and the road-surface was slippery. Pone's front feet kept sliding, and John began to sweat. He knew that the road could be dangerous; he also suspected he should have had Pone re-shod, but thrift had persuaded him to try and get another week out of the current set of shoes. Not clever!

Just as he was cursing himself, Pone collapsed under him! Very fast.

Just down on one knee and up again. More of a stumble than anything, but… John slipped off his back and led him. He peered down at his knees. On the near one was a pink graze where the hair had been removed. No blood … John led him the rest of the way home.

"Am I really this stupid?" he asked himself.

When they got home John sprayed the knee with disinfectant and left it alone. The graze didn't seem to be much, and it didn't seem to worry Pone. The damage proved to be purely superficial. John made sure Pone was re-shod the next day, and was sick with himself for a lot longer.

A week before the end of February a sequence of rainclouds settled over Hampshire. One afternoon, sparkling and bright after a morning of downpour, John rode Pone along the road towards the circular all-weather. A milk-lorry came down the Shipley road towards them. The answer was to go into the field, while it passed. The gate was open, but the gateway was a lake of bright water. Still, there seemed to be no alternative. As the tanker slowed down, Pone walked to the edge of the water and stopped dead, and John found himself, in the last week of the campaign, on the verge of "a fight", which he had sworn not to have.

"About Turn!" he cried, trying to sound cheerful, and turned Pone round. He then squeezed with his thighs, and sang out loudly, "Come Back! Come Back! Back! Back!" At the same time he applied a steady pressure to Pone's mouth, first one side, then the other, and so on... just like the routine he remembered from the breaking-in days, when Harry Bridger had wanted Pone to walk backwards.

Puffing and splashing, Pone walked backwards into the lake and out the other side. Meanwhile an understanding tanker driver crept past and waved as he went on. John waved back, congratulated Pone profusely, turned him round and sent him on his way as though nothing out of the ordinary had occurred. He had to grin, almost triumphantly. At last he had got something right. Pone's little ears were waxing and waning in a show of uncertainty, and he wasn't sure quite what had been going on - but by this time it was all over. No Fight! At the far end of the field a gap in the fence let them back onto the road – all quiet on the Western Front!

By now Pone was as hard as nails, and as fit as a flea. On the debit side was one slightly blemished knee. A small patch of black skin had formed, but the hair didn't seem to want to re-grow.

On the last day of February, after lunch, Patrick O'Malley drove his smallest horsebox, with John as groom, and Pone as cargo. They headed north-east, and their destination was just outside a village called Wickham, the far side of Hungerford.

Part Two

CHAPTER NINETEEN

Joan Ferris, well wrapped up in an old green windcheater and her brown corduroy trousers, stood under the porch at the back door of Glebe Farm Cottage, Wickham, which was in fact three red brick Victorian cottages skilfully converted into one residence under a grey slate roof. Her back door was once the front door of the cottage nearest to her stables.

She and daughter Kate had mucked out and watered the three resident horses at first light. Three filled haynets were ready in the barn. Breakfast was history and Kate had been carried off to school.

It was nine o'clock; the weather was drab and overcast, but dry. In front of her was the back-garden: a strip of unkempt grass framing a narrow rose-bed in a state of hibernation. Beyond, the view was frustrated by a tall privet hedge. To her right a grey flagstone path led to the gate. Beyond the gate, on the far side of a gravel track, was one dark brown creosoted wooden building, and beside it another dark brown creosoted wooden building, with a tributary gravel path between the two. The right-hand building consisted of three loose-boxes facing towards the house. Just one was occupied. A small chestnut head, cocked on one side, peered over the half-door - two intelligent eyes watched Joan as she stood and listened. She was listening to a sound like the ticking of a clock in 2/4 time; a steady click-click.... click-click.... click-click...

Feeling a pressure against her right leg, she looked down and the dog Brownie rubbed her ear against her mistress's thigh a second time, then looked up at her with intense, almost lunatic, amber eyes. Brownie was a curly-coated, liver-coloured Irish Water Spaniel. Her mad eyes were no indication of her character or her state of mind, which was loving and intelligent, but gave her a certain authority as a guard-dog, especially on dark nights. Now, the message her persistent ear was conveying was, "Please let me back into the house; I've had quite enough fresh air."

Joan accommodated her, then stood in the hall for a moment. Hanging on the wall in front of her were a multitude of outer garments, including two smart blue back protectors, her own and her daughter's. After a moment she took off her windcheater, discarded the next layer (a pullover), and the back protector took its place. On again went the windcheater, and there she stood, slightly chubbier.

Once outside, she made her way down the path and through the gate. She stroked the chestnut pony's nose as she passed, and went into the tack room, which was next door. She selected a set of tack from those lining the walls, the saddles perched on steel frames, the bridles hanging from hooks underneath. She picked up a grooming kit from the shelf beneath the tack. Emerging, she turned down the passage between the two buildings. Ahead of her a bay head appeared and disappeared in time to the ticking, as the new pony weaved from side to side on steel-shod hooves.

"Now then, little man."

The bay head stopped weaving. The hooves were silent. Joan and Pone looked at each other.

The second block of three boxes faced away from the house, towards a schooling-area, or manège, which measured sixty metres by thirty; it was enclosed by solid wooden post-and-rail fencing, with a gate on the far side. It consisted of a sand surface on which were a variety of coloured poles and barrels and tyres and upright standards, which could be used to create jumps of various shapes and sizes, and other bits and pieces, including several little oil drums, painted white and each bearing a capital letter in black. These could be arranged for practicing dressage.

On the left of the manège was a row of ten pigsties, a relic of a previous age. Each comprised a small yard in front of a kennel into which the former inhabitants could retire for a lie-down between meals.

Beyond the manège was a large field that stretched away to a belt of woods. In the corner nearest to the stable yard, beside the gateway, stood a wooden field-shelter, its rear facing the stables. Another head, a stationary chestnut head, was peering round at the yard. This was old Dalesman, Joan's eventer, in his sleeping quarters.

Joan patted the new pony on the neck, let herself into his box, and put her tack on the straw in the corner. She tied the pony up and groomed him, talking all the time. She was pleasantly surprised by how fit and well he looked. He also pleased her by his manners in the box - going across when she told him to, and picking up his feet properly when she wanted to clean them. He was just as polite as he had been when first they met. She squatted down to have a good look at the blemish on his near-fore knee. She clicked her tongue in a way that suggested that she wasn't entirely satisfied by what she saw. At the sound the bay pony looked down at her and pricked his ears.

When the tack was on, she left him tied up, while she moved one or two of the bits and pieces in the manège to create some space. She then attached a lunge-rein to his bridle and took him into the manège by the gate on the far side. Another good mark for the pony: on the way out of his box he showed no inclination to rush through the doorway. Once in the manège, Joan lunged him for about ten minutes, walking and trotting, first anticlockwise, then clockwise.

"Good," she said, as she brought him to her and detached the lunge-rein, which she coiled up and deposited on a barrel. She patted him on the neck. Then she tightened the girths, let down the stirrup-irons and gathered up the reins.

"Stand still," she said. The pony stood still.

Joan raised her left knee, and put her left foot into the stirrup. Then she took hold of the pommel of the saddle and raised herself smoothly off the ground. Whereupon the pony stood straight up in the air and pawed the heavens, knocking Joan back onto the sand, where she just managed to stay on her feet and keep hold of the reins. The pony came back down to earth, then soared up again, and when he came down the second time he flew round Joan like a dervish.

"That bloody John!" said Joan to herself. "That bloody John told me he was all right to mount!"

Then she banished that bloody John from her mind and applied herself to more immediate problems. "Come on, little man," she said to the pony, "it's not the end of the world." But he kept on cantering round, puffing and hot, ears flickering, eyes red-rimmed and anything but happy.

She talked to him, and cooed at him, and eventually he stopped his antics. The red disappeared, but the worried look didn't. Joan led him round the manège until he calmed down. Then she led him round the stables, inspected the pigsties, and showed him the barn (at the other end of the manège, facing towards the track down to the road), and the muck-heap, which was beside the barn, within the confines, on three sides, of its low brick wall.

Speckled black-and-white chickens cocked their heads as they passed, and then went on picking over the muck-heap, which was adjacent to their enclosure, to which they were seldom confined. On the track opposite the muck-heap, she introduced him to her blue Bedford 2-horse horse-box. Then she led him down to the road which led to Wickham. Across the road, a couple of hundred yards up a lane, was Glebe Farm itself, to which the Ferris home once belonged. Then she led him back again. All the time she talked to him, and this went on until she found he was listening, and saw the worried look in his eyes diminish, then disappear.

Eventually she took him back into the manège. Still talking quietly, she stood by the saddle and lengthened the left-hand stirrup-leather, until she could comfortably put her foot into the iron, without having to stretch up on her right toe. Then she checked the girth and tightened it one hole

"Now you be a good boy and stand still," she said, and put her foot in the stirrup and stood there, making no attempt to mount. "There, nothing wrong with that, is there?"

The dark ears conveyed only qualified agreement.

She did it three times, talking and patting as she did so. The fourth time, after putting her foot in the stirrup she took hold of the saddle and lifted herself off the ground. This put pressure on to the saddle, and thus on to the pony's back, and the signals from his ears registered that he felt the difference.

"Stand, stand, stand," she urged quietly, and he did. So she stepped down, gave him a pat, and did it again.

The third time, she raised herself smoothly off the ground as before, then quietly put her right leg across the saddle, and settled into the sitting position. The little ears went mad, but the pony stood like a rock.

"Well done, little man, well done."

She patted him, and then remembered that she was going to kill that bloody John.

*

Dusk was falling. Kate Ferris got out of the big blue Volvo. The yard light was on.

"Thank you, Mrs Clarke," she said. "Bye, Jen. 'Bye, Stevie."

The car reversed, turned round by the muckheap and headed back towards the road. Kate crossed the back garden towards the house. She was fourteen, and long in the leg. Her brown hair was cut short, her eyes were grey. High cheek-bones framed an elegant nose.

She greeted Brownie with a hug in the kitchen, then went to her room and changed out of her school clothes into a pair of blue jeans, a blue sweater, and a windcheater. In the porch she put on her Wellingtons. She found her mother in the field-shelter, fastening Dalesman's rugs.

"Hello, dear. Good day?"

Kate wrinkled her nose. "According to Mrs Shewring my attitude towards physics is really bad. I don't think my attitude's bad at all, mum – I just can't do physics. But Mr Ayres gave me 85% in the English test."

"That sounds all right. Your father will approve."

"How did you get on with the new pony?"

"That bloody John might have told me that it's still funny about being mounted. If I'd known, I could have…" She paused as she saw a smile flit across Kate's face. "What are you thinking?"

"Did you put your foot in the stirrup?"

"Well of course I did!"

"You know how racing people always use those very short leathers. They can't put their foot in the stirrup to mount. It's too high up."

"I know," said her mother. "They leap aboard, don't they? Jump up across the neck and then wriggle."

"Either that or they get given a leg-up – straight up into the saddle. Today could be the first time he's ever felt pressure on the stirrup, and the saddle shifting sideways a little bit."

Joan thought about it for a moment. "I'll still kill John. He should have reminded me that racing people are weird."

"What's he like?" Kate asked.

"John? Paddy O'Malley tells me that he's a bright boy and works hard. And I suspect he worries too much. But very nice to talk to."

"So did you solve the problem?"

"Mounting? Yes, eventually - after he had tried to do me grievous bodily harm. Only the grace of God saved me from landing on my backside." She gave Kate every detail of the contest.

"And how was he afterwards?"

"One thing I noticed - when he got upset, he was *really* upset. Sort of … 'Oh, dear, something's gone wrong! It's terrible, terrible, terrible!' He took it very seriously, and it was quite some time before he calmed down. Once I managed to get on him, I just rode him round the place for a little while and didn't do much." She thought for a moment and laughed. "Actually, he's had a pretty traumatic day."

After Joan had ridden Pone for a little while, she put him back in his box, and he started weaving again, as she expected he would. Joan then tacked up Dalesman, took him for a walk and a trot down the lane, and then spent twenty minutes in the manège, practising dressage. While they were in there, the pony stopped weaving, and watched.

When she had finished with Dalesman, she put a New Zealand rug on him, and turned him out in the field. This made the pony weave twice as hard as before.

Joan got a smaller rug from the tack room. Two minutes later the pony was turned out as well. Dalesman was grazing at the far end, under the wood. When he saw what was going on, he cantered back towards the gate.

The pony stood still. The big chestnut towered over him. Dalesman stuck out his head and sniffed; the pony sniffed back. Whereupon the chestnut giant stood up on his hind legs and began to spar. Then down. Then up again, and more sparring. The pony was horrified. He stood rooted to the spot. Then he picked a likely moment and galloped off as fast as he could, looking backwards all the time in case of pursuit.

"I'd completely forgotten," said Joan, "that Dalesman always used to box with that other pony ... what was its name?"

"Coriander."

"Coriander. Thank you. It was their game. But this poor creature had no idea what was going on. Anyway, Dalesman desisted after that, thank goodness. By the time I brought them in, they weren't exactly the best of chums, but they were almost grazing together."

Through the dusk came the regular beat of steel on concrete. The trauma of the day had had no effect on the pony's regrettable habit.

"Is Dad back tonight?" Kate asked.

"No. Not till Saturday. Let's just do the haynets and feed, and then I'll get you your tea."

CHAPTER TWENTY

The next morning Joan took her time over mounting the pony. She made certain he knew what was happening, what to expect, and when to expect it. He stood like a rock while she got on, and tossed his head in pleasure when she made much of him.

Joan emitted a sigh of relief and took him off for a walk and a trot down to the road. Wickham to the right, woodland to the left. They turned left. Two or three cars and a lorry passed them, and the pony didn't turn a hair. Half a mile down the road they turned left up a track into the woods, a track which curved gently left-handed and would bring them to the gate into the far end of Joan's field. Under the trees the dark brown leaf-mould lay thick, moist and bouncy, and Joan asked the pony to canter. He enjoyed stretching out across the dappled sunshine that filtered through the branches, and the way he moved pleased her. A pheasant clattered out of the undergrowth, complaining loudly, and he hardly shifted off course. Just the merest hip-switch and then on again. He stood still while she opened the gate. Once through it, he was most helpful when she asked him to walk it shut with his chest.

When they got back to base, she took him into the manège and did some simple schooling. They walked, trotted, and cantered round the arena; first one way, then the other, with figures-of-eight round the jumps and poles to relieve the monotony. Immediately Joan was impressed by the balanced way in which he moved.

His little ears were pricked as he set off on yet another left-handed circuit of the outer perimeter. He reached the end of the straight nearest to the boxes, began to turn to the left, and then stopped dead.

"Come on, little man," Joan encouraged him. No response. She clicked at him, and squeezed with her knees. The little ears went back, the neck twisted slightly to the left; she saw him watching her out of the corner of his eye. His eye wasn't nasty, just non-cooperative.

"Come on, little man," she said, and gave him a gentle kick in the ribs with both heels. His front end left the ground, as he resisted. It wasn't a full-blown rear, just a warning.

"Oh dear, oh dear!" said Joan. "I wonder what we can be thinking." In her right hand Joan carried a schooling whip; about three foot long, and very slender. Fibreglass shaft under a braided buff-coloured covering. The grip was dark brown suede.

She raised it and hit him twice hard, on his right hindquarter. Then switched hands and gave the left one the same treatment. The pony went straight up in the air, nearly fell, clattered down to earth, up again ... down again. Then he ran backwards until he hit the rails, bounced off, staggered, and stood shivering.

"Well, what a little swine we are – at times!" said Joan mildly. The pony stood still: tense, red-eyed, suddenly awash with sweat, waiting for the next move - so she did nothing; just sat on his back and thought about it, and looked at the red rim which she could just see in the corner of his eye. Then she twitched her right wrist and the end of the slender whip tapped the pony (more like a tickle, really) round the hocks.

He didn't respond by going forward - or by going up. He merely lashed out at it with one hind leg, and when it kept on tickling him, he gave it both barrels. But it didn't do any good, because Joan sat quiet as a mouse, saying, "Oh dear, what a silly little man!" and the stick kept tic-tic-tickling. Not enough provocation to make him lose his temper again, but irritating. And all the time she talked to him, pleasantly.

The minutes passed, and nothing changed very much: the occasional half-rear, the occasional kick, flying sand rattling off the fence, the friendly voice calling him a silly little man, and the inexorable whip, tickling. In the background, far away, life went on: rooks talked to each other high up in the woods as they repaired last year's nests. From higher still, the tiny warble of an invisible skylark. God's in his heaven, and all's well with the world – except in the manège.

After fifteen minutes Joan heard and felt a heartfelt sigh from her mount, and his neck relaxed. Then, without being asked, he walked forward. When she asked him to trot, he sighed again - and complied.

*

When Kate got back from school, Joan told her all about it.
"He really is a swine, you know."
"Poor Mum."

"Saturday tomorrow, unless I've lost count," said Joan, "you can ride him, and see what you think."

They were filling haynets in the barn. They gave one to Dropshot, the chestnut pony whose box looked out onto the back garden.

"Which reminds me, "Joan went on, "Mrs Perry's coming tomorrow, to see this chap do his stuff."

"Are you expecting problems?" said Kate.

"I'm sure he'll perform beautifully – for you. That may not be enough for Mrs Perry."

She patted the pony on the neck. "Still, that's not entirely your fault," she told him.

They took the other two haynets round to the other boxes. Kate looked into the first on the left, and said, "He's disappeared!"

"Follow me."

Dusk was falling as Joan led the way into the field and round to the front of the field-shelter. Double rails restricted traffic in and out to a four-foot gap that was secured by slip-rails. Peering out over the rails stood Dalesman, with a jute rug on. In the shadows at the back Kate made out the figure of the bay pony. Rugless, because he still had a thick winter coat. He walked over to the rails and looked at her; then reached out and nibbled at the haynet she was carrying. He looked tiny beside the big chestnut.

"I see," said Kate slowly, "and I don't notice any weaving. Could this be Mum being brilliant?"

"I thought it was worth a try. They seemed to get on well enough when they were turned out. No boxing today. They've been in here for an hour, and so far no weaving, no fighting; in fact I think they quite like each other. You hang his net up that end, and Dalesman can have his here. Good old man!" she said to the big horse. "You teach your new friend. Teach him how to behave!"

They fed the three horses and went indoors. After supper, they crept out into the yard and made their way under the stars past the chestnut pony and out to the back of the field shelter. From inside came the tug-tug and crunch-crunch-crunch of two sets of teeth making much of the hay. Of weaving there was no sound. Silently mother and daughter made their way back to the house.

CHAPTER TWENTY-ONE

After breakfast on Saturday morning Kate Ferris emerged from the house wearing dark blue jeans and light brown jodhpur boots; blue quilted body-warmer over a blue back-protector and a dark grey shirt; on her head a crash helmet, secured by a chin-strap and covered up by a red silk jockey-cap.

Mother had brought the new pony into the yard and tied him up in a box. Now, chatting quietly together, mother and daughter dressed him over and tacked him up, punctuating the conversation with compliments, endearments and caresses for the object of their attentions – and he seemed to enjoy the experience.

Then out into the manège, where mother Ferris stood at his head and daughter tightened the girths.

"What do you think, mum? Shall I jump up and wriggle? Or will you give me a leg-up?"

"Oh, I don't think so, dear. Neither. Remember, I was alone when I had my problem. Now he has me at his head, and we're quite relaxed – aren't we, little man? So just do the normal thing and all will be well."

"Here we go!" Kate put her left foot into the stirrup ever so quietly, rose into the air like thistledown and landed in the saddle as light as a feather. Before he knew what had happened, she was patting the pony's neck and paying him compliments – and to all intents and purposes he appeared to have no complaints whatsoever.

Now he was cantering, balanced and cooperative. Kate gave the signals with hand and thigh, and he curved away from the rail and across the middle of the arena, and then changed legs for her as he started to follow the far rail in the opposite direction. And on, and on – until Kate pulled him up where Joan was standing, and patted him on the neck.

"Feels really good, Mum. Really good."

"You seem to get on very well with him, dear. Fingers crossed!"

While Kate walked the pony round, Joan put up three sets of poles, about two-foot-six high. One halfway along each side of the enclosure, and the third between them, across the middle.

"Just pop over the outside ones."

Kate squeezed the pony into a trot. He came round the far end, saw the poles, cantered two strides and popped over.

"Good boy, good boy, steady," Kate murmured, and reined him back into a trot for the bend at the other end. Trot-trot-trot.... canter, canter, pop.

"And now the one in the middle," Joan instructed, and Kate turned him left up the middle, jumped the poles, then trotted round to the right and jumped the first obstacle the reverse way. As she came back to Joan she said quietly, "He's really good!"

Mother and daughter made a fuss of the pony, and he seemed pleased that they were pleased.

Joan said, "Pop over the one on the far side, then this one, and that'll do."

Kate trotted off, left-handed, the same way as she had started off originally. She turned into the far straight, cantered into the obstacle and popped, slowed to a trot, went into the bend – and the pony stopped dead.

She clicked, squeezed, and kicked, and the pony backed two paces and half-reared.

"Don't be soft," she said. The bay ears flickered.

"Come on," she said.

She kicked and squeezed some more. The pony tossed his head several times, lifting both his front feet off the ground. From halfway up the arena Joan watched and said nothing.

"Mum, shall I give him a crack?"

"No."

Joan strolled over to them.

"Get off him, dear. Lend me your crash-hat. Thank you. Hold him while I get on with my magic wand."

When Joan was in the saddle, with her slender schooling whip in her right hand, Kate said, "Do you want me to chase him?"

"Don't you dare," said Joan. "You'll frighten the life out of me – never mind him! No, you go and make us both a cup of coffee. Bring it out here."

"What are you going to do, Mum?"

"I'm going to sit here, very gently reminding him of his duty with this not-very-offensive weapon.... until something happens."

Joan liked real coffee freshly ground, so it was about fifteen minutes before Kate came back with two dark-brown steaming mugs. She was just in time to see the pony heave a great sigh and walk on, and then trot on, and then jump the jump on the other side of the arena.

"Well done, little man – wasn't that easy?" said Joan. She rode him round to where Kate was standing. They drank their coffee, and discussed the juvenile delinquent in very light-hearted terms, with a great deal of giggling, and the occasional shriek, and the juvenile delinquent didn't know what to make of it all.

*

At three-thirty that afternoon a purple Range-Rover pulled up outside the yard. Brownie went to the garden gate and peered at it; then growled emphatically and made for the back door to announce visitors. From the vehicle emerged Millicent Perry and her daughter Emerald. Dressed in an expensive-looking tweed trouser suit, mother Perry was petite and pink, with blue eyes and blonde hair, not one tendril of which was out of place. She opened the back of the car and swopped her shoes for a pair of green mini-Wellington boots.

Thirteen-year-old Emerald was a smaller version of her mother, and just as pretty – maybe even prettier. White shirt, blue Barbour jacket over her back-protector, dark blue breeches and black boots. She was carrying a crash-hat covered by a black-and-white check silk cap.

Together they made their way over to the chestnut pony's box. Dropshot was saddled and bridled. Joan was brushing out his long flaxen tail.

"Hello, Millicent. Hello, Emerald. How are you?"

"We're both very well, thank you," mother Perry replied. "And how's Dropshot? He looks very well – he really does. Do you think you've managed to sort him out?"

Joan heaved a sigh. "Nothing is simple in this life," she replied with a smile.

At that moment Kate came out of the house, crash-hat in hand. While she was greeting the visitors, Joan brought out Dropshot. Fourteen and a half hands high, bright chestnut, very handsome, his pale mane and tail made him look rather dashing.

Joan led him round to the manège, and the others followed.

"What I'd like to do," she said, "is to have Kate ride him first. We'll see how she gets on, and then we'll see Emerald ride him."

"It's no good to us if Kate can manage him," Millicent Perry protested. "I mean, it's Emerald he's got to go well for. Otherwise, you know… it's a complete…"

"I quite understand," Joan said lightly. "But I think we'll do it the way I suggest, just to give ourselves a general impression of the parameters within which we're working. Let's find out what he's capable of first, and then we can judge the rest of his performance against that."

Joan wasn't entirely sure what "parameters" were, so she concentrated on tightening the pony's girth, and holding him while Kate mounted. Then she came out of the arena and joined mother and daughter as they leaned over the rails.

The manège was laid out to offer four jumps. Two small arrangements of poles along the side nearest the field; a bigger spread of poles on the side nearest the boxes, and a similar one down the middle.

Kate loosened Dropshot up with a walk and a trot, twisting and turning to left and right, and he answered her signals easily and willingly. Then she asked him to canter and did a sequence of figures-of-eight. Finally, she returned to the walk, and made him stop and stand, and do various little drill sequences, which he seemed to understand very well.

"Jump the two on the far side," Joan said, "then the big one, then the far two again."

The chestnut pony set off, and popped the first, and popped the second. Then he cantered slowly round the far bend. As they came out of the bend Kate squeezed him into two long strides. No hesitation, no ambiguity. Two long strides will be fine, she was suggesting – and it was. Over the poles they floated. Then she eased him back and they hacked round the bend, and popped the two little ones again, before trotting over to where the watchers were standing.

"All right?" Joan asked.

"Fine," Kate said.

"Jump round again, and end up with the one in the middle."

Kate turned away and cantered off.

"You've no idea how jealous I am of Kate," Joan said.

"Oh, why's that?" mother Perry asked.

"She has this gift of being able to see a stride so early that she very seldom meets a fence wrong, because she's had time to adjust, if need be. I never know I'm wrong till it's too late to do anything about it!"

As she spoke the object of her envy had popped over the little ones and floated high above the bigger one. She then turned up the middle and cleared that one as well. There were no obvious signs of adjustment, but somehow the pony met all the jumps exactly as Joan had predicted.

Kate rode back to them, and dismounted.

Joan said, "Now then, Emerald. Up you get."

Emerald mounted and adjusted her leathers; she was shorter in the leg than Kate.

"Hold him together," said Joan quietly. "Squeeze him with your legs. Let him know you're there. Have a trot round, while you warm yourself up. When you're ready, just jump the outside ones."

As Emerald rode away, Joan's spirits sank; not that she didn't know what to expect, but seeing it straight after Kate was a bit depressing. Where Kate had looked like part of the machinery, Emerald seemed no more than a passenger – worse, a burden, loosely attached and all the more burdensome for that. They jumped the first all right, and the second; then took the bend, and faced the third. There the chestnut pony cocked his jaw and ran out into the middle of the arena, and Emerald raised her stick and started belabouring him.

"You see!" her mother snorted, her petite nostrils flaring with indignation. "He's as bad as ever! And you know he cost a fortune…I think Gavin must sue the chap who sold him to us! What on earth possessed him to…?"

"Emerald, stop doing that!" Joan raised her voice above the stream of complaints. "Stop it at once and bring him over here. On second thoughts, stop it and stay where you are!"

She ducked through the rails and walked over to where the pony stood. She put a hand on the rein, and looked up at Emerald's scarlet face.

"No need to go mad. One crack would have been enough," she said quietly. "One crack. On the backside. For being a bad boy. Understood? Now, what about you?" Joan's gaze was very direct, and Emerald had to look away. "Keep hold of his head, and use your legs, and _ride_ him."

She spoke very quietly, but with a certain emphasis. "Don't – just – sit - there – like – a – pudding! All right?" She smiled.

Emerald sniffed twice and nodded. Joan patted her knee. "Go on. Give it a go. Do it properly. It might work."

She went back to where Kate and Mrs Perry were standing. Emerald and Dropshot set off again; jumped the first, jumped the second, came round the bend with Emerald bouncing up and down and squeaking. "Go on! Go on! GO ON!"

The pony kept straight this time – and stopped dead at the take-off stride. Emerald flew over his head, and demolished the poles with a most impressive cartwheel.

"That pony's dangerous," her mother announced.

"Catch Dropshot," Joan said to Kate. She herself went and rescued Emerald, who was winded and tearful, but not damaged. Joan brought her back to the ringside, and made her and her mother watch Kate do two more faultless rounds on the pony. Then she offered them tea, which Mrs Perry refused. So she escorted them back to the Range-Rover.

"You see," she explained, "that is a very good pony. But it needs riding."

"Emerald's a very good rider," Mrs Perry responded stoutly.

"I am sure she was, while she was competing among the babies," Joan conceded, "and while she had a pony that did everything for her. But now she's moved up a class, and more is required. And she now has a pony that needs riding properly. Unless she realises that she has a lot to learn, she'll never be any good. And until her riding improves she will never ride that pony. He has no respect for her, so he does exactly what he likes."

Mother Perry informed Joan that the pony would be collected the next day, and the purple carriage departed, Emerald pale, tear-stained and silent, her mother a perfectly-turned-out example of high dudgeon.

"Poor Mum," said Kate, who had heard the end of the debate.

Joan shrugged. "I can't stop myself from telling the truth. It's a weakness – I must grow out of it. Never mind. Teatime?"

CHAPTER TWENTY-TWO

Literature was James Ferris's passion. If there was one thing he enjoyed more than discovering new writing talent, it was devising schemes for selling as many of their books as was humanly possible, and then several million more. It was with these two objects in mind that he travelled the world, and he seldom came back without having considerably boosted the share price and the reputation of the firm which employed him.

James Ferris had lived in England for twenty-five years, but the melodious tone of his voice still owed much to County Tipperary. There his parents (now advanced in years) had a small farm which James, Joan and Kate visited every year. It was his and Joan's firm intention to retire to this earthly paradise "one day", and in the meantime there were always a few horses on the farm to keep wife and daughter occupied during their visits.

His eyes were blue, and the fair hair that was beginning to thin out on the dome of his head had developed touches of grey distinction about his ears. He had the body of a prop-forward, and had once been in contention for the green jersey. It was only a very few years since he retired with honour from the "veterans" level of club rugby. It was all very well laying his body on the line for Newbury RUFC, but when it became a struggle to get back up again it was time to pass the torch to younger and suppler bodies.

Apart from literature, "wine, women and song" were his passions. His appetite for wine was there for the long haul, and well disciplined - he wanted to stay healthy. His respect for strong, attractive, intelligent women was typical of the Irish. His wife was a fine example of the brand and daughter Kate looked like taking after her. As for singing, he possessed an excellent baritone voice and was easily persuaded to let it rip. Father and daughter were both accomplished guitarists.

Although Irish, James was not a dedicated horseman. At weekends he would drive the horsebox, heave the bales and fill the buckets. He would offer a handkerchief, or even a shoulder, to cry on, but he never interfered with this strange religion which had possessed his wife and daughter.

On the evening of the day when Mrs Perry threw her tantrum, James Ferris sat in his chair in front of an idle fireplace, surrounded by his nearest and dearest, nursing a long Scotch and soda. He told of Paris on Monday, Rome on Wednesday, London Airport on Saturday afternoon, and, yes, it was very nice to be home. At his slippered feet the hairy sphinx that was Brownie gazed up at him with amber eyes which said how pleased she was to see him back. From time to time she rolled over and waved to him with all four paws.

"So... how's life?" James asked Kate.

"Mum's got this very odd new pony..."

"Pony? Pony? What about school?"

"Oh, that! I was in trouble with my physics, but I'm trying to do better," Kate replied. "Everything else is fine, dad, especially English. Oh, and I'm in the play."

"I should know what it is, but I've forgotten."

"Henry the Fifth. Shakespeare. Are you familiar?"

"I practically wrote it. Who are you?"

"Fluellen."

"A good-looking girl like you, playing a grubby Welsh coward – why?"

"I'm an actor," Kate replied loftily. "I disappear behind the mask of – in this case – a grubby Welsh coward."

"How's your Welsh?"

"Improv-ing," said Kate, in Welsh.

"Go on then. Let's hear what you can do!"

Kate's brow furrowed.

"Captain MacMorris, I think, look you, under your correction, there is not many of your nation..."

"Of my nation?" James broke in, in very passable Scottish. "Who talks of my nation?"

"Look you, if you take the matter otherwise than is meant, Captain MacMorris, peradventure I shall think you do not use me with that affability as in discretion you ought to use me, look you..."

At this point Kate ran out of words, and James was with some difficulty dissuaded from completing the scene on his own. Whereupon he questioned her closely about the whole of life's rich pageant, before allowing her to tell him about the new pony, and the weaving, the stopping, the rearing and the fact that they hadn't a clue what made him do what he did.

Then Joan took over, and told him about Mrs Perry and Emerald. This was a tale that called for a sedative, so Joan had a Scotch and James had a second to keep her company, and that helped the family to see the world in a more agreeable light.

*

On Sunday morning a small turquoise horsebox with chocolate trimmings stood outside the Ferris stables. The ramp was down. Up it the boy who had come with the driver led Dropshot. The ramp was raised and secured. Joan helped load rugs and tack into the compartment behind the driver. She was sorry to see the chestnut pony go. In a way, she was sorry to see Emerald go, because she wasn't a bad girl – but as long as mother Perry lived in a dream world there was no point in going on.

*

"Hi, Mum," Kate said on Tuesday night. "How was he today?"

"Really nice... one stop, and it only took a little while for him to get going again. No big sulk, no tantrum. And I must tell you - when I turned him out at lunchtime, Dalesman stood up on his hind legs for a spar, and the little fellow gave as good as he got. And when he'd had enough of boxing, he'd whip round; up would go his backside and he'd pretend to kick! I think they really like each other now... perhaps he's even feeling more at home.... and, touch wood, still no weaving since they started living together!"

*

"How was he, Mum?" Kate asked on Thursday.

"I don't know, I just do not know. He was good yesterday, and he was being good this morning. Jumped really well, and schooling on the flat lovely, perfect. Then suddenly the brakes went on. I thought, well, he's improving all the time and he's enjoying life in general, so he can take a bit of discipline and toe the line... we're friends, aren't we? So I gave him just one crack, not particularly hard, sort of 'Go on, you silly ass!' Well, my dear, he went absolutely potty, just like that, in a split second. Up in the air, spinning round, and running backwards into the rails."

"Oh dear…"

"Oh dear, in spades," Joan agreed. "It was so quick, and so intense. Sweating and shaking, and really, really upset. A bit angry, a bit bloody-minded, but most of all *upset*. And those eyes - all red round the rims. It took me ages to get him to relax and forget it, ages! After that, we did a little bit more, but then I stopped him, because I could feel he wasn't over it."

She sighed. "I don't know what sets him off, but he takes an awful lot out of himself when things go haywire. When I turned him out, Dalesman came over for a game, and the little fellow just mooched off by himself, looking really low."

She shook her head. "It would make life a lot easier if horses could talk. Have I said that before? Which reminds me – John Dunne and the O'Malleys are coming to supper next week. There'll be no shortage of talk that evening. It's Decision Time for young master Dunne."

CHAPTER TWENTY-THREE

In the middle of the oval table stood a silver fox on a black plinth, looking over its left shoulder, showing a lot of teeth. Had there been more room on that plinth, John Dunne speculated, no doubt several hounds would have been closing in.

"Now let's get down to business," Joan said, as Kate came back from the kitchen where she had deposited the last of the main course's plates and dishes.

"And no one's to start fighting till I give the word," added James.

He rose from his chair at the head of the table, opposite his wife, picked up the fuller of the two bottles of red wine and began to refill glasses, going round the table in a clockwise direction. First Judy O'Malley, then John Dunne, on one side, then Joan at the end. On the other side: a generous half-glass for Rachel O'Malley, a full one for her father, and another half-measure for Kate.

Joan waited till he had topped up his own glass and seated himself.

"It's perfectly simple," she began, "or rather, the first bit is perfectly simple." She looked across at Judy O'Malley, then Rachel, then Patrick.

"Patrick, you've always said that this animal was not suitable for any young rider, and certainly not suitable for Rachel."

He nodded. "I did, and I'm more than ever of that opinion."

"Well, you're quite right. This pony is very talented in every way. But he stops, he gets hysterical, he rears, he's dangerous. If by any chance we got him going, I cannot ever envisage being able to recommend him to a young rider with any confidence that he wouldn't... what do dedicated criminals do?"

"Re-offend?" James volunteered.

"Exactly.

"They are recidivists, and...."

"Thank you, dear," said Joan firmly. "We don't need any more. Re-offend is the concept we have to think about."

"Only trying to help," James muttered, rolling his eyes.

"If he improved and was sold and then re-offended, all I could say would be, 'Send him back to me and I'll try again'. And that's no good to anybody. And if he were to re-offend, who knows what damage he might do?"

A smile lit up Patrick's face. "Have you met your match, Joan? Has this slip of a pony got the better of you?"

His wife and the two girls combined to subject him to a volley of not-so-gentle abuse. When more wine had calmed the troubled waters, Joan said, "I'm not ready to admit defeat, Patrick, not quite yet, but for the moment I'm not winning the argument."

She paused, then fixed her gaze on John, who raised his glass and sipped nervously.

"As I say, John, he has bundles of ability, bundles! But he has this quirk...whatever it is... which really makes him quite useless, because you never know when he's going to have one of his... fits."

John nodded. "I know - from painful experience."

"Exactly. However, if you keep him with us for the summer, I might find out what makes him tick. I might get him going. In that case Kate would be ideal to ride him in Pony Club and Junior competitions, which would suit him. Kate likes him, she gets on with him, all things considered, and she's had a lot of experience for her age. It might work. In which case you might be able to sell him and come out of the deal with a profit. Might..."

"I would love to keep him with you, Mrs Ferris," John replied. "But I can't afford to keep a pony anywhere, except at Mr Fearnley's. There it costs me virtually nothing; it's a perk that goes with the job. Even the chance of a profit at the end of the road doesn't make the deal sensible for me. Too much of a gamble."

He saw Joan glance towards Patrick O'Malley, from whom she may have received a look which in some mysterious way confirmed that John was telling the truth, and was not trying to pull a fast one.

"But," John resumed, "I have a suggestion to make."

"Go on."

"If you think what I am going to say is a bit cheeky, just say so, and I'll forget it."

"Understood."

"I give you half the pony!"

Silence, while his words sank in.

"If you like the idea, half of him is yours," John resumed. "You keep him, you campaign him, you do what you like with him. If he learns how to behave and can do stuff that would help Kate's progress – perhaps that would justify his existence. But I don't pay a penny. I really can't afford it. If we end up selling him – which will be your decision - we split the money, fifty-fifty. On the other hand, if things don't go the right way, you can throw him back at me any time, and I'll be responsible for tidying up the mess. It's my mess."

John drew breath, relieved to have completed a speech which owed much to various conversations he had had with Rosemary during the previous week.

"It's not the worst idea I've ever heard," Joan said. "As of now he's worth nothing, so you're giving me half of nothing – as a present. Free. If I managed to perform a miracle and make him worth something... well, my nothing becomes an asset. If that happened, I might find myself quite pleased to be his half-owner. We'll certainly give the proposition some thought."

"And of course I must pay you for the month he's been here," said John.

She thought for a moment. "Let's leave that for the time being. If we take the half share, one might say that we've had him here on approval, allowing us to assess what sort of a proposition he represents. If we like the proposition, we could forget the month's keep. Which reminds me," she added, inconsequentially, "why did you tell me that he was all right to mount?"

"He was...he is... he should be..." John stammered. "He hadn't given me any trouble for months. What did he do?"

"The first time I tried to get on him, he went straight up in the air, all but knocked me on my backside, and then sprinted round me in ever-decreasing circles!"

"I told her," interposed Kate, "that racing people always jump up, or get a leg-up, so he wasn't used to the foot-in-the-stirrups-and-heave."

"You're quite right," John confirmed. He raised an apologetic hand. "Sorry about that, Mrs Ferris. I should have told you. I never thought." He paused and then pointed an accusing finger at Kate. "Hey! If you knew what was likely to happen, why didn't *you* warn your mother?"

Shock! Horror! Uproar! Then the light-hearted counter-attack was led by Patrick O'Malley. How dare John try to put the blame on an innocent schoolgirl whose mother was working her fingers to the bone to rectify mistakes for which John himself was solely responsible? John regretted and retracted, then apologised profusely to the Ferris ladies, who generously forgave him. Peace was restored and celebrated with another bottle of wine.

*

After the business came the music. It had been quite an experience, John reflected as he drove homewards alone – the O'Malleys were staying the night. Kate had produced one guitar, her father another. Some of the songs were familiar even to John. No one can spend any length of time in the racing community without picking up one or two Irish hymns of praise. As he drove, he began to sing.

"I love its cathedrals and cities,
Once founded by Patrick so true,
And I know that it bears in its bosom
The ashes of Brian Boru."

He fell silent and forced himself to look stern and respectable. He knew the importance of looking stern and respectable when driving home late at night with, by his standards, a skinful!

*

At about that time, over a thimbleful of brandy, Joan said, "Can we afford another horse that we have to finance ourselves?"

James thought about it, and then said, "How long will it take to find out if you can do anything with him?"

"A few months… a few months should give us a pretty good idea."

"An extra horse for a few months is not going to break the bank. I'll bail you out."

"Yes, but…"

"And if this pony went the right way," James continued, "how good might he be?"

"He's got a lot of talent,"

"There you are, then. If he goes the right way, you could end up making money. And you'll have another pony for Kate to ride. If she's serious about horses in the longer term, we want to give her all the help we can. One question…"

"What?"

"Would we be putting our daughter at risk?"

"What about me?"

"Our daughter and my beloved."

"Thank you, dear. I think it might just be all right. As long as we stick to the no-fights policy. Plus, Kate gets on really well with him."

"Give it a go," said James.

"What shall we call him?" said Joan.

"What does John call him?"

"Pone, if I remember rightly... short for Al Capone. The notorious Chicago gangster," Joan explained.

"Sounds like it suits him down to the ground! What about Alcapony? James suggested.

"Alcapony?"

"Yes. When he's bad he's Al Capone, gangster – through gritted teeth. When he's good he can be 'Alca-pony!' uttered in a tone overflowing with tenderness, forgiveness and good humour!"

CHAPTER TWENTY-FOUR

Skyline Drive (Skyline for short) was a big chestnut horse with a white blaze above his nose and two white feet in front. Four years old. Too immature to run at two or three, he had a rubber neck and no tolerance of restraint.

"How should I ride him?"

"Well, don't do what you did last time," said Harry.

The last time John Dunne had ridden Skyline, Harry had been a close observer – but not for long. They had started the gallop together, close against the boundary hedge of the Weyhill gallops, but before they had gone fifty yards the chestnut went clear and they didn't meet up again until the string was walking back home. Mr Fearnley was not best pleased with John and told him so. Ten days had passed since then, and they were walking down towards the derelict old starting gate which marked the beginning of the seven furlong gallop to do the same bit of work.

"How should I ride him?"

"When he gives his little buck and kick, don't grab hold of his head and try to strangle him. You can't win that game. Sit on your arse for two... three strides, play with his mouth, whistle a tune, talk to him. I'll wait for you. When you feel him relax ..."

"If...."

"*When* you feel him relax, you can drop your hands onto his withers, cock your dock, adopt the position, and prepare to have a good time. Watch his ears. If he starts paying attention to you, he might forget about breaking the world record for seven furlongs!"

"But he carted Jamie Kavanagh as well as me. Jamie's a big, strong lad."

"Yeah, but he's got no subtlety, no fin... something...."

"Finesse?"

Harry didn't answer. His mind was back in the here-and-now. "Are you ready?" he grunted

"Yes – as I'll ever be!"

Harry clicked gently with tongue in roof of mouth. His horse trotted on, and John sat on his arse as Skyline's buck and kick attempted to dislodge him. He began to talk in the plaintive tones of a suppliant and his eyes never left the flickering ears of the bouncing chestnut.

Skyline shook his head and then dropped it down towards his knees. He pranced off a bit sideways, but reasonably sedate. John dropped his hands onto the chestnut withers. He kept talking like mad and did his best to conceal his insecurity.

They hacked sideways up to where Harry was still trotting.

"Well done! Now you can ease yourself into the position, and off we go. Play with his mouth, don't fight him!"

John lifted his bottom from the saddle, balanced himself over the withers and off they went.

"Rubberdy-dubberdy-dubberdy-do!"

"Meaning?"

"It's just the rhythm that we're dancing to," Harry explained. "I want my beast, and yours, to know that I'm happy about it. And when I whistle" (he did so) "I keep to the beat. Must I teach you everything?"

"Yes," said John, chuckling. "Blimey!"

"What?"

"When I laughed, his ears did a double-take!"

"I'm not surprised. Laughing equals 'All's well.' Now let's do the business. Click-click, gently does it, and we move up a gear."

And they did, and John listened to the muffled beat of hooves on turf, and to the muted thump-thump of the bellows that powered the machines they were bestriding.

Now they topped the rise and were on a gentle downhill slope, striding over the green turf, every half furlong passing between the two white plastic markers that signposted the way they should go. One furlong, two furlongs, three... A gradual left wheel, camber dropping away to the right, which caused Skyline to nudge Harry's mount as he drifted off line before changing legs and balancing himself. Then the ground levelled out for a furlong before starting to rise again. As they passed the overgrown hedge on the left, the trainer came into view, standing beside his Range Rover, puffing at a small cigar and watching intently. Behind him they glimpsed the string of horses that had already galloped, quietly heading for home.

With a growling "Let's go!" Harry gave the order to make the horses work. Hands and heels applied the pressure, strides lengthened in response, eating up the ground for the last two furlongs, showing what the horses could do as they raced past the watcher.

With a "Whoa!" and a "Whoa! Whoa!" and a "Whoa! Whoa! Whoa!" they pulled up, without too much trouble, for the horses were familiar with the territory and the procedure. They walked back to Mr Fearnley. As they circled round him, he questioned Harry about the way the work had gone, all the time watching the horses' nostrils - blowing hard, then not so hard as they got their breath back. Eventually he dismissed them with a smile and a "That's better!" for John.

When the latter had recovered from that speechlessness which comes from an experience that has created amazing pleasure, he turned to Harry and said: "Do you think he'll ever ride out with us again?"

"The boss?"

"Yes. I thought he used to enjoy it. When I used to ride the pony..."

Harry nodded. "I know what you mean. Mind you, he's not a young man any more. Over sixty-five, I'm pretty certain. Another thing.... there's more horses in the yard than there was, and more horses mean more office work and stuff like that for the boss."

"I see."

"I asked him about it, must have been a year ago. He said that he can sit in that juggernaut watching the work and talk to his owners on his mobile. He can ring his own office from down here and discuss stuff with Mrs Stuart, while he's waiting for us." He paused. "But he admitted that breakfast after an hour in that motor was rubbish compared with breakfast after ninety minutes on a good sort of horse."

"I agree," said John. "It's the best meal in the world."

"There's a lot to be said for being workers rather than bosses, young John. And there's quite a lot to be said for the job you've done this morning - thanks entirely to my tuition. Don't you forget that!"

"I wouldn't dare!" John smiled. "What's that you're on?"

"Will Rogers."

"So that's Will Rogers." John had never ridden him. "He's been a bit of a dead loss, hasn't he?"

"Eleven years old. Hasn't won for seven years," said Harry. "Flat or jumping, he hates going racing. But he can work!" He paused, then pointed a threatening forefinger.

"I shouldn't have said that. Understood?"

"If you say so."

"Good lad. Let's trot on. We've got a bit of catching up to do."

CHAPTER TWENTY-FIVE

During the holidays, the riding of Alcapony, half of whom now belonged to the Ferris family, was shared between Kate and her mother. This was sensible, because one person, alone, might easily have given up. The pony would go well for weeks, until they began to believe that the miracle had been achieved. Dressage? He was like a happy dancer. Jumping round the manège? Effortless. Popping over the jumps they created through the woods? As if it was the greatest fun in the world.

Then suddenly for no reason - stop, resist, refuse! It appeared that his tolerance of discipline, even the mildest discipline, was strictly limited, so that he simply could not remain co-operative for any length of time. In that situation, someone to share the workload was essential.

Because they were a charitable family they gave him the benefit of the doubt as regards his name. As James had suggested, "Alcapone!" could be made to sound full of disgust, when he deserved it. But most of the time he was "Alca-pony", or "Little Man", or "Little Al", or just "Al", all four soubriquets employed as terms of endearment.

When he had his tantrums, there was very little anyone could do. Joan already knew that if they punished him he got really, really upset, and it had become obvious to her that the bolshiness was the least of her worries. The big, damaging, scarring problem was the fight that followed, if one allowed a fight to develop. So they didn't. Whenever he began to act up, his rider would sit still as a mouse, and just quietly tickle him up with the long slender schooling-whip. And in the end he would sigh, and plod on, like a deflated balloon.

In mitigation, it could be said that he was more upset by his own tantrums than Joan and Kate were; and he never bore a grudge or got any worse than he was in the beginning. But time passed, and the pattern remained the same - just marking time at a level which had bags of potential, but was of no immediate value. You don't win things or become more valuable if you have a hysterical fifteen minutes whenever the spirit moves you.

It helped that both Kate and her mother had plenty of other horse-work to distract them. A steady stream of riders of all ages, and their horses, descended on the stables for tuition each week. Joan and Kate taught the riders and schooled their mounts: their joint reputation for getting the best out of both had been quietly growing, in spite of the odd failure – as in the case of Mrs Perry and Dropshot.

As a form of investment Mother Ferris also liked to buy and "make" (educate) young horses, which she would cash in when she or her bank manager thought it appropriate.

Kate was an essential part of everything her mother did. She was also in great demand in her own right, as a rider. At an early age good judges had noticed that she was exceptionally talented, and as such highly desirable. Parents would ask if she would ride ponies that weren't going well for their own children, and dealers regularly requested her services because good performances meant higher prices.

So it was that, when Alcapony was really driving mother and daughter mad, they could thankfully turn him out for the day, and concentrate on other aspects of their equestrian interests. It was a good arrangement: it allowed all concerned to be patient – no pressure.

*

Not many miles away, pressure was very much in evidence.

"Just sign it!" said Mr Fearnley. He passed the pink form across his magnificent desk.

"Are you sure, sir?"

"Beyond the shadow of a doubt."

John signed.

"Thank you. That will go to the BHA with a letter from me, confirming that I wish you to be granted an amateur jockey's licence, and that I intend to give you a few rides on the flat."

"But..."

"Don't argue, John. In the last month, have you or have you not become number one jockey to Skyline Drive?"

"Yes, sir. Thanks to Harry, sir..."

"That's the way it goes in racing. If you listen and learn, and treat the right people with respect, you make progress, and you become useful. Now I want you to ride that horse in his first race. If you do well, and give him a nice introduction, it'll be another feather in your cap. That's all."

"I see, sir."

"He's an animal with too much character. He could go the wrong way if he takes against the game. So the first race is important. There is no need for him to have a hard time: just a pleasant introduction to travelling in a horsebox, the racecourse scene, the crowds and all the hustle and bustle. And more of the same during the race itself. He's been through the stalls here a couple of times. Harry rode him. I imagine he told you - he was very good."

"Yes, sir."

"Harry will tell you how to ride him, how to look after him, how to bring him back in one piece."

"Could he win?"

"No chance. First time out, fat as a pig, ridden by a debutant jockey. No chance. If he enjoys himself and does a clear round, and maybe beats a few - that'll be good enough."

"No pressure, sir?"

"Exactly."

*

Three weeks later, the evening before the race, John sought out Harry, and the latter went through the routine with him.

"When you walk into the changing room looking lost, one of the valets will introduce himself. It'll probably be Cyril that looks after me. The guv'nor will have told him to expect you. He'll see that you appear at the right place, at the right time, looking like a jockey!"

He then went through every stage in the race, emphasising the need to give Skyline a good first taste of competition; to relax him and get him to settle at a comfortable pace, to encourage him to enjoy himself.

"If you get that bit right, you'll have done a good job. If he's full of running at the business end of the race you can shorten up your reins, click with your tongue, give him a slap down the neck, and "Come on, my son!" Just like we do when we're riding work. See if he can run a bit. Late on - last three furlongs. Got it?"

"Thank you, Harry. I'm very grateful."

*

"Why are you biting your tongue?" Mr Fearnley inquired.

John's tongue disappeared. "It's the only way I can stop my teeth from chattering, sir."

"Shall I offer him a noggin?" asked the big American in the Panama hat, reaching for his inside pocket.

"Please don't, Homer," said Fearnley, "or they'll lock us up and the horse as well."

Homer Langhorne's hand resumed its "at ease" position. "Now listen to me, young man," he said. "You are here to have fun, riding my horse. This is not your funeral, nor are you about to be hung. Geddit?"

"Yes, sir. Thank you, sir. I'll try, sir."

The paddock at Kempton Park featured fifteen groups of "connections", each group containing a splash of colour in the shape of a jockey in black boots with mahogany tops, white breeches, a multicoloured jacket and cap, carrying a whip with which he might well be slapping his lower leg from time to time to show that he was confident and paying attention to what his owner and trainer were saying. None of the other riders was biting his tongue.

John's jacket was bright green with pale grey sleeves and cap. They had done sterling service in America, where Homer Langhorne was a considerable player in the racing world. They had also featured in England, where for the last several years he had entrusted two or three horses to his English second cousin, Richard Fearnley.

One of these was Skyline, who was to be seen, prancing happily with pricked ears, one of fifteen horses walking round the outer edge of the paddock, close to the racegoers who filled the three steps, or levels, designed to enable as many people as possible to see the runners. Each horse was led by a lad or lass, and some had two attendants. In the case of Skyline, Morgan strode out on his right and the lad on the end of the lead rein was Ken Hardy.

The race was over ten furlongs (a mile and a quarter). It was for 3, 4 and 5-year-olds which had never run on the flat, to be ridden by amateur riders. Such races were designed for big, backward babies, perhaps destined to become jumpers, perhaps simply so slow to mature that they had only just achieved sufficient strength and fitness to justify an exploratory outing on the racecourse. A few of the riders were also backward babies, but the majority were veterans of numerous point-to-points and steeplechases.

A bell rang. "Come along, John."

Fearnley led his jockey to where Skyline was waiting for them. Ken had removed the light sheet which had covered the saddle and the horse's loins, and stood at his head. The trainer checked the girths, tightened them one notch, and did the same to the surcingle.

At a glance from him, John stepped forward, gathered up the reins and raised his left foot behind him. A Fearnley hand took hold of his shin down by the ankle. He was lifted off the ground and landed gently on the saddle. He slipped his feet into the irons and gave Skyline a pat.

"Get him balanced, keep hold of his head, make him enjoy himself. Do not ask him for any sort of effort till you get to the three furlong pole, as you come into the straight. Understood?"

"Yessir, yessir!"

"On no account bite your tongue!"

"No, sir. I mean Yessir."

*

"Get him balanced," said Ken, as he led Skyline out of the paddock. "Get him to settle."

"Will he run away with me going down to the start?"

"No. He'll not know where he is. You watch – he'll canter off sweet as a nut. When you get down there, pay attention to the starter and his assistants. In the stalls, if you have to wait a bit, keep talking to him. Watch what's going on. When they're nearly all in, make sure he's facing his front, facing the gates. He doesn't want to be poking his head over the side when the gates open. When they open, you just concentrate on getting him balanced, and settled. Nice rhythm. Talk. Whistle a tune. If he travels well, you'll find yourself mid-div..."

"Mid-div?"

"Halfway down the field or thereabouts. Stay there. When you turn into the straight, you can ask him the question..."

"The question...?"

"See if he can go a bit, learn something about him. Hands and heels. Don't hit him, and don't expect too much. If he enjoys himself and comes back in one piece, the guv'nor and the owner will be chuffed. Good luck! And don't bite your tongue!"

*

Crash went the gates, and out flew the runners. John sat on his backside for the first stride, then up into the crouch with the second. Skylight felt bigger and more electric in his movements than he ever had on the gallops. But he wasn't pulling hard, just coasting along, with his ears going fifty to the dozen as he clocked the strange scene of which he was now a part. Ahead of him John saw four of his competitors. Two by two. White cap over a red jacket, alongside black jacket and blue cap next to the right-hand rails. Next came a wasp (yellow and black hoops) riding a bay upsides a grey horse sporting dark green and white stripes. Skylight was next, and between him and the rails was another grey, ridden by a black and red harlequin. John didn't dare look round, but he could hear lungs and hooves, ahead and behind, beating out the rhythm of the gallop.

They were approaching the end of the back straight when John was tempted – because Skyline was going so easily – to make a forward move. He had just started to whistle and edge to the left when the space he was edging into was filled as the front end of a horse moved up beside him and then forged past. Shocked, John resumed his place beside the grey.

A furlong later they went into the long right-hand bend that led into the home straight. John tried again, and again he was thwarted by the sudden appearance of a horse on his left hand side. It happened a third time as they started up the short home straight.

Surely it's my turn now, John said to himself. He risked a glance round. Nothing coming! Here we go! A little bit of left hand down and a double-click of the tongue; and at last Skyline was out in the clear. Ahead was a vast expanse of straight. Featuring in the right-hand part of that expanse seven horses were fighting for supremacy - and Skyline was closing the gap between him and them.

The three that had passed John paid the price for their impetuosity. They had gone too soon. Their riders were kicking and shoving, their whips flailed – to no avail. The beasts were "cooked" and Skyline overtook them as if they were standing still – which they nearly were.

Three lengths ahead, the original leading pair were being challenged by the two that had followed them into the straight. All four were under pressure – not because they were "cooked". They simply wanted to beat each other.

As the one furlong marker flashed past him, John suddenly remembered Ken's injunction – he must ask the question. Hands and heels. Don't hit him.

John shortened up the reins and double-clicked his tongue. Further encouragement proved unnecessary. Skyline became a Ferrari. His stride lengthened, his rhythm accelerated, and the three length gap reduced, and reduced, and reduced to such effect that he sailed up to the leaders, and passed the winning post half a length clear of the toiling quartet.

*

When John dismounted in the winner's enclosure, his knees very nearly gave way, and he had to cling on to the saddle for a moment. One of his borrowed lightweight boots had escaped from the elastic band that was meant to be supporting it just below the knee. The boot was now hanging round his ankle, revealing an expanse of skinny white shin.

"What on earth's the matter, boy?"

"Sorry, sir, but my knees jolly nearly gave way."

"Well, you must get fitter, mustn't you?"

"Give him a break, Richard," chipped in Mr Langhorne. "It was a masterly exhibition of the art of riding. Well done, young man, I'm delighted, and if my trainer is an old Grinch, well, that's his problem. Wonderful job, boy, wonderful!"

"You're quite right," said Fearnley. "John, you were masterly!"

"Well, I'm not sure about that, sir. You see.... "

"Enough of this chatter," Fearnley commanded. "Get that saddle off, and get weighed in. Victory is ours! Glory is ours, provided there are no slip-ups. Off you go!"

They watched him stagger away towards the weighing room, clutching the saddle, one boot up, one boot down.

*

That evening Rosemary came to supper in John's flat. In fact she brought the supper with her, in the shape of fish and chips. The domestic arrangements (a small Belling with one ring and an oven, plus the bathroom basin for washing up) were more than adequate. She insisted on kissing John, in his role as conquering hero. Happily success had not gone to his head.

"I tried to tell them the truth, but they wouldn't let me. They kept saying I was masterly."

"Well, you were. You won."

"Before the race, in the paddock, the guv'nor told me not to make a forward move until well into the last straight. I had three goes at it, long before the last straight, and each time I was stopped by someone charging past me. If I'd had my way, I would have challenged much too soon, and poor old Skyline would have fallen in a heap before we got to the finish... which is exactly what happened to the three that came past me."

"I see!" said Rosemary. Her eyes sparkled with laughter, and she raised a forefinger to her lips. "Just don't tell anybody. Your secret is safe with me, and I am going to spread the word that you were.... masterly! Give us another kiss, O masterly one!"

As they did the washing up she asked about the pony.

"I've not heard a word since we did the deal," he said. "I'm not going to bother them, while they're sizing him up and feeling their way. They'll let me know when there's any news."

He looked at his watch. "I think we should be down at the pub. I believe I'm going to be pumped full of alcohol if the lads get their way. I told you - this jockeying is a terrible mistake!"

CHAPTER TWENTY-SIX

The morning after John's triumph, Joan Ferris stood by the rail of the manège at Glebe Farm Cottage, gazing across the field. After a few minutes she spotted movement. The distant gate opened and closed as Kate rode Al into the field. He had done the circuit – down to the road, turn left, trot for half a mile, turn left again into the woods for a canter. Kate walked him across the field and Joan went round and opened the gate for them.

"What next, mum?"

"We'll turn him out."

"No more exercise?"

"That's enough for today."

"Are you sure?"

"Perfectly sure."

"What are you up to, Mum?"

"Tomorrow, we'll go show-jumping at Michelham."

"Really? How exciting!"

"He's been fairly good recently. Strange surroundings might surprise him into producing..."

"His best behaviour?"

"We shall see. I remember something Patrick O'Malley said at supper that night. It's not unknown for some racehorses to be bolshy at home and angels in public. Something like that. Maybe he knows something we don't. Don't tell him I said that, mind!"

"Never," said Kate with a smile.

"Anyway," said Joan, "we've cut short today's exercise before there was any chance of a tantrum. We want him to go to Michelham on good terms with himself and with us."

"I hope he doesn't understand every word we say," said Kate.

"I never thought of that," said her mother.

Both of them looked at Al in silence. To no purpose. He was giving nothing away.

At that moment James hove into sight between the buildings. He was carrying a newspaper.

"How about this then?"

"What, dear?"

"Kempton Park, 4 o'clock, 1st Skyline Drive (25-1) ridden by Mr J. Dunne. Isn't that John?"

"Trained Fearnley?" Joan queried.

"Trained Fearnley."

"That's John," said Joan. "Well done him! We must ring him tonight. Now tell me, James, is there any possibility that horses understand every word we say?"

*

Michelham Equestrian Centre had once been an aircraft hangar on the edge of a Second World War aerodrome. A gigantic grey turtle shell of steel and concrete, it sat a mile from an exit off the M4. When the RAF decamped, the authorities were delighted when the farmer on whose land it stood offered to take it off their hands. Since then it had assumed a number of roles. For several decades it provided a home for almost all the grit that treated the roads in the south of England. Global warming gradually took the icing off that particular cake and the owners turned in several different directions in order to make the structure financially viable. The most recent of these was its adaptation to equestrian uses.

Its concrete floor had been replaced by a deep carpet of wood chips, heavily rolled to provide a good, sound, springy surface. It was available for horse business of all sorts, in conjunction with local Pony Clubs, Riding Clubs and Hunt Committees. On Sunday afternoons it provided three hours of Clear Round jumping, over obstacles that were always attractive and never too big. The customers turned up, paid their £5 fee and were divided into a succession of classes. They waited their turn, and had a go. If they wanted to do more, they paid more and repeated the exercise. It was an experience which was good for young horses and ponies, and for their riders, without most of the pressure associated with more formal equestrian events. In addition, it was weatherproof.

*

At 2.30 the following afternoon James drove the horsebox slowly through the gate and on to the tarmac of the car-park. Nearer the imposing building, a variety of horses (ridden or led) were pacing to and fro on a wide strip of gravel. James parked among about thirty horseboxes and trailers of various shapes and sizes. The Ferris family left Alcapony and went over to the huge sliding doors into the building.

An office was tucked away in the corner on the right hand side. Straight ahead was a practice area, defined by wooden posts linked by white ropes, in which several horses were schooling on the flat and popping over two jumps. The wood-chip floor was light brown, with just a touch of pink. In the further left-hand corner of the practice area, a gap in the rope provided access to a buffer zone (twenty yards of bare woodchips), beyond which a small collecting-ring served the main arena, which occupied the rest of the building.

The main arena was fifty yards wide by eighty long. It contained a course of coloured jumps. There were three rows of seats up the two sides and along the far end, many of them empty. On a Sunday afternoon they were occupied almost entirely by participants and their camp-followers.

The Ferris team had arrived during an interval between sessions. The public address was announcing the numbers of the starters for the next class - the words echoed clearly off the high roof. The office was queue-free and in no time at all Alcapony was inscribed in Class F at approximately 3.15. Three refusals and out. A rosette for all clear rounds.

Mother and daughter sent James back to his newspaper in the horsebox. They crossed the practice area and the buffer zone and set off round the jumps in the arena beyond.

"In from the collecting-ring and turn right," said Kate, almost to herself. "Jump the rustic poles. Round to the left, along the straight, under the stands... two ... three strides to white pole over black barrels..."

"He's seen plenty of barrels," Joan said.

"One... two... three... four strides to a red and blue parallel... Then a little double of crossed poles, one stride in between... and left again under the Royal Box." Kate was fantasising a little bit. "Upright poles... quite big... it would be nice to meet them right... then steady, steady, and pop the little gate... left wheel again back towards the collecting-ring... red and black poles over tyres... then crossed rustic poles... very small... left again by the collecting-ring..... left again up the middle ... and the last is a small spread... three foot, is it, Mum?"

"Just about, and about three foot wide."

*

Alcapony stepped neatly down the ramp, and looked about him. Alert, inquisitive, unworried. Kate held him beside the box while Joan brushed him over and tacked him up. When horses trotted past behind him, he followed them out of the corner of his eye, but they didn't bother him.

When he was properly dressed, Joan held him while Kate mounted. On her head was her crash-hat with the red jockey cap. The number 4 on her back (black 4 on white card) stood out against the dark blue of her windcheater. She wore blue jeans and tan jodhpur boots.

The partnership went for a walk and a trot round the car-park, and Kate could feel that Al knew this was a bit of an adventure. Not for the first time she was aware of the way he moved. When he trotted, he floated.

She walked him over to the big doors, where her parents were waiting.

"Quarter of an hour," James said.

"I'd better let him have a feel of the wood chips."

She walked onto the artificial surface and waited for a reaction, but there wasn't one. Little did she know that Al was well accustomed to an artificial surface. She trotted off in a big circle round the practice area, threading her way through several other horses loosening up and popping over the trial jumps. Two strapping young ladies in trousers supervised and repaired. In the main ring, beyond the great divide, a class was coming to an end. Al viewed the scene with equanimity. He heard the thuds, the creaks, the jingles, the clatters, the chat, and didn't seem to object to any of it.

Kate walked him back to her parents.

"What now, Mum?"

"Pop the nearer of the jumps. Walk along the side of the main ring. Let him have a good look. Then jump the other one, and have another walk. Give him a chance to see the first two going round."

Off she went. Trot, trot, trot, canter, canter, lift-off! And when he landed he bucked.

"Steady, Al," Kate said. "Steady, steady, good little man!"

She walked him along the rope barrier, and he looked into the arena, taking it all in.

*

The Public Address announced the start of the class. In the collecting ring the first two competitors waited, one steady as a rock, the other sidling impatiently. Kate rode past them and turned. She waited behind two horses for a go at the second jump, and Al cleared it nicely. As she walked round again, the first competitor, a piebald pony, was just jumping the first rustic poles. Al stopped and pricked his ears, and Kate let him stand there. His head shifted as he followed the pony down the line on the right hand side, across the end, back up the left hand side, and then back up the middle. The piebald made the jumps look very small.

She took him for another circuit of the practice area, keeping her eye on the collecting-ring. When the bell rang and the second horse set off, she took another turn. Another clear round, and as the second horse came out Kate was in exactly the right place.

Number three went in, and Kate took his place in the collecting-ring. Number three was a large grey cob, ridden by a teenage boy wearing a white crash-hat. They went clear to the upright poles at the far end, where the grey refused. The boy gave him a crack, and sent him at it again. The grey blitzed through it, leaving destruction in his wake; did the same at the little gate, and refused thrice at the next. A klaxon sounded, and out of the ring he came.

It took some time for the ground-crew to reassemble the furniture. As the seconds passed, Alcapony began to sidle and dance, toss his head and hump his back. He seemed to understand that his moment was due… and he wanted to get on.

"Steady, little man," Kate whispered, stroking his neck.

Then "Off you go" the starter called, and Kate trotted Al into the arena. She trotted down the centre and then circled round to her left, checking out the fences and giving Al a look at them. Underneath her, he felt balanced and strong. The bell rang. Still trotting, she turned him towards the little rustic poles.

She clicked and squeezed him into a canter and his ears pricked as he lengthened his stride. They met the fence wrong, but it didn't matter. When Al thought he was near enough he launched himself and flew, floated back to earth and went on his way.

"Good little man!" said Kate, and steadied him into the left-hand bend. She saw they were "right" for the pole over the barrels, so she sat still and let him go in and jump: another effortless effort. He was relaxing now, and responded to the brakes when she asked him to balance himself before the red and black parallel. He cleared it easily, and then skipped neatly over the double of crossed poles.

Left at the far end. Once again Kate asked him to balance himself and pay attention to the upright white poles, and once again he listened to her. He was just as neat and tidy over the little gate.

Left wheel in perfect accord, and Kate was beginning to enjoy herself. Over the tyres they floated, and on to the crossed rustic poles. Easy! Left again… and then left again up the mid…

The steering locked, the power failed, the brakes were on. As the pony skidded to a halt, Kate burst out laughing.

"Alcapone!" she exclaimed. She watched the black ears flutter "thither and from" as he listened to her. "You are really bad! Bad! Bad! Unbelievably bad! In fact you're good for nothing!" But she said the last bit with just the hint of a smile in her voice.

Then she bowed to the imaginary Royal Box to signify the end of her five-pounds-worth, and rode out of the ring.

*

On the way home Joan said, "Can you think of any reason?"

"There was no excuse," Kate replied. "Unless… well, he did stand in that collecting ring rather a long time, while they repaired the course. Maybe it was a mistake to let him get his bearings - he had a good idea where the Exit was. So we go once round, nice as pie, and then, just as he's expecting me to pull him up and give him a kiss, I ask him to turn up the middle. Shock! Horror! Help! But at least we didn't have a fight. And it is just possible that he is now feeling a bit stupid."

The head that was making mincemeat of a haynet just behind her was registering hunger fortissimo, but not even a suggestion of embarrassment.

So nothing changed at Glebe Farm Cottage. Patience and laughter continued to be the keynote of the Ferris philosophy towards Alcapony, and there were days when it seemed that progress was being made. But there were also days when the message was different. On balance, however, the good times seemed to be lasting a little bit longer, and the crises seemed to blow over rather more quickly– all forgiven, friends again. At least all concerned were fond of each other. That was important.

CHAPTER TWENTY-SEVEN

"Tell me about Will Rogers?" said John.

A fortnight had passed since that glorious day at Kempton, and John's thoughts had wandered back to the conversation about the lead horse which hadn't won for seven years but could catch pigeons on the gallops. Harry had told him to keep the matter a secret, and he had complied, but he was eager for enlightenment.

They were alone, walking along a green lane after cantering at Weyhill. Skyline and Will Rogers, side by side but not too close. Skyline was still having an easy time after his race, and Will Rogers was there to keep him company. The rest of the string was a hundred yards ahead.

"Like I told you, going racing used to upset him so much he couldn't cope. By the time he got to the course he was a wreck. That was when I started looking after him. No one else wanted him, and I was curious to find out what made him tick. I'm a thinking jockey, you know."

"I had noticed."

"The old boy became a lead horse: When I wasn't riding work, I would sometimes lead the work on him, and at a certain point the serious horses would go about their business and leave us behind.

"The thing was, once he stopped racing he started to thrive, and his work improved. One day, I was talking to the guv'nor - after a bit of work – just him on his feet and me on Will. The others had set off for home.

" 'Guv'nor,' I said. 'How good were the three I was leading?'

'I think a lot of them, Harry. I'll be disappointed if they can't win good races in due course."

"So I said to the guv'nor, 'Will Rogers could have gone with them

116

when they went past us. He was cantering at the time.'

'Surely not?'

'Cross my heart, guv'nor!'

'He must have improved.'

'Exactly, sir. And it's only you and me know about it.'

'That's very interesting, Harry' (says the guv'nor) 'D'you know who owns him?'

'One of the Americans, sir? Mr Langhorne?'

'Yes. And he likes to have a bet.' "

John interrupted the flow of reminiscence. "The same chap that owns this fellow?" He gestured towards Skyline with a finger.

"Correct, young John!"

By the time they got back to the yard, John's education had taken a further leap in the right direction. He already knew that Mr Fearnley invested money on fancied horses for the benefit of his staff, on the understanding that they didn't broadcast vital information to the undeserving, thus ruining the odds. Usually these bets showed a profit, which was paid out to the staff at Christmas.

Now Harry explained that most yards (and Fearnley's was no exception) had one or two lads who wanted a little bit extra, and attempted to get it by feeding hot tips to "punters" in return for a share in any profit that might accrue. This might well ruin the price for the rest of the world.

"What about the owners of the horses?" John asked.

Good question, Harry had replied. The good trainer considered that betting owners were entitled to the best odds when they backed their horses. So the ideal arrangement would be an owner who possessed, not only a good horse to bet on, but also another, which would lead the good horse in its work, and which was so celebrated for being useless that nobody paid much attention to the gallops it took part in. Thus your good horse slips under the radar, and everybody is surprised when it wins – apart from Messrs Fearnley and Langhorne, and jockey Harry Bridger. That's the idea, anyway.

By this time they were filling haynets in an empty barn.

"You don't think Mr Langhorne backed Skyline at Kempton?"

"I'm sure he did."

"And Mr Fearnley?"

"Certainly. I did too!" said Harry.

"But you said he had no chance. And so did the boss. I'm glad I didn't know! I'd have died of nerves! Bloody hell!"

"There you are," said Harry. "What you don't know can't upset you. I was looking after you – so was the boss!"

A week later, John was summoned to Mr Fearnley's office.

"Ah, John, there you are!" said the trainer. He picked up a brown envelope from his desk and passed it over. "Well done. Mr Langhorne was highly delighted. Say nothing to anyone – apart from Harry, I suppose. Try not to spend it all at once."

Inside the envelope was £100. Five twenties. John took it round to the flat and looked for a secure resting place. The bottom drawer of his chest of drawers seemed promising. In it were a jumble of long johns and knee-length woollen socks for protection against the worst of the winter weather. Sometimes they were used several times, then put back in the drawer and forgotten – avoiding the visit to the laundry that might have been quite a good idea. He chose one of the socks, inserted the envelope and put the sock at the bottom of the heap.

CHAPTER TWENTY-EIGHT

"Everybody looks at me sideways," James Ferris complained one Friday evening, as he shared a drink with his better half.

Joan looked at him sideways.

" You see. Even you. You're as bad as…"

"I was trying to work out what on earth you were talking about."

"Maybe that's what they're all doing."

"Who all?"

"I go to feed the chickens... Six eggs tonight, by the way…"

"That's more like it."

"… come on, chuck-chucks… din-dins for chuck-chucks - and they all cock their heads on one side."

"I'm not surprised."

"I exchange words with the mad dog…"

He prodded Brownie with his foot, and she fixed him with her lunatic stare, her head tilted. "See what I mean?"

Joan laughed.

"I give Alcapony a pat on the neck and half a carrot. Does he take the carrot? He docs, but first he cocks his head like a chicken and eyes me almost with distrust. Why me? Am I not his friend in spite of everything?"

"I don't know about the chickens and Brownie," said Joan, "but I think I can explain Al. Once upon a time that little fellow somehow developed reservations about us - the human race."

"It's us that should have the reservations about him."

"I'm just telling you what I think he's thinking. He has reservations about us - misgivings, uncertainties. Anything we suggest is somehow suspect in his eyes. John had endless problems. I tend to think that perhaps he was the author of his own misfortunes, because he worried too much, and possibly sowed the seeds of uncertainty in poor Al's head. But maybe the beast had had problems before he got to John. We'll probably never know. So just keep giving him the carrots, dear!"

*

The following afternoon, Joan put down the telephone, left the house and walked through to the manège.

"Paragon can't get here," she announced.

"Oh, bugger."

"Really, Kate."

"Sorry, Mum."

Kate was sitting on Al, whom she had just brought home after a hack round the woods. His fresh summer coat glittered with wellbeing.

The manège had been cleared of the jumps and laid out for dressage. A rectangle, forty metres by twenty, had been defined by the lettered white oil drums in their correct positions: "A" at the centre of the short side to the right; "C" opposite, at the centre of the short side to the left; "K", "E" and "H" defined the long side nearest to the boxes, "M", "B" and "F" the long side nearest to the field. That was the framework within which the action would be contained. The very middle of a dressage arena is known as X, but there is no marker because it would interfere with traffic.

Paragon was the name of a pony Kate was due to ride the next day at nearby Addington. It was a Pony Club Combined Training event – just dressage and show jumping. Paragon was going to do the dressage, and the plan had been that Kate would have a practice on him this afternoon, to get to know him, and to rehearse the test. Paragon lived with his owners. Now a problem with their horsebox meant that he could not be delivered for the rehearsal. The Sunday arrangement, however, was still on.

"I spent all last night learning that test," Kate said. "It would have been nice to have had a run-through."

"Do it on him."

"What?"

"On Al," said her mother. She went round and opened the gate. "Where's the test?"

"In the tack-room."

When Joan got back with the printed sheet, Kate and Al were walking up to the start at the "A" marker.

As they set off, Kate commentated on their progress:

"Enter at A, working trot... at X, halt and salute...."

"Keep him straight," Joan reminded her.

"Proceed working trot... at C turn left.... change the rein......H...X....F... Where to now, mum?"

"A...K...E...H...C... working trot....between C and M canter right... "

From time to time Kate needed help, but mostly she knew the programme. Joan watched them as they went through the various figures. Not for the first time she noticed the harmony that seemed to exist between horse and rider.

It took less than five minutes from start to finish. It involved going over the same ground again and again. As it went on, Joan wondered whether constant repetition would eventually spark off one of Al's outbursts. He looked happy enough. Trouble was, he always looked happy enough, until it happened - whatever "it" might be.

For once there were no crossed wires. Kate rode back to the gate, patting Al's neck and stroking his ears all the way.

"Wasn't he good?"

"Perfect," Joan agreed.

"Hey, why don't we take him tomorrow?"

"Do we dare?"

"If I'm going to ride Paragon, I might as well ride Al too. A little easy dressage could be just what he's..."

"We could... It's not far. And we're going anyway..." Joan paused. "We could just do the dressage."

"Play it by ear?" Kate suggested. She patted Al's neck. "It's time you did something, beast. Isn't it?"

Alcapony's demeanour remained relaxed, correct – and, it has to be admitted, inscrutable.

CHAPTER TWENTY-NINE

Sunday morning found the Ferris horsebox parked under a row of trees that bisected a sloping green meadow – one among a long line of horse conveyances of every sort. Behind them, beyond the trees, was a car-park, and next to it a warm-up area, in which a dozen ponies were going about their business. Silent hooves, creak of leather, distant shouts, laughter, the thrum-thrum-thrum of engines. The dew was off the grass already and the sun shone; as it should, in early June.

Below the horseboxes was the Secretary's office (another horsebox), and a mobile canteen selling hot-dogs, egg and bacon sandwiches, tea and coffee.

Lower still, the ground levelled out. There were two dressage arenas, contained within low white boards and decorated by the lettered markers. There was a pony performing in each of them. A few spectators looked on. Outside each arena, behind the "A" marker, the judge sat in a car, judging. Beside the judge sat a "writer", recording scores and comments.

Fifty yards to the right of the dressage was a show-jumping course. A bay pony was methodically knocking down whatever got in its way.

Paragon was a bonny grey pony - neat, handsome and willing. The trouble was, he would buck every time he went round a bend or corner, and every time he changed gear.

He belonged to a Mr and Mrs Page, whose son John was constantly being fired into orbit by this exuberance. Not quite into orbit, in fact, but in that general direction. Compulsive and continual bucking plays havoc with a pony's dressage scores. That's why they had asked for Kate's services. Now, three Pages and Joan stood beside the relevant dressage arena and giggled uncharitably as they saw Kate suffering the identical indignities.

In the fullness of time her ordeal was over. She saluted the judge, and the pony bucked as they came out of the ring.

"I could kill him!" Kate whispered as she dismounted.

Joan smiled, the Pages sympathised. They all walked back to the Pages' newly mended horsebox, and de-tacked the pony. Joan looked at him. "He's quite fat," she said. "You might try cutting down his grub. Particularly on dressage days. Too much food can make horses – you know - hyperactive. And dressage is just a little bit repressive. Restrictive, anyway. Maybe they don't like that."

She walked round behind Paragon and gazed at him from that angle. Then she went up to his shoulder and ran a hand down his spine. As her fingers gently followed the line between his hindquarters, Paragon swished his tail.

"Was that a fly irritating him? Did anyone see a fly?" she murmured. Nobody had seen anything remotely like a fly. "Perhaps he's just ticklish, but on the other hand maybe something is pinching a nerve. Not necessarily hurting, but itchy enough to make him hump his back. Might be an idea to get a "back" man to have a look at him."

"Batman?" said Mr Page.

"B-A-C-K," Kate clarified.

"No supernatural powers?"

" 'Fraid not," said Joan. "But worthwhile, none the less. I know one or two.... But I'm only guessing. At this stage I really haven't a clue why he does what he does. All we have learnt is that it's not John's fault."

"Which makes me very happy," said John Page, giving Kate a grin that conveyed, "I know how you're feeling!"

They talked for a few more minutes. Then Paragon was boxed up and the Page family went in search of refreshments.

Joan looked at her watch as she and Kate walked back to base.

"Twenty past ten. What time's Al's dressage?"

"Eleven-o-five."

At the foot of a tree James Ferris and Brownie were guarding horse, horsebox, tack, picnic, and the Sunday Telegraph crossword. Joan and Kate unboxed Al and tacked him up. As Kate rode away to warm up, Joan followed them with her eye.

"Will he behave?"

"Of course he will," said James. In situations like this loyalty was paramount. Besides, his brain was busy thinking about a four-letter word beginning with "S" for "Prison can cause disturbance."

At six minutes past eleven o'clock, Al trotted into the arena. At the centre he stopped and stood quite still (and straight) while Kate saluted the judge. Then he trotted away. Track left, change rein, left wheel, diagonally across, trot, trot, trot, then left and left and canter. Then back to the trot, and up and down, and round and round in circles. Trot, trot, canter, canter, circle to the left, circle to the right.... On the sidelines, James and Joan stood and watched - with fingers crossed.

Finally Al turned down the centre line at the trot, changed down to a walk. Halted. Stood like a stone, straight as a ruler, while Kate saluted. Then they walked out of the arena. Just like that. Joan let out a long sigh.

James nudged her. "What did I tell you?"

"You never told me anything."

"You just don't listen, do you?"

Kate rode up to them. She dismounted and kissed Al on the nose. He didn't seem to mind. In fact, with ears pricked and steady gaze, he looked thoroughly pleased with life.

"Wasn't he great, Mum?"

"Did he ever feel as if he was going to explode?"

"Not once! In fact, the beast was showing off. Did you see the way he was pointing his toe as he trotted?"

They walked back to the box, and removed Al's saddle. Kate took the reins and let him have a pick of grass. Joan started unpacking the lunch basket.

"Hey, Mum."

"What?"

"Let's do the show-jumping."

"Do you think?"

"Why not? It's a very small course. And the entry fee covered both."

"Shouldn't we quit while we're in front?"

"He felt so... so good, Mum. Almost, almost as if he was keen to please."

"What do you think, James?"

James peered over the top of his newspaper.

"Go on, Dad, tell her!"

"Push your luck," he said with a smile. "Go for it!"

He pointed a finger at the munching pony.

"Don't let me down, little man!"

Al went on munching. One ear twitched, but that was in response to a fly. Possibly the same one that may or may not have caused Paragon to use his tail as a propeller.

Kate handed the reins to her mother and went to the Secretary's office. When she came back, she said: "Twelve noon, fifteen declared. Clear rounds jump off against the clock."

"Right," said Joan. "In for a penny, in for a pound. After what happened at Michelham, I think it's vital that you spend as little time as possible in the collecting-ring. Remember what you said? We don't want him to get wound up, and we don't want him knowing where the exit is, just in case that was what caused the trouble. So - we'd better get organised."

She made a few suggestions. James and Kate paid attention.

*

Major Rodney Stackpole wore a brown and black check tweed cap that matched his jacket, under which was a yellow suede waistcoat. His legs were a vision in beige cavalry twill, narrow cut, immaculately creased. Dark brown shoes glittered fiercely in the sunlight. As did his ginger moustache. As did his rather bloodshot blue eyes.

At twenty-five minutes to one o'clock, Major Stackpole looked at his list and called out, "Number 11, Kate Ferris and Alcapony, into the collecting-ring! Please!"

A pony came puffing out of the arena, and he sent the next one in. Then he consulted his list again and was preparing to make more noises, when his eyes lit on Joan, standing at the corner of his collecting-ring.

"Mrs Ferris!" he called over the backs of two ponies that were now waiting to perform. "Mrs Ferris, Kate should be here!"

Joan favoured him with a wide and enchanting smile. "Under no circumstances is Kate coming here until the last possible moment."

"Then I'll have to disqualify..."

"If she gets here too early, her pony will probably walk all over you!"

"But that's simply not..."

"Don't worry, Major. She will be here when you need her. Trust me!"

Major Stackpole glowered.

"On your head be it!"

Joan smiled again and transferred her gaze towards the ranks of horseboxes. Beyond, in a gap in the trees stood James. He waved at her. Beyond the trees she could see Kate warming up Al. She had jumped the low poles set up for practice purposes, and was now trotting round the perimeter. On the far side of the warm-up area stood young John Page. The signal, when it came, would go from Joan to James to Kate, if she was on the near side; or from Joan to James to John to Kate, if she was on the far side.

Major Stackpole sent another pony on its way. Kate was next but one.

Joan waved. James waved. John could be seen to be shouting. Kate steered Al left-handed. The partnership came trotting through the trees,

125

and changed down to a walk. Kate could see the pony in the ring finishing its round and coming out of the arena. She saw the next one (a grey) go in and start. She set off on a semicircular detour to waste a bit more time.

In due course the grey came to the last obstacle, cleared it, and headed for the exit. Major Stackpole looked at his list and scowled. His expression was still radiating irritation when Kate rode into his jurisdiction, smiled, and went straight on into the arena without stopping.

"Off you go!" Major Stackpole ordered grimly. This sort of thing made him feel redundant. Bad for discipline, too. Still, Kate Ferris did have a very jolly smile. And so did her mother. Fine looking woman. By Jove, yes!

CHAPTER THIRTY

The first fence was a confection of coloured poles. Alcapony half-hesitated, then lifted over with ease. The second was an upright. He cleared it by about a foot and Kate felt him take hold of the bit. "Good little man!" she said, and the dark ears signalled that he heard her. They turned left-handed into a line of three: a small spread, a white pole over black tyres, and a double over rustic poles. No problem. Left again at the top of the arena and over two little obstacles along the far end. Left again, into three fences down the left hand side. Still clear, still feeling good as they turned left ... *past the collecting ring.* Kate was praying that she wouldn't feel the dreaded sideways pull, dragging them off course, all systems dead... but Al had seen the fence in front of him and went for it, soared over, ears pricked, full of running.

"Brilliant!" said Kate. She had never felt so relieved in her life.

The next series of obstacles required one more left turn and then a succession of right turns as the course took them diagonally across the centre of the arena and then diagonally back in the opposite direction. Round the bends Al was as quick as a polo pony, his jumping remained faultless, and his determination never wavered.

When it was all over, Joan, James and the three Pages escorted pony and rider back to the horsebox. Kate slipped off Al's back. For a while she was speechless, but her smile said it all. The others were more effusive. Pats, strokes, kisses, and "Good little man!" many times over. All Al wanted was a chance to grab a mouthful of grass. He had just about managed it when real life intervened.

"Call it a day, or go in the jump-off?" Joan asked.

Kate thought about it for less than a second. "Let's have a go. We'll never have him in a better frame of mind."

"He'll be going into the same arena," Joan warned, "and he'll know his way around the second time. So there'll be plenty of provocation, if he feels like throwing a wobbly... I don't know what to..."

"It's against the clock," said Kate, who seemed oblivious to her mother's misgivings, "but I vote I just go for a clear round, without hurrying."

"Yes, of course," said Joan, doubt swept aside by her daughter's enthusiasm.

"Well done, Kate," said a voice. They looked round. It was Emerald Perry. Rather shy and a bit red in the face.

"Hello, Emerald, nice to see you. How are you?" said Joan.

"Very well, thank you, Mrs Ferris. Hello, Mr Ferris."

"Good to see you, Emerald!" said James and introduced her to the Pages.

"Have you got Dropshot here?" Joan asked.

"No. Actually that's what I wanted to talk to you about. Maybe later on, if you have the time?"

"Of course, dear. In a minute. As soon as we've sorted ourselves out."

"Did you notice the dressage scores?" Kate asked.

"Yes. That's why I said well done."

"What?"

"You were third."

"I don't believe it!"

Kate looked down at the handsome bay head, cropping turf beside her right boot.

"Alca-pony!" This formal address resonated with pride as well as affection. "Alca-pony! Third place. Not bad! Plus one clear round show jumping! What d'you think about that?"

"Munch, munch, munch!" seemed to say it all, as far as he was concerned.

In due course Joan took Emerald off with her. Her first port of call was Major Stackpole. She gave him yet another seductive smile, and thanked him for his help with an intensity that was almost gushing. By the time she had finished, he found he had agreed to extend the same latitude to Al for the jump-off.

This was over the same course, minus a few of the jumps, each of the remainder having been raised by several inches. There were seven clear rounds, and this time they went against the clock. So there was an element of urgency now which there hadn't been before: more kick and push into the jumps and away from them; the shortest possible line, and every corner cut to the bone. And those who overdid the speed paid the price, as flying poles earned them the appropriate penalties.

When Al's turn was imminent, even more sentries were posted. Joan at the collecting-ring, James under the trees, Emerald at one end of the warm-up area, John Page standing halfway along, and finally Kate, wherever she was. The timing again worked to perfection. As the previous contestant came out of the ring, Al was on his way in - no hanging about.

At the bell, Kate turned him towards the first obstacle, and clicked with her tongue. He cantered into it, measured his take-off and soared over. Unlike the opposition, Kate was in no hurry. All she wanted was for Al to enjoy himself. She let him stride along at his own pace.

They jumped the first circuit without fault, and then prepared to turn away from the exit. Once again Kate said a prayer, once again it was answered. Al showed no desire to down tools - on the contrary he went for the next obstacle as if he would eat it... and the next, and the next, and the next.

There were only four clear rounds, and Al was third fastest. Third in the dressage, plus third in the jumping – second place over all. More adulation. He took it in his stride, even though nothing like this had ever happened to him before. Nothing, not even an earthquake, was going to distract him from devouring as much of the grass as he could get hold of before the chattering classes returned him to solitary confinement in the horsebox, with only a haynet to comfort him.

*

"I'll tell you something, Mum," said Kate. James was driving, and Kate sat between her parents. "He must be pretty fast."

"Why do you say that?"

"We were going as steady as you like, and the first two only beat us by a few seconds. The other clears and those with four faults were all going for their lives."

"And?"

"Only a couple of them went faster than us, and, as I say, we could have gone much, much faster."

She contemplated the red rosette lying on the shelf below the windscreen. Two ribbons, hanging down, fluttered to the rhythm of the engine.

James said, "What did Emerald Perry want?"

"Very interesting," said Joan. "She asked if I would have Dropshot back, and could she come and stay for a bit, because she really, really wants to improve her riding. And dad will pay."

"Good for her," said James. "Good for dad. But what about mother?"

"Well, we went over and had a word with dad, who had brought her. He's called Gavin and he's rather nice. It sounds as though Emerald and dad have ganged up on Mum and given her a hard time. She wanted to get rid of the pony. They say it isn't the pony's fault, and they want to have another go."

"What did you say?"

"That I'd think it over." She glanced at Kate. "What do you think?"

"I like her a lot. She'd give anything to ride well. The trouble was, her Mum kept confusing her. Blaming the pony. Stirring up trouble."

"Stir," said James.

"Stir?" Kate asked.

"Four-letter word meaning prison can cause disturbance."

"Aren't you the clever one," said Joan.

That evening a phone line between Berkshire and Hampshire was red hot for about ten minutes. "Really? Wow! Terrific! Incredible!" This is a savage abridgement of what John Dunne had to say to Mrs Ferris, when he received the news that, for the first time ever, a certain bay pony with a bare patch on one knee had completed not just one, but two tasks on the same day (three if you count the jump-off) and had emerged smelling of roses.

Part Three

CHAPTER THIRTY-ONE

"What on earth do we do with him?" said Mr Fearnley. He beckoned to John to come into his office and sit down, then continued with the conversation he was having on the phone.

He was talking about Skyline Drive's three-year-old full brother, another flashy chestnut with the same white markings, called Shenandoah (Shen, for short). He was talking to his American cousin Homer Langhorne, the owner and breeder of both horses.

Shenandoah, who had outgrown his strength as a baby, had been "broken and ridden away" the previous autumn, as a two-year-old. The process had been incident-free. Since then he had devoted his life to inventing more and more ways of making a nuisance of himself: ask him to walk and he would dance; to trot, and he would buck; to canter, and he would leap sideways, park his head between his knees and attempt to bury his jockey. Perversity seemed to run in the family.

On a Thursday, when the horses had an easy day, the string would go for a good long trot along the road to Monxton. On the way back they would arrive at the top of the hill by the gate into the schooling field. The drill was to go into the field, past the fences and hurdles, and through the gap in the hedge into the lower field. All they had to do was walk down the slope to the gate which gave access to two hundred yards of road back to the stables. This detour was to avoid walking down a steep and slippery stretch of road. Simple? Not for Shen. As soon as he felt the downhill slope under his hooves, he would stop dead and rear: once, twice, three times, with a single pace forward between each elevation. Nothing particularly dangerous, because he seemed to know what he was doing, but there was no apparent reason for it, apart from sheer bloody-mindedness. Eventually he would capitulate and consent to go home. John had never ridden him, but had been watching his antics for some weeks.

Mr Fearnley replaced the receiver and stared out of the window. Then he turned back to John, "Any ideas?"

"About Shenandoah?"

"Yes."

"No, sir."

"Well you should have! He's full brother to your Skyline Drive. You should be full of ideas! That's why I invited you to come and talk to me."

"Can I have a day or two to think about it?"

That evening John sat at a table in the Bell Inn at Grately. Opposite him sat Bod, who tested the beer, then put down his glass with a smack of the lips and said, "Well?"

John told him about the conversation with Mr Fearnley. When he had finished, Bod said, "So this horse... he's a monkey?"

" Yes, that's exactly what he is... from a family of monkeys, judging by the way his full-brother used to be."

"And he seems to be bored by the routine?"

"That's all I could think of."

Bod glanced round the room. They were alone. He leant forward and spoke in a whisper.

"Don't ever repeat what I am about to tell you."

John nodded almost imperceptibly. Secrets seemed to have become part of his racing education.

"One good way of training racehorses involves a routine which is boring, on purpose. Most horses like it. The same routes, the same timetable, the same bits of work on the same days every week. Why does it work? Because sameness is reassuring, the horses don't get stirred up, they don't get upset, they know what to expect – no surprises. They don't come back to the yard with their eyes popping out of their heads. When they get home after exercise, all they can think of is their grub. They get stuck into their mangers and they lick the pot clean. You only get out of horses what you put into them – that's the saying. Within reason the work makes them hungry and the food makes them bigger, stronger and faster. Are you with me?"

John nodded.

"Mr Fearnley does it that way, the quiet way, and it suits the vast majority of his horses, which is why he is among the top trainers year after year." He paused, looked round again and lowered his voice still further. John leaned forward.

"But... he is not so good with the mavericks... the ones who don't conform. The ones who require something different. It's understandable..."

"It is?"

"If you have no money and you try to make a living training horses, you have cheap bad horses to work on, so you either learn all the tricks or you go out of business. The rich trainers don't get that experience. With well-bred, good class horses to train, with good lads to look after them and rich owners to replace them, they don't need it. So, most of their horses will thrive on the quiet routine, and the oddballs can be got rid of."

"So what should I suggest for Shen?" said John.

"Take him out of the string. Take him off on his own, maybe with an old jumper for company. Go somewhere different. Do something different."

"I could do that," said John, pensive. "I know a circuit which is very different from where the string normally goes... what else?"

"Challenge him. Test him... "

"Mr Fearnley?

"No, you fool! The horse. If he wants to be a smart-arse, give him a few problems to sort out. Something to think about."

"How?"

"You're worse than a rich man. You want it on a plate! Use your brain!"

"I could ask Ken..."

"I shouldn't. He's not best pleased with you since that business with the pony."

"I was forgetting. Harry, then?"

"That's more like it. But don't tell him what I said about Mr Fearnley. That's between you and me."

*

"About Shenandoah, sir..."

"I wish I hadn't asked." Mr Fearnley raised an apologetic hand. "Sorry, John, that was very rude. Go on..."

"I think he's bored, sir. And he hates being in a string of horses, sort of in a queue. He thinks he deserves more from life."

Fearnley snorted. John persisted.

"I think he finds life much too easy, because he's smart, and that's why he plays the fool. He might stop messing about if we made life a little bit more difficult for him. If we challenged him. As things are he's learning to say "No!" all the time, which can't be a good idea, can it, sir?"

"That bit makes sense. What are you suggesting?"

"Well, if Harry could ride him, sir - I've spoken to him and he's up for it - and I could ride one of the old jumpers.... be his nanny, his escort. A few weeks of special treatment, no queuing up, away from everything to do with the normal routine ..."

"And what are the challenges you're going to confront him with?"

"We'll work something out, sir. Harry will think of something."

Fearnley frowned and gave two thoughtful grunts.

"Worth a try... He's certainly not doing himself any good as things are – that's very true. But no stupidities," he added, "as in the case of that bloody pony... I don't want anybody getting hurt."

"That's why I want Harry, sir. If I come up with anything stupid, he will say no."

"Good thinking, John. How long?"

"A month, sir?"

"Do it! Start on Monday."

*

On the Monday of the third week in July, after breakfast, the experiment began. Ten minutes before second lot pulled out, Harry Bridger was legged up on Shenandoah, and John on Troy (King of Troy, to give him his full name), the winner of eleven steeplechases, and due to be retired at the end of the upcoming jump season. The duo set off along the Shipley Road. They walked past the small all-weather, and then trotted up the road which climbed steadily. When it levelled off, they walked.

"Well?" John asked.

"So far so good," said Harry. "This fellow appreciated not having to hang about in the yard while second lot was forming up. That's what usually starts off his nonsense."

When they got to the lane that led to the Appleton gallops, they turned in and walked beside the big all-weather until it curved to the left. On the other side of the track was the old gate on to the downland. It was open. John pointed.

"Is that our route?" Harry asked.

"Yes," said John.

"The other day I noticed the gate had been cleaned up."

"I did it for the pony."

John led the way across the track and through the gate.

"OK?" he said.

"Better shut the gate," said Harry.

"I'll drive up later."

"Not good enough."

Harry jumped off and shut the gate with one hand while holding Shen with the other. John held his breath and waited for disaster, but the horse didn't turn a hair. Job done, Harry led Shen to where Troy was standing, stood him facing John's knee and was back in the saddle like lightning – so smooth that his mount hardly noticed.

"Well done," said John.

"If we'd left that gate open, and one of the others got loose up here and went through it and died a terrible death on this dangerous mountainside, who would get the blame?"

"Me?"

"You see?" said Harry. "I'm looking after you! What now?"

"We trot, trot, trot up this dangerous mountainside. When you feel like, come upsides – the track's wide enough, isn't it?"

"Yes. OK, let's go."

They climbed steadily across the hillside on the drovers' road (going in the opposite direction to the one John had originally followed on Pone). The stiff slope soon had the horses blowing hard. After a bit, Harry brought Shen alongside.

"Look at that," he said, nodding to the right. A hundred yards below them, second lot had arrived and was cantering in line astern, well spread out, along the all-weather.

"What a sight!" said John.

"What about this fellow," Harry replied. John switched his gaze to the chestnut head bobbing along beside him. The ears were pricked, the neck was arched, and every few strides Shen was glancing at the horses down below.

"What's he thinking?"

"This is the life, and those poor bastards don't know what they're missing!" said Harry. "Something like that?"

When they reached the top they walked along the crest of the hill. Lapwings rose into the sky with melancholy cries to greet them. Sheep raised silent heads and stared. John explained how he had found this area when he had been preparing Pone for his visit to Mrs Ferris.

They followed the track down to the "isolation" boxes, then turned round and trotted back up to the top again. Second lot had cantered back along the all-weather and gone home. They walked down to the gate, which Harry dealt with. No problem.

The change of routine went well for the next three days, and on the Friday they sallied forth along the same route – but only up to a point. When they got to the lane to the gallops, they ignored it. They took the next right turn, passed the isolation boxes and the paddocks, then negotiated the gate onto the open downland.

Instead of taking the right-hand drovers' road across the hillside, they kept going along a narrower track that led straight up the hill. A little jog until it got too steep, and then a steady walk. At the top they paused and took in the view. This wasn't really "big" country, but big enough to make quite large pylons seem fairly insignificant. Down below was the beginning of the Ministry of Defence's Salisbury Plain estate. Mother Nature and the Military held sway for miles in every direction and seemed to enjoy each other's company. From time to time they hoisted red flags and made loud noises, but the real enemy, Man in large numbers, was kept at arm's length.

Fifty yards further on, the track began to slope steeply downwards and the gallops came into view below. Immediately below them was the western end of the all-weather. At this point they were walking downhill side by side, both keeping hold of their horses' heads and reminding them to be careful where they put their feet – because the ground was steep and the going a bit loose – flints and chalk breaking through the turf, treacherous at the best of times.

When they reached the bottom, Harry patted Shen on the neck.

"Not bad, eh?" he said.

"Not bad at all!" agreed John.

It was a small thing, but possibly significant. Shenandoah had never previously consented to walk down a steep slope without using it as an excuse to make a fuss, a drama, a song and dance. So his behaviour on this occasion was interesting... Time would tell.

CHAPTER THIRTY-TWO

"Damned good for the character!" muttered Major Stackpole, twirling the ends of his ginger moustache between fingers and thumbs. Major Stackpole, like many a retired soldier before and since, was seldom idle. Acting as starter at Addington had been a minor item on his agenda. Far more important were his responsibilities on the first of August as Chief Steward of the Hucklebury Pony Club Combined Training Competition. Major Stackpole was proud of the fact that, under his direction, Hucklebury had become one of the best of its kind in the South of England. This year the programme included Cross-Country, as well as Dressage and Show-jumping.

Like a latter day Wellington, Stackpole surveyed his battlefield, which was a hive of activity at least as busy as Waterloo, if not more so: two dressage arenas, one show-jumping ring, all three in full swing. On the far side occasional glimpses of galloping ponies, and the intermittent sound of whistles, as competitors progressed round the cross-country course and jaywalkers were encouraged to jump for cover.

Major Stackpole adjusted his gaze downwards towards Mrs Sweeny, who sat at a trestle table outside the horsebox which was the Chief Steward's office. In front of her were entry-forms, schedules, dressage test sheets, and number cloths, all anchored to the table by terracotta bathroom tiles. Beside her chair, supported by boxes and leaning up against the horsebox, were two large blackboards on which were inscribed the names of competitors and their scores in the various sections of the event.

Mrs Sweeny was black-haired and sharp-eyed. Organising was her speciality, equestrian events her passion, and Major Stackpole of the ginger moustache and the cavalry twills the object of her intense admiration. Her tweed jacket hung from the back of her chair; her white short-sleeved shirt shone in the sunlight. She had capable arms and plenty of heart room.

"Good day for it, what?" said the Major.

"Isn't it just, Major."

"Plenty of entries."

"Even more than last year."

"Some damn good young riders."

Mrs Sweeny agreed, and reeled off a list of names.

"... and of course there's Kate Ferris." She looked at a list. "Riding something called Alcapony."

"Yeee-ss," said the Major slowly. He frowned. "Hard to know what to think, really."

"How d'you mean, Major?

"She's won this event the last two years."

"Awfully good, isn't she?"

"I'm not sure…" the Major revealed solemnly, "…that it's good for a young person to win things too often. Can be bad for the…"

"Character?" Mrs Sweeny hazarded.

"Exactly!"

*

At about that moment Alcapony was completing an excellent dressage test with his pale pink tongue hanging out of the left-hand side of his mouth. To the rhythm of the trot, it flapped; when he cantered, it swung; when he walked, its movement was imperceptible. He was walking now, on the way back to the horsebox, with Joan at his head and Kate on top.

"Did you see his tongue?" Joan asked.

"Yes."

"How long has he been doing it?"

"Just this last week."

"Why's he doing it?"

"No idea. Is it bad?" Kate asked.

"I don't think so," her mother replied. "But some judges are funny about it. They call it 'Resistance' and you get penalised."

"He certainly wasn't resisting," Kate said. "I think it's a sign that he's getting more and more relaxed."

"Try convincing judges," said Joan darkly. "We may have to play about with a noseband."

"Whatever you say, mother," Kate replied, and she gave the bay neck a gentle pat. Since Addington, Al had taken part in four more competitions of various sorts, and had performed well, with no tantrums. And the same could be said of the team which followed him across the south of England, shepherding him down to the start of the various disciplines as late as possible, but not late enough to be disqualified.

A hundred yards to the west, Emerald Perry rode Dropshot in the practice area. She and Dropshot had only been back at Glebe Farm Cottage for three weeks and the signs were encouraging. They had done quite a good dressage, and were soon to set off on the cross-country course. Emerald turned her pony in towards one of the jumps, an inviting little obstacle consisting of three rustic poles, the bottom one providing a ground-line, the top one not more than two-foot-six-inches high.

Dropshot cantered prettily towards it and stopped. Even before he had ground to a halt, two black leather boot-heels crunched his ribs, and a pair of vengeful knees were all but squeezing the life out of him. At the same time out of the corner of his eye he caught a glimpse of a stick twirling into the offensive position before descending on his right hindquarter. Crack!

Dropshot leapt forward from a standstill, and took all three rustic poles with him. He stayed on his feet on the other side, but only just. Above the clatter of falling timber he heard a stream of low-pitched and quite adult vitriol emerging from the mouth of his young rider. Dropshot was shocked to the core. He had forgotten that Emerald was no longer to be trifled with.

She rode him away, after apologising to the boy whose job it was to repair the damage - partly for destroying the jump, and partly for her language. Then she circled round and approached again. Dropshot jumped it perfectly. Emerald was generous with her congratulations. Dropshot couldn't quite understand what it all meant, but he reckoned he had better be careful.

"Well done," said the boy.

Emerald grinned.

When her turn came, she took Dropshot round the cross-country course slowly and carefully, and Dropshot jumped every fence, without even the semblance of an attempt to stop or deviate. The combination picked up time faults, which did nothing to detract from Emerald's delight. Ecstatic is not too extravagant a word to describe her mood.

*

"Don't hurry," said Joan.

Kate nodded. She rode Al into the starting pen for the cross country. The members of her escort held their breath.

"Five ... four ... three ... two ... one ... Go!" said the starter, and Kate clicked Al into a canter.

"Good little man," she said as they approached quite a solid log. Al looked at it carefully, then jumped high over the top. He landed on springy turf, moved on, felt a hand patting his neck, and began to enjoy himself. The size of the obstacles didn't bother him, and his rider seemed to have no doubt that this was rather fun and not at all hazardous, so let's enjoy... Every time they approached an obstacle Kate's voice would say, "Steady, now!" or "Concentrate!" or "On we go!" and on they went. There was also a fair amount of "Good little man!" in a tone of voice which did no harm at all to Al's morale.

After a bit, Kate let him stride on a little faster. Once or twice he came into a fence all wrong, and an adjustment had to be made fast and late; which he achieved, quick as a cat, and his confidence grew.

Steady progress on good ground, on a flat track that wasn't very tiring. And the not-so-easy jumps gave him a chance to show how smart he was. This, Al decided, was all right; in fact, maybe better than all right. It was almost too soon when he found himself going through the finish line.

"Whoa! Whoa, little man! Good little man!" Al changed down to a trot, then a walk, and felt her hand on the left side of his neck. He was hardly blowing.

Kate looked at her watch and turned in the saddle.

"Was I all right for time?" she called.

"Yes, well inside," replied the lady who was checking the finishers. Kate patted Al's neck some more as they walked off towards the horsebox.

*

"What about that, then?" said the man, pointing. He was fair-haired, thinning on top, grey round the edges, and solidly built. Major Stackpole followed the line of the pointing finger. His eye scanned the nearer of the two scoreboards, now full of figures as the event moved towards its close.

"What about what?" he responded stiffly.

"Number 26, Alcapony, rider Kate Ferris, Dressage: 16 penalties, Show Jumping: Zero penalties, Cross Country: No Jumping Penalties, but..."

"But 20 penalties for being over the time allowed," Major Stackpole completed the sentence.

"She wasn't over the time allowed," said the man. At his side, on a lead, an Irish Water Spaniel cocked her head and favoured Major Stackpole with a demented look that might be misinterpreted as hostile.

Major Stackpole chuckled. "I assure you, my dear chap, that we don't make mistakes." He looked fondly at Mrs Sweeny. "Been at the game a long time, haven't we?"

"Indeed, Major," she confirmed with a roguish smile. She loved watching the Major dealing with lesser mortals.

The fair-haired lesser mortal said, "Number 26 tells me she had no Time Faults. The Timekeeper told her she had no Time Faults."

He pointed to a sheaf of papers. "There are the sheets from the Timekeepers. Do me a favour and check what they say about number 26, there's a good fellow."

Major Stackpole drew himself up to his full height, which was not all that full. He didn't enjoy being labelled a "good fellow" by a chap who wasn't wearing a jacket. On the other hand, his full height did not allow him to look down on the complainant, and the chap's forearms were distinctly robust. And that dog...

*

"Well, I'm amazed!" Major Stackpole announced, when the error had been identified and corrected. "I've never known anything like it. It's very, very unusual indeed for Mrs Sweeny to make a mistake. Isn't it, Mrs Sweeny?"

"Very, very unusual", agreed Mrs Sweeny, through gritted teeth. Her tension was caused by inner turmoil. On the one hand she wished to be loyal to her leader; on the other, she was tempted, sorely tempted, to remind him that *he* had been responsible for recording Time Faults.

*

Before Al's show-jumping, the usual precautions were deployed. The starter was a friend of Joan's, which made things easier, and the system worked well. Al was a model of calm decorum as he walked into the ring, viewed the obstacles, waited for the bell and did the clear round which was all that was required.

Late in the afternoon, outside the Chief Steward's horsebox a semicircle of well-trodden turf had developed round the trestle table. Beyond it stood a multitude of parents, children, and camp-followers.

With the aid of a megaphone Major Stackpole called up the prize-winners, who received their rosettes and trophies from a handsome blonde lady packed solidly into a green tweed suit. Very small children went up first; the smaller they were, the more the gallery applauded. They were followed by their elders, class by class.

"... and finally, the over-all winner of the Combined Training Competition, Mrs Joan Ferris's Alcapony, ridden by Kate Ferris – Kate winning this particular competition for the third year in succession! Well done, Kate!"

Kate stepped forward, the blonde lady congratulated her, Mrs Sweeny joined in the applause, and so did Major Stackpole. He just hoped Kate Ferris's character could stand all this success at such a tender age.

*

The shadows were beginning to lengthen. Most of the cars and many of the horseboxes had left. Under the trees beside the Ferris horsebox the family and Emerald Perry sat on the grass.

Dropshot had done a reasonable dressage, had gone clear (apart from time faults) across country, and had had only one show-jump down. It was the first time that rider and pony had achieved respectability, after two years of trauma, despair and a home life riven by discord. Emerald reckoned she was in Heaven.

The side ramp was down. In his stall Dropshot was steadily converting his supply of fibrous nutrient. Beside him Al, leaning over the partition, was peering out round his haynet.

"Do you think he's a reformed character, Mum?"

Joan smiled. "I doubt it."

Kate picked up a silver tankard and waved it under Al's nose.

"You won this, and you never put a foot wrong. Tell her you've seen the light."

Al cocked his head on one side. His ears pricked. He looked down at Kate with steady eyes.

"I wish I knew what goes on inside that little head," said Joan.

"Talking of which," James said, "what about that Major Stackpole, then?"

"What about him?" Joan asked.

"The Phantom Time Faults ... Why d'you think he...?"

"You're not suggesting he did it on purpose, are you?"

"I wouldn't be at all surprised. There's something about that man..."

"Daddy, really!" said Kate. "You cannot be serious!"

"Can I not?" said her father, darkly. An occasional tendency towards the dark side was something that he had caught from his wife early in their marriage.

*

That night, after the girls had gone to bed, Joan wandered out to the yard with Brownie. It was warm and still, and the high heavens glittered merrily. "The silence, the shine and the size, of the high, unexpressible skies," she murmured. Brownie went off on patrol, while Joan checked Dropshot's hay and water. Then she went out to the field-shelter. Dalesman heard her step and peered round to greet her. She rubbed his nose. Then from the shadows at the back of the shed came a soft musical nicker (a sort of muted version of a neigh) and the straw creaked as Al came across. He pushed against her arm with his nose.

She gave them each a Polo, and checked their hay and water. Then Brownie collected her and they went back indoors.

"He spoke to me," she said to James.

"Who?"

"Al. It's the first time ever."

"What did he say?"

"Sort of 'Hello, friend. Nice to see you.' "

"Do you think he means it?"

"Hope springs eternal."

In more immediate terms, Joan watched and waited for the flapping tongue to reappear, so that she could experiment with nosebands, but it turned out to be a one-week wonder. It never appeared again, and no explanation for the phenomenon was ever supplied by any of the several experts she consulted on the subject.

CHAPTER THIRTY-THREE

Ten days after the mighty Shen abseiled down a steep slope without turning it into an argument, John knocked on the door of Mr Fearnley's office and went in.

""Sorry to bother you, sir. It's about Shenandoah..."

"Have you killed him already?"

"No, sir. He's been going well. We want to start jumping him."

"What?"

"Harry's idea. Poles, and loose school.... something new. 'Get on with it and do as you're told' – that's how Harry describes it. 'He won't know what's hit him at first' - that's another quote from Harry. I thought I'd better double-check with you before...."

Fearnley reflected for all of ten seconds.

"So this is the challenge, is it?"

"Yessir."

"If Harry's in favour, so be it! You'll have to explain to Mr Langhorne if you mess up!"

*

The following day, when he returned from exercise over hill and dale, the mighty Shenandoah discovered that more was required. Wearing "boots" to protect his front tendons, he was lunged by Harry over a pole on the ground, and then a pole off the ground, which he kicked out of his way the first time, but not the second.

Next he was allowed to watch a rider-less King of Troy perform in the loose school before being asked to follow suit. Did he go mad? He did not. With minimal encouragement (two cheerfully clicking tongues and a prodigious growl from Harry) he trotted towards a monstrous obstacle (a pole ten inches from the ground with another lying on the surface a foot in front of it). As he approached this impediment his neck bent, his ears pricked and his eyes were fixed on the challenge. Pop! And over he went. He trotted round to the other side and repeated the performance. Immediately, unmistakably, this was a sober student concentrating, concentrating on the job in hand – quite different from the beast he had been all his life up to this "Eureka" moment!

Over the next few days he was good without a rider and even better when Harry was on board. The partnership was a joy to behold, and this was only the beginning. When the team emerged from the loose-school and faced the real world, good times got even better.

Day by day, obstacles of various shapes and sizes appeared where no obstacles had been before. The three flights of hurdles beside the Number 2 all-weather became five. A weak spot in the hedge between the two fields was trimmed and tidied and became a miniature fence. Then a Landrover and trailer trekked up to the level stretch at the top of the drovers' road. When it left, its load had been transformed into two inviting little post-and-rail fences – wings and all. And wherever a fallen tree trunk could be turned into an obstacle by a judicious adjustment of its position, John sweated blood to achieve that judicious adjustment. Small obstacles, but testing in one way or another. Led by Troy, Shenandoah could not be faulted. He took to jumping like a duck to water, and his sensible demeanour surprised even Harry.

*

On the 7th of September Mr Fearnley leant against his Range Rover and watched two horses devour five hurdles at considerable speed. When they got back to him, he quietly clapped his hands.

"Well done, well done indeed! A bit of a change, what? Shenandoah might even make a racehorse one day!"

"If he's too slow for the flat he'd make a jumper," said Harry, who was aboard the animal in question. "I wouldn't mind riding him!"

"And so you shall. Before that, however, I suggest we find out if he can gallop. Is he ready to do a bit of work, John? I imagine he's fat as a pig after his holiday."

John started to say something, but Harry got there first. "He'll be fine, sir. He hasn't been idle. In fact he's done more than you might think. I'll look after him, and if he gets tired I'll see he doesn't do too much."

As they walked away from their trainer, Harry looked across at John and winked. The gesture was so quick and so miniscule as to be almost invisible, but Mr Fearnley didn't miss it and he knew that his favourite jockey was playing games with him – not for the first time. He chuckled.

*

Two days later, at eight o'clock in the morning, the Range Rover trundled down the eastern side of the Weyhill gallops, heading towards the wild and inexplicable length of hedge beyond which Mr Fearnley was in the habit of watching horses work. On his way he passed six horses gently ambling in the same direction. The last two were Shen (Harry Bridger) and Troy (John Dunne).

By the time Mr Fearnley had gone past, the six horses had reached a marker: a rather dirty white pole, less than perfectly upright thanks to many years of exposure to the elements, standing at the junction between the Straight Mile and the Round Gallop and supporting a grubby white wooden disc that said "10" in big black numerals. The 10 referred to the number of furlongs the horses would have to gallop if they turned left on to the Round Gallop at that point and set off. To begin with, three furlongs on a left-hand curve which would find them sweeping past the old starting gate and joining the Seven Furlongs. Three and seven make ten, so there one had a test of a mile and a quarter (or 10 furlongs).

As the six horses approached the marker, the leading four adopted a two-by-two arrangement, three lengths or so between the pairs, still walking. They were respectable 4-year-old handicappers, due to run the following week.

The orders were that the four should work two by two for the first six furlongs. Then the second pair would join the first (if they could) and they would finish four abreast, doing their best work but "not going mad" – as the trainer was fond of reminding his riders.

Behind them would come Shen on his own – following as best he could and being nursed by Harry if he ran out of puff.

As the five turned left on to the Round Gallop and prepared to set off, John wished Harry good luck, then steered Troy away from the others and continued on towards the spot where Mr Fearnley would be waiting.

Over his left shoulder John watched the two pairs set off three lengths apart with a bigger gap separating them from Shen, who seemed to take a moment or two to get going. The horses stretched out at a steady pace between the white markers and followed the left-handed curve. Once they had passed the old starting gate and straightened up (John was now looking over his right shoulder) the pace increased, and Shen must have been a good ten lengths adrift as they disappeared over the rise. John

146

trotted on for fifty yards and saw them reappear at the bottom of the slope, where their line curved left again and headed towards the independent hedge. He watched the second pair join the two in front and noted that Shen had halved the gap between himself and those in front of him. Not too bad, he thought, as the five disappeared behind the hedge. He continued on his way. Four or five minutes later he met the four "serious" workers on their way home, and greetings were exchanged. When he reached the Range Rover, he found Shen circling it. Mr Fearnley was on his feet and deep in conversation with his jockey. He heard Harry say, ""If I was devious and sly, guv'nor, as you are suggesting, I would never have told you that I gave them a ten-lengths start."

"I suppose there's something in that," Mr Fearnley agreed. He turned to John. "Your friend Bridger here is five lengths behind at the bottom of the hill. When the others accelerate, he just cruises up behind them till he's on their tails. Then, when he gets to me, he grins, virtually pulls up, and canters slowly after them, finishing twenty lengths behind. Don't you think that's rather devious, John?"

"Not really, sir. As long as he tells _you_ the truth, that's what matters. There's no need for everybody to know what's what – and you did ask Harry to look after the horse, with him being so fat after his holiday."

"You buggers always stick together...You want to be careful about the company you keep, John. Too much time spent with Harry and you'll never tell the truth again!"

"Yes, sir. I'll remember that. So you were pleased with Shen, sir?"

Mr Fearnley smiled. "In spite of Harry's efforts to conceal the fact, he worked really well, and took the job seriously. Excellent - and he wouldn't have blown out a candle when he pulled up." He paused. "I'm amazed how fit he is and I want to see this holiday camp of yours!"

*

At lunchtime the following day the Range Rover crept across the Appleton all-weather. Wooden pallets had been strategically placed so that it would not break down the bank at either side of the track. The old gate was open. Mr Fearnley drove, Harry sat beside him and John perched on the back seat between them.

"See what it's like, sir?" John said, pointing out of the window as they started up the drove. "A good sound turf surface and a real uphill pull. Three quarters of a mile, we reckon."

"The first time," Harry said, "by the time we got this far, Shen was looking down at the string on the all-weather as much as to say, 'You poor sods! Just look at me – I'm having fun!' Little did he know that he was working just as hard as they were – if not harder!"

"Harder, I would say," said Mr Fearnley, "judging by the way he galloped yesterday. He's a fit horse!"

"There you are, sir. John done well to discover this circuit."

"That makes me an idiot," said Fearnley, "for not having spotted it myself. I've been here twenty-five years."

"Not an idiot, guv'nor - never! This sort of route is for the odds and sods, and you don't train many of them, nor would you be wanting to. Besides, you employ John. If he occasionally gets something right, most of the credit must go to you, sir. John agrees with me. Don't you, John?"

"I certainly do, sir," John confirmed. "Whose idea was it in the first place? Who said that something must be done? You, sir."

"Gentlemen, I had forgotten that," said Mr Fearnley, smiling broadly. "I feel much better. Thank you for the vote of confidence, and thank you for a good job well done."

CHAPTER THIRTY-FOUR

As the mists of autumn began to shroud the land at dawn and dusk, John's involvement with Shenandoah was looking good. The same could be said of the time he had spent with young David Sayers. Head Lad Tom Cribb reported positively. "He's a good kid. He does his work. He's quiet around his horses." The boss was equally positive. "The horses like him. They go well for him. I hope he stays with us.''

That was not all. During the summer Skyline Drive had moved on to bigger things, winning a "Listed Race" and then a "Group Three" and John had ridden him in all his work. Then he lost him, as the horse was whisked off to America. Mr Fearnley and Homer Langhorne were trying to win the Arlington Million, a prestige race at Langhorne's home track in Illinois.

*

One morning John returned to his flat at lunch-time. On the mat he found a letter in an unknown hand.

"Dear John,

Mum suggested I write and tell you what's been happening.

Since Hucklebury, Al has done:

Ferndale East Pony Club Event: 1st (won a trophy!)

Pony Club Horse Trials Qualifier: 1st

Then we registered him with BE, and finished second in the South Wilts Event (BE80)."

John read the sentence a second time, but BE and BE80 were terms with which he was not familiar.

"Plus I should nearly have won a 2-day event on him. I jumped a cross-country fence incorrectly and got eliminated, after leading in the dressage. I was sick with myself.

"At the Horse Trials qualifier it was a very wet day. I was warming up for the show-jumping, and Mum said to jump the practice jump once more before I went into the ring. I headed for it, and no way could I see a stride, so I sat still and left it to Al. We hit the top bar and took it with us as we tipped up and skidded along the ground for about ten yards, one on top of the other! Just about to do my show-jumping, and we were both plastered all down one side with very wet mud! What I didn't know was that Mum had asked a friend to come to the practice area to see how it should be done! Anyway, we went into the ring and did a clear round, and we won the competition, so only my pride was injured!

"Must go now. Mum wants to talk to you. Can you come to supper on Sunday week? Bring a friend if you like, she says – I think she's been talking to the O'Malleys. Much love, Kate."

*

Seven p.m. on Sunday week found Joan Ferris sitting on one side of her fireplace. Kate sat opposite. John shared the sofa with Rosemary. James was hovering over the gathering with a bottle of wine. When no glass remained unfulfilled he sat himself down on the armchair beside Kate.

Rosemary and the Ferris ladies had recognised each other instantly, from various equestrian happenings over a number of years, though they hadn't met before. John had told them about Rosemary's point-to-pointing and the Ferrises were duly impressed. They were equally impressed to hear that something called "Shen" had won its first hurdle race ridden by someone called "Harry".

"What you've done with Al is a miracle," said John, guiding the conversation back to the reason for this reunion.

"You exaggerate," Joan replied. "The O'Malleys warned us."

Alcapony's record on the Pony Club circuit spoke for itself, and the report on his deportment was equally good. The previous week he had been involved in a long-drawn-out show-jumping competition. Two rounds, followed by a jump-off against the clock. It was quite an important competition, and the officials were making no concessions. Al had been obliged to present himself on time, and to behave himself. Not just once, but three times. His nerve had stood the strain, and he had added another victory to his record.

"A miracle!" John insisted. "How else do you account for the transformation?"

"Square peg in a round hole," said Joan. "Nothing miraculous."

John looked perplexed.

"You racing people," said Joan, "you break-in horses as yearlings and you race them as two-year-olds. Too much, and much too soon." She paused. "Too much and much too soon," she repeated. "And when things go wrong, you get rid of them... the ones that don't fit into the system. Am I right?"

John turned to Rosemary. "She is, isn't she?"

"Not entirely."

"What?" exclaimed John.

"Too much hurry-hurry is a factor in racing, but not all the time, and not in every yard," said Rosemary. "I've heard you and the boss and Tom Cribb - and Harry, of course - discussing different ways to get difficult horses to see the light. Changing this and trying that... slowly-slowly. Mr Fearnley never hurries. What about Shen?"

"That's true," said John, feeling rather foolish. "Why didn't I say that?"

"Just because the pony's going so well," Rosemary added with half a smile, "it doesn't mean you have to agree with everything Mrs Ferris says."

"Quite right!" said Joan. "I was wrong to generalise, especially on a racing matter, about which I know little. However, your chap..."

"Our chap," John reminded her.

"Our chap - with his Connemara blood, and Welsh, and Arab - is a real person, who requires time, and understanding, and slowly-slowly, as Rosemary said. He's strong-willed, too, with a lot of character. That sort calls for diplomacy. It took a bit longer than it should have, because he'd had a bad time before he came here."

John winced. Rosemary nudged.

"I'm not suggesting one needs to be soft," Joan went on. "We've never been soft with him. We just have to go steadily, a step at a time. If necessary, give him a break. If necessary, go back and repeat a lesson."

"Reculer pour mieux sauter," James interjected. "I want you to know, John, that I am on your side against these women. *Reculer etcetera* means to take a backward step in preparation for a leap forward that will be all the better for it."

"*I* knew that," said Kate.

"But did your mother?"

There was a moment of disdainful silence before Joan resumed her thread. "He's a lovely little horse now - most of the time! We've just got to pray that nothing awful crops up and destroys the *entente cordiale* before it has had time to become rock solid." She gave her husband a meaningful glance. "French, James. It means friendship."

Once this skirmish had run its course and the dust had settled, John looked across at Kate.

"Has it really been as simple as your mother says?"

"I promise you. It took a lot of patience, and Mum has had the worst of it, when I've been at school."

There came a thumping sound from the hall. The door opened, and John found himself gazing at a medium-sized figure in a blue tracksuit. From its top protruded a very pretty face framed by a head of blonde curls.

"How far?" Joan asked.

"Three and a half miles."

"This is Emerald Perry," said James. "She's our secret weapon. Emerald, this is John, of whom you have heard much, and his friend and colleague, Rosemary."

Greetings exchanged, Emerald turned to Joan.

"I need a shower. Is there enough hot water?"

"More than enough – help yourself."

When Emerald had gone, Joan explained her. "She spends a lot of time here nowadays, in the holidays and at weekends. She rides Dropshot."

"That little chestnut pony in the box facing the house," Kate reminded John. "Dropshot used to live here, until Mother Perry took umbrage. Now we're back in favour and Dropshot's back – so is Emerald."

"And she's become a real asset," her mother confirmed. "Now let's get back to Al, John. We've registered him."

"Ah, yes, is that the mysterious BE? I was going to ask you. What is BE?"

"BE is British Eventing, the governing body of the sport. To take part in BE competitions, he had to be registered. That's all."

"What's a BE competition?"

"Virtually all the events in the UK are BE-affiliated."

"Like Badminton, Burghley, Gatcombe...?"

"That's the top end.... and right down to much humbler levels. Any BE event has to conform to the rules and standards that the governing body requires."

"And do they run sort of pony classes as well as the important stuff?"

"Not specifically," said Joan.

"But surely he's too small?"

"Horses have to be at least fifteen hands," said Joan. "Which he is. So far this season he has shown himself one of the best at Pony Club level, and ready for the next step up. Quite a big step, mind you. Finishing second in his first BE 80 shows that he's comfortable at that level. So we move upwards and onwards. 90 next and then 100. If he gets that far he becomes suitable for Novice classes."

"I see," said John, but he was lying, and Rosemary knew it.

"Don't worry," she said with a grin. "I'll explain it to him. A bit at a time, I think."

John grinned and nodded vigorously.

"90s and 100s are the levels just above what he has been doing," Rosemary went on. "Bigger jumps, more complicated tests. Tougher cross-country. That's right, isn't it?"

"Correct," said Joan. "If he could do reasonably well in a BE 100 this year, it would greatly increase his value."

"She's thinking about your finances," James said to John. "How are they, by the way?" he added in a stage whisper

John smiled. "Improving. Quite a lot better than they were."

"Good," said Joan. "Alcapony – fingers crossed - is on the verge of becoming a bit of an asset - top Pony Club animal, as I said, and capable of introducing a young rider to BE Novice Events."

"Top Pony Club... and capable of introducing *a young rider* to BE Novice Events!" John repeated solemnly. "And I nearly finished him off! Bloody Hell!" He paused. "Sorry about the language."

"*Errare humanum est,*" said Joan with a smile. "*Parcere divinum.* That's Latin. Be kind enough to translate, James!"

But James and Kate had disappeared into the kitchen to ensure that the preparations for supper were going according to plan. They were, and the quality of the feast contributed significantly to the pleasures of the evening.

*

"Are you happy with our agreement?" John asked, three hours later, as he and Rosemary prepared to leave. "Or does it need to be revised?"

"Perfectly happy," Joan assured him. She picked up a torch from the table in the hall, and led the way out into the dark. "Don't go without saying hello."

They went across the back garden, greeted Dropshot with a Polo mint, walked down the passage, round the manège, through the gate and over to the field-shelter.

The torchlight made the shadows of the horses loom huge on the back wall: Dalesman on the left, Al on the right. John looked at the little bay with his jute rug on. As Al walked towards the rails, the light glinted on one of his knees; on the patch of black skin where the hair had never regrown after that stumble. It seemed like a long time ago. John's gaze moved to his withers, and he remembered how Al had tried to kick Rosemary's mum when she put her hand on the spot that had been rubbed by the misplaced saddle. He remembered many things, and then he looked into Al's eyes and saw no sign of the worried look which had once revealed his state of mind. He doesn't know me, John found himself thinking, as he gave him a Polo. As if the past had never happened.

"And the weaving?" he asked.

"Almost never," Kate said. "Provided he's turned out for a little while each day, he's perfectly happy in a box. At shows, he stands in the horsebox all day, half asleep most of the time."

"Why don't you ever come and see him perform?" Joan asked, as they started back towards the house.

"I don't dare. I might bring him bad luck."

"You dramatise everything. No wonder you got in a muddle!" She turned to Rosemary. "Can you not sedate him?"

""I'll think about it," Rosemary replied. John glanced at her. Her eyes sparkled happily in the darkness.

As she drove him home, John told Rosemary about Sir Noel Murless, eight times champion trainer in Britain in the 1950s and '60s.

"In his biography he says that he learned more about horses from Mary Jane than from anybody else in his whole life. She was his first pony, which he got when he was eight. I wish I'd got Al when I was eight – I wouldn't have made so many mistakes."

"Well, he's going in the right direction now."

"If it works out, one day I might be saying, 'I learned more about horses from my first pony than I did from anyone else - but I did it the hard way!'"

The easy way seemed to be the option preferred by the pony in question. Alcapony was second in a BE 90 2-day contest a month after the dinner party, and notched up a good third in a BE100 a fortnight later. A mistake in dressage (Kate was adamant that the mistake was hers, not his) prevented him winning the former, and there wasn't much between first and third in the latter - and in neither contest was there any indication that temperament or lack of size was going to hold him back.

CHAPTER THIRTY-FIVE

Major Stackpole, who may or may not have had a weakness for inventing time faults, certainly had a good eye for promising riders. He also had a friend called Colonel Bailey – retired soldiers both. Colonel Bailey's 18-year-old daughter Joanna had finished 6th in the European Junior 3-Day-Event Championship the previous year, riding her horse Prospero. In due course Joanna celebrated her 19th birthday, which meant she was no longer a junior, and went to university to study medicine, which was going to keep her hard at work for the next seven years, and perhaps for ever. As a consequence, she decided not to compete on Prospero at senior level.

One evening the Colonel asked the Major to recommend a good young rider to team up with Prospero, with a view to more European Junior glory. And Major Stackpole (all credit to him, if this was another case of a sinner who repents) unhesitatingly recommended Kate Ferris, who had just turned sixteen.

Consequently, by the spring of the following year, Prospero, a large gelding (sixteen hands and one inch at the withers), 12 years old, three-quarters thoroughbred, dark brown, very laid-back and very genial, had taken up residence at Glebe Farm Cottage, where he settled in well and pleased his new connections.

Otherwise, arrangements in the yard were much as before. Al (now a six-year-old) lived with 13-year-old old Dalesman; Dropshot continued in residence, Emerald came to stay for the holidays and most weekends in term time, and Joan had started working on a five-year-old called Roscoe, a thoroughbred gelding which had proved too slow for racing. Joan had picked him up cheap at Brightwells Horses-in-Training sale. The plan was to make something of him as an eventer and then sell him on.

Two extra horses and a few inquiries about future liveries suggested to Joan that perhaps, sometime soon, a few more boxes would have to be considered. She talked to the farmer across the road about renting some unused stabling, if the need arose.

Meanwhile over at Weyhill a certain amount of attention was focussed on Shenandoah, unbeaten after three hurdle races. Mr Fearnley showed that he too had a devious side to his character by only running him in modest races at comparatively humble tracks, and his jockey, the redoubtable Harry Bridger, made sure that these races were as educational as possible. Shen was put into crowded spaces and encouraged to cope, to stay cool, and not to get carried away. He was required to be bold and swift when he met his hurdles on the right stride, and to play it safe when he met them wrong. He took to the business cheerfully and with confidence.

Harry also arranged things so that he never won by more than half a length. Consequently, his arrival on the racing scene was almost entirely "below the radar" and nobody identified him as a contender for major honours. However his next engagement would be the Triumph Hurdle at Cheltenham, the richest and most prestigious prize for four-year-old hurdlers.

*

In early March Joan said, "Crookley."

Kate said, "Prospero?"

Joan nodded. Crookley provided a programme of One-Day competitions which had become a popular place to start the eventing season, because the course was good and so was the management, and a one-day test was quite enough for a first outing.

"Colonel Bailey says that there's going to be a section for horses that the selectors want to have a look at with this year's Junior World Championship in mind. The hardened warriors mainly. I think Prospero's just about ready... what do you think?"

"He's fairly fit, mum."

"He doesn't have to win... Just show that he's still in good order. The Championships aren't till August."

The next day Joan said, "I think we might as well take Al to Crookley too. Enter him in a Novice class."

"Hooray!" said Kate. She had said nothing to influence her mother during the winter, but had been longing for the day when Al moved up to another level. "The moment of truth, mum!"

"It's one of the easier cross-country courses."

"I remember," said Kate. "Twists and turns, but smallish jumps."

"The nearest thing to a gentle introduction that we're likely to get," said Joan.

*

Black skies, a chill wind and the threat of rain. Huddled under the overgrown but leafless hedge were the usual collection of horseboxes, trailers and cars. Horses, riders and camp-followers – all well wrapped up -went about their business to the rhythm of chattering teeth. February is said to be the cruellest month, but March can run it close on occasions, and this was one of them.

Behind the horseboxes was the warm-up area, its right-hand side defined by two tents and the horsebox that served as the Secretary's office. Beyond this encampment was the dressage arena. A respectable distance to the right of this, the start of the Cross-Country course sent the competitors off into the surrounding woods, then out over open countryside along a three-mile track which ended right next to where it began.

Behind the Ferris horsebox, partly shielded from the elements, Emerald was holding Al while Joan finished tacking him up – Al looking rather small and windswept, with his tail between his legs. No sign of James or Brownie today. They were on duty at home, walking, earning money for the Church Roof Fund, no doubt suffering and no doubt uncomplaining. On second thoughts, James wouldn't complain – Brownie was another matter entirely.

In the cab, rugged up in two sweaters and a Puffa jacket, Kate decided to give herself another five minutes. One thing about Al - he didn't take long to warm up before his dressage. He was naturally supple and never (touch wood) started the day moving stiffly. Everything depended on his mood, and that was ultimately out of her hands. Besides, he was a reformed character, she reminded herself.

Behind her, Prospero, who would perform later, shifted in his stall. His ears flickered as he listened to the sounds from outside and tried to work out why he had been left alone in the box.

When the last of the five minutes had come and gone, Kate swopped three layers of insulation for her back protector and a black riding jacket, climbed down from the cab and shivered as the wind extended a greeting.

"What do you think, little man?" she asked Al, patting his neck as they trotted off towards the practice area. His toes flicked out and his shoulder muscles rippled beside her knees in an easy rhythm. Once he was on the move his pricked ears suggested he was in good heart, in spite of the weather. In fact the chill may easily have contributed to his eagerness to get on with the job in hand.

Kate was just a little uptight as she rode into the arena, but she needn't have been. Al went about his work in copybook fashion, and the extra complications that a Novice competition served up failed to bother him or his rider. Halfway through, he suddenly bucked, and Kate couldn't help laughing. Was he feeling well, or was it the wind under his tail? Either way, it showed that he wasn't overawed by the occasion and that helped her to relax and enjoy herself. And it didn't do too much damage to his test, which was not bad at all. Mid-div, she guessed; maybe nearer the top than the bottom. Good little man!

*

Crookley's cross-country test was not too demanding, but the organisers compensated for that by having quite a big show-jumping course. Kate timed her arrival at the start so as to get there as late as possible, but this was a BE event and she knew that taking liberties was not an option. In addition, on this occasion she didn't have a team to help her. However, for reasons which cannot be explained without some reference to divine intervention, Al arrived at the collecting ring a bit too early, but didn't turn a hair.

He went into the ring, and positively devoured the course. The single fences he cleared with ease; and he made nothing of the doubles and combinations; because his "little" legs had more spring, power and elasticity than even Kate and her mother had given them credit for.

There followed an interval, during which Kate walked the cross-country course, and she did so with mixed feelings. She had no worries about Prospero, for he had a fine record at a very high level of competition. Al however was a different kettle of fish. At this level the jumps were a bit tougher and the speed required was greater than he was used to. So... fingers crossed! The good news was that the rain had held off and the underfoot conditions would not be too deep, heavy and taxing.

As they waited to start, Alcapony got really excited, because of the proximity of the end of the cross country course. A finisher galloped past just as he was waiting to set off. He plunged, twisted and turned, but only because he wanted to get on with it, not because he was trying to duck out.

"Three, two, one, GO!" chanted the starter. Al shot off, going too fast, and for half a dozen strides Kate gave him his head, so that he could work off the tensions of waiting. Then "Steady, little man! Steady, little man!" and pressure on his mouth, and he came back to her, and settled to the pace that she wanted.

Over the first, over the second, round the first bend and over the third. No problems. The fourth was a hedge with a ditch in front, the first ditch in front of an obstacle Al had ever met. He looked at the black hollow, and looked again, neck bent, ears pricked. He braked marginally with each of his approach strides ... Prop, prop, prop! Then he saw what it was and knew how to cope. He launched himself and cleared the hedge by a foot.

"Wheeeee!" sang Kate as they came back down to earth and galloped on. One dark ear twitched back and forth in response.

The next fence wasn't big but it was complicated. Up a bank, pop over a log to land on a down slope; two short strides down to a coffin-shaped ditch. Over the ditch, up another bank and away over a second log. Al made it look easy.

He got to halfway without having made a mistake. Up to that point Kate had set only a steady pace, to allow him to find a comfortable stride that gave him every chance of meeting the obstacles correctly. Now she let out an inch of rein. She felt him accelerate easily over the springy turf, and still his jumping remained effortless and precise. They completed the second half a good deal faster than the first, and still without a serious mistake.

"Good little man!" Kate said, as they cleared the last. "Good, good, good little man!"

They galloped past the Finish, and pulled up. She felt the rhythm of his lungs beneath her; she listened to the sound from his nostrils. He was hardly blowing and his ears were pricked. Kate was delighted, and in the back of her mind regretted having not let him go a little bit faster early on.

*

Half an hour later she was on Prospero, in the special class the Colonel had mentioned. It was interesting, swopping horses like this. She was further from the ground on Prospero... yes, and each stride covered more distance... yes, but both Prospero and Al moved with the same athleticism. Was Prospero wider to sit on? No, actually he was no broader than Al - but there was much more neck and head in front of her, which made her feel very secure.

Prospero did a good dressage test, as a championship contender

159

should, and Kate was pretty sure he would finish close to the top of his section. She handed him over to her mother and Emerald, and trotted over to the scoreboard to see how many time faults Al had got on the cross-country. She found his name, saw his score, checked the rest of them… and was delighted.

Only six time faults, many less than most of the others. He had finished 5th out of a field of 40! He was in the money… a prize-winner… in his first grown-up Novice event! A delighted Kate hurried back to base reminding herself that her day's work was not yet over, and that rejoicing must not be allowed to distract her from the job in hand. After all, Prospero was the main reason for being there.

Prospero took care of her. He followed up with an effortless clear round in the show-jumping, and then there was the cross-country. This, on such a horse, proved to be the equivalent of driving a Rolls-Royce. Prospero was smooth and rather majestic in everything he did, and in addition he could turn on a sixpence and react like lightning if ever he found himself in anything like trouble. So Kate helped when she could, and tried not to hinder when she couldn't. The result was a clear round in a very respectable time. He finished second in his class, and showed that he was as good as ever. Mission accomplished.

On the way home, Kate never stopped talking. It was like the singing of a very delightful and delighted bird. A lark, possibly – on a high! And all she could sing about was Alcapony. Prospero and international honours wouldn't have got a look-in, had it not been for Joan and Emerald's sense of fair play. But most of the time they were content to sit and listen; very occasionally they were allowed to join in the chorus.

In their stalls, Prospero and Al stood side by side, legs slightly splayed for purposes of balance; warm, contented, steadily munching at their haynets, and apparently paying no attention whatsoever to the birdsong.

CHAPTER THIRTY-SIX

John Dunne was walking towards the office when Mr Fearnley emerged from his front door and stood for a moment assessing the heavy black sky. It had just stopped raining.

"Good morning, John."

"Good morning, sir."

"There's one thing I want you to know, John..."

"Yes, sir?"

"Whatever happens today...?"

"Yessir?"

"It's all your fault!"

"If you say so, sir."

"I do."

With a smile and a wave he got into the front passenger seat of the black Bentley. Sitting behind the wheel, Harry Bridger shook a friendly fist in John's direction. The car slid quietly down the drive and away. As if by arrangement, it started raining again.

Five hours later Rosemary closed a file, switched off her computer and rose to her feet. She turned the sign hanging on the inside of the office door. "Back in 20 minutes" became its message to the world. She locked the door and went through to the house, where Mr Fearnley's large TV screen was silent, but alive with colour and movement. Rosemary sat in an armchair and reached for the remote.

In the hostel at the back of the stables the lads were in front of their equally large screen. A sofa, several chairs, and much of the carpet were fully occupied, leaving standing room only for the latecomers. Here the sound was on and the audience was paying close attention. Conversation was low key. Anything louder was nipped in the bud.

In his flat, John crouched forward on his one armchair and gazed unblinking at his small screen. The sound was on, but very low, and the picture, though in full colour, was using much too much black and grey, because the scene it revealed was overcast and rain was falling. It wouldn't help Shen, John reflected glumly. His concern was ninety percent for the horse, but there was also the small matter of his £10 win bet at 10 – 1. Harry had insisted that he took this bold step, but removing the money from his winter sock had caused John considerable anguish.

*

As Ken Hardy led Shenandoah down the walkway from the Cheltenham paddock to the track, the chestnut horse pricked his ears and took a lively interest in the densely-packed ranks of spectators to left and right. Year after year, it seemed, jump racing's faithful proved indomitable. The worse the weather, the braver they became. If the horses and jockeys must suffer, we'll suffer with them – the Cheltenham Festival did that to otherwise rational human beings.

Ahead of Shen, a number of horses were already cantering down to the start. A dozen more were following him. Twenty-four runners in this year's Triumph Hurdle, the jump season's ultimate challenge for four-year-olds.

Ken unbuckled the lead rein as he reached the narrow all-weather track down which the runners went – so as not to cut up the turf.

"Good luck," he said, patting the horse and letting him go.

"See you later," said Harry. He clicked his tongue, and Shen was away, cantering gently down the slope.

Only one thing was bothering the jockey. As Shen bounced elegantly along the all-weather, there to his right beyond the white rail was the wide expanse of the racing surface: green grass, luxuriant in its healthy growth, but so sodden with rain that the ground would ride very heavy, especially up the final hill, and those who could handle it would prosper and those who couldn't wouldn't.

That expanse of turf represented one of the great tests in British racing. The Grand National has its fences and its distance, the Derby has the switchback which is Tattenham Corner and the camber of Epsom's last two furlongs. Cheltenham had its constant undulations and its unforgiving uphill finish. And Harry was riding a horse whose best form had been shown on "top of the ground" (alias "good to firm"). Shen had never run on anything else.

Down at the start the horses circled this way and that in the "holding area", just off the track, while the starter's assistants checked their girths.

Vets and blacksmiths were in attendance, quietly hopeful that their intervention would not be required. Runners in twos and threes trotted up to the practice hurdle to remind their mounts of the nature of the contest.

As the clock ticked and start time came closer, the runners were ushered on to the track, and formed a great circle, walking nose-to-tail, totally relaxed and perfectly comfortable. For many years the starting of big fields under jumping rules had been a mess, until the 2013 Grand National when senior starter Hugh Barclay showed how easy it was to persuade thirty-eight horses to walk gently towards a starting-gate in a reasonably straight line. The key was simply not to upset the runners. This came as a shock to the British Horseracing Authority, which had for some years been wedded to certain preliminaries that were guaranteed to send horses and jockeys mad. Nevertheless, slowly slowly, big-field starting began to improve, and this twenty-four runner Triumph Hurdle looked like being one of the better examples.

In due course the starter mounted his rostrum and raised his yellow flag to indicate that the runners were under his orders. A furlong up the course another yellow flag was raised: the recall man was ready, in case of a false start.

The starter then invited the runners to break the circle and walk towards the starting gate. The line they formed was comfortable and unhurried.

"Steady, jockeys! You're looking good. Very good. Gently does it!"

As the line advanced, any horse that wanted to be in the front rank early on had every chance of being there, and any horse that wanted a slow start and some cover would have no difficulty in losing a length or two in the first two or three strides. And all could see the first hurdle - which helps.

"Steady, lads! Steady! You're looking good! And OFF YOU GO!"

Flags fell. Tapes rose. Crowd roared.

Shen jumped the first hurdle cleanly, in fourth place, two away from the left-hand rail. Two horses in front of him, and one half a length ahead on his right. On his left was an animal that he had ridden for a trainer who was a neighbour of Mr Fearnley, and knew to be moderate. As the field landed over the first, the muted rumble of hooves engaging with saturated turf was punctuated by the crackle of wood as the top rails of hurdles were clattered.

Two went past Harry as they came to the second. He let them go and looked to settle down in about sixth place, still maintaining his line, one off the rails. Uphill towards the stands and the enclosures the twenty-four runners headed, before a left-hand bend took them away from the human roar and into the tranquillity of the back straight.

Harry glanced at those in front. The first two he knew well: one was a very hard puller, the other was ridden by a wild man – both could be guaranteed to go too fast early on and pay the price when push came to shove. So far Shen had handled the ground without any sign of discomfort and was moving easily. Harry began to hum a tune and take a gentle pull on the reins. Two horses ranged up on his right, not hurrying, but reacting to the fact that he had slowed his pace just a little bit. Further from the inside rail, they would have an extra few yards to cover, on ground which made every yard a punishment.

Third hurdle – Shen was meeting it wrong: if he took off too soon he might land on the timber; if he took off too late he might clip that top rail. Harry sat still and left it to the horse, and the horse showed how much he had learnt. He didn't try to beat any long-jump record. Instead he got too close to the hurdle for comfort. No problem: he simply bounced skyward and tucked up all four legs. Didn't touch a twig, landed safely and sauntered on – lost a length, but no damage done. The fourth he met perfectly and he took back the lost ground with interest.

As the field climbed towards the top of the hill at the far end of the course, the watchers in the stands could see changes taking place at the head of affairs. The weaker brethren were found out by the pace, the uphill climb and the testing underfoot conditions. Inevitably their lungs wilted, lactic acid clogged their limbs, their strides shortened and they began to go backwards. At the same time there appeared on the scene a number of horses whose energy reserves had been prudently managed by jockeys familiar with the dangerous battlefield which is Cheltenham. Those who were advancing had to negotiate those who were retreating. As jockeys reacted to traffic problems, the runners spread out across much of the width of the course.

At the top of the hill the track curved to the left and started down a slope towards home; a slope that featured two hurdles and would soon usher the competitors into the final and brutal uphill examination.

After the fifth, Harry glanced to his right. In the leading group he recognised five of the half dozen or so that he expected to be concerned in the final stages of the race, every one of them top class, every one of them ridden by a jockey with no weaknesses. He was pleased to see that horses and riders were working quite hard. They had had to work to get into contention, whereas Shen had maintained a handy position from the start without having to be asked to go into overdrive. The one he couldn't see was a grey horse, Diamond Crown, the best of the Irish contingent, ridden by the Irish champion jump jockey, Denis Cassidy, an old friend and rival of Harry's.

Shen jumped the sixth in fifth place and jumped it well. As the course curved to the left again and met the rising ground Harry changed his line fractionally to the right, aiming for the gap which had appeared between two horses ahead on his left and two which had come past him on his right.

As Shen shot through the gap and started up the hill, a grey head appeared beside Harry's right knee. Diamond Crown had been directly behind him all the time, had followed him through the gap and now drew alongside. His jockey, in green and gold, had time to flash a smile before his mount carried him into the lead. No fool, that Cassidy, Harry said to himself as he went in pursuit.

Shen was half a length behind when he met the second last all wrong. This time he took off a stride too soon and had to stretch to get his front half over the birch-lined timber. As he landed, his hind legs caught the top of the hurdle a hefty blow that wiped out much of his momentum.

For a split second Harry knew for certain that all hope was gone, but a further split second revealed that Shen's internal combustion engine was still alive and kicking. Power flooded back and serious business was resumed. The grey was now two lengths ahead. Both horses met the last on a good stride and jumped it well.

The run-in at Cheltenham may only be 440 yards or thereabouts, but to the horses and jockeys in a tight finish it might as well be four miles – especially on soft ground. Yard by yard and grimly, the playboy Shen reduced the deficit. On his back Harry swung his whip and didn't hit him. He simply squeezed, pushed and begged. He took up the rhythm of the horse's stride, he encouraged the rhythm of the horse's stride, he demanded the rhythm of the horse's stride. He was a chunky muscular nugget of a man, and every ounce of his strength was helping Shen up that hill.

Ahead, approaching the end of an unforgiving ordeal, and without the incentive of an opponent in front of him, the grey horse began to wander off a straight line, to the right, towards the roaring stands, away from Shen. That helped the English cause. Every yard of deviation is an extra few inches for the deviant to run.

Three strides from the line the grey nose was still ahead and Harry gave Shen one good crack. Three strides later it was anybody's guess. And that was it.

It took no time at all before both horses were walking with their heads lowered and their lungs pumping as they began to enjoy the fact that the race was over and screaming muscles need no longer scream, while their jockeys shook hands, then waited.

The rain had stopped. The sun appeared. One by one, the rest of the field left the course. The chestnut and the grey had it to themselves. To themselves, apart from a long-legged blonde with a microphone on a stick, and her cameraman. The two horses walked round in a big circle, one on one side, one on the other. The blonde squelched across to Harry and stuck the mike in his face.

"What do you think?"

"What about?" Harry enquired, poker-faced.

"Well, did you win?"

"It was very close..."

"But, Harry, you've been in close finishes before. You jockeys get a feeling, don't you?"

"Not this time. We were too far apart. Didn't you notice?"

She snorted with frustration and paddled away to interrogate the Irish jockey. Cassidy was no help at all. The thing was, she was there to interview the conquering hero, and that iconic figure was not available until the wretched judge announced the result.

Time passed. The crowd stood silent until the mega TV screens began replaying the finish. That made them cheer... and cheer again. Cheering probably relieved their tension. No help at all for the delightful blonde.

Eventually the Public Address addressed the issue. A voice from on high announced a dead-heat, and the roar of the crowd must have been heard in Gloucester. When two horses give their all in horrible conditions over two miles and one furlong of undulating terrain and then up a very steep hill, the decision that both of them are winners is an "oh be joyful" moment for the vast majority of the sporting public.

*

Shen came out of the race unscathed. Within ten days he was beginning to look like himself again, his appetite was back to normal and he was behaving like a lamb in springtime.

The financial consequences of the result for the betting public were in accordance with rules that were firm but fair. In the event of a dead heat, the backers of both the dead-heaters get paid out, but they have their dividend halved. Thus £10 pounds at 10 – 1 becomes £10 at 5 - 1. In John's case £50 was added to the winter sock, and the envelope began to feel the strain. £150 in cash is no small matter.

The word from on high suggested that the Americans were delighted, as was Mr Fearnley, as were the lads in the yard, apart from Morgan the travelling head lad, who railed at the injustice which had reduced his dividend by such a vast amount.

Mr Fearnley presented the pub with enough money to finance a night of song and huge amounts of alcohol, a festivity to which all the villagers were invited. He himself partook of the entertainment for an hour. His parting shot was that of a man who accepted full responsibility for the welfare of his employees. "Don't be late in the morning," he said.

*

In due course, Mr Fearnley summoned the confederates to his office and sat them down to plot Shen's next endeavour. Mr Homer Langhorne had enquired whether he might do something at Royal Ascot in the third week of June. He was bringing a few friends over from America for the occasion.

"You very kindly allowed me to find out," said Mr Fearnley, frowning fiercely at Harry, "that Shen has plenty of speed, and probably stays long distances. Would that be about right?"

"Yessir. Any horse that runs up the Cheltenham hill in the mud like he did has all the stamina you could wish for. Plus, I think he will be even better on firmer ground. Plus, he has a good mouth. Push-button gears, sir. He'll not be wasting energy."

"John?"

"I second that, sir."

"Good," said the trainer. "I like harmony among my troops. How about the Queen Alexandra on the last day of the Royal Meeting, the Saturday?"

"Perfect," said Harry.

"Two and three-quarter miles. Do you want to ride him?"

"Wish I could," said Harry with a sigh. "But nowadays nine stone is a weight I cannot get down to – can I?"

"Try," said Mr Fearnley.

CHAPTER THIRTY-SEVEN

On and off, the wet weather persisted, and Joan was in two minds about sending Alcapony to the Trensham Horse Trials, where another Novice Class was next on his agenda. A week beforehand, however, the rain stopped, the ground began to dry out, and the horsebox made the journey south to the Surrey/Hampshire border.

Al did a dressage which put him in the top third of his section of Novices. He then did a clear round show-jumping, one of a very few. Soon afterwards the rain began again, and got harder and harder. Kate was glad she was one of the first to go in the cross-country, before the downpour turned the ground into a quagmire, and before a lot of competitors had cut it up; but the more the rain fell, the worse grew her forebodings. In deep sticky mud she feared that the "little legs" would struggle.

Once again, Al got very excited at the start, and charged off when the starter let him go. Kate took a hold of his head and steadied him, and then steadied him again, to a pace which she hoped would enable him to get round without getting too tired.

He was going very well till about halfway, where they started up a long climb to the eighth fence, a double coffin, just like the one he had dealt with so cleverly at Crookley, only this time with two ditches to negotiate between the log-in and the log-out. Al was foot perfect, but Kate felt the effort he had to make – the ground was turning into glue. The course continued uphill, and soon his ears were flicking backwards and forwards, and she knew that he wasn't enjoying himself one little bit; nor was she. Two more fences, which he jumped well, and then the course levelled out at last.

Suddenly a man jumped out on to the course ahead of them, waving his arms. It was a fence-judge, so Kate pulled up. There had been a problem ahead (a horse had crashed through the next obstacle, which had to be repaired). Kate was delighted. This was one time when a delay was just what the doctor ordered. It lasted about twelve minutes. The procedure was that the fence-judge would take note of the length of the delay, and the times of delayed competitors would be adjusted accordingly once the round was completed.

Kate walked Al round and round, to stop him getting cold and stiffening up. Gradually he got his breath back, until finally he was comfortable again. But the rain would not relent.

When the order was given for them to carry on, Al had no trouble with the next few fences which were on level ground. Then another hill faced them - short, but rather steep and very sticky. At the top was the final obstacle, a telegraph pole over a wide ditch. Alcapony scrambled up the hill - but the last few yards he found very difficult. Somehow or other he launched himself at the jump, and somehow or other made it to the other side. He stumbled as he landed, and Kate had to cling on like a limpet.

*

Back at the horsebox, James was waterproofed up to the eyes.

"Well done!" he said from under the dripping brim of an Australian drover's hat with a certain amount of age to it.

"Oh, Dad, he's so tired. I think I should have pulled up."

"He'll be all right," said James. "He's from Connemara!"

Joan unsaddled Al, threw a sweat rug over his back, and then a waterproof over his loins. James led him off to the shelter of some trees to dry off and cool down. Kate climbed into the back of the box, where her mother tended to her needs with hot coffee and dry clothes.

Half an hour later Al was in his stall in the horsebox, damp and steaming a bit, but apparently none the worse. In fact he was savaging his haynet with a ferocious appetite which could certainly be described as healthy.

The rain eased, and finally stopped. From time to time the sun peered through the clouds and then disappeared again. In one of the brighter moments, Kate and her mother went over to look at the scores. Al had had a good dressage and gone clear show-jumping. In addition, most of the others had done their cross-country after him, and the ground had been deteriorating all afternoon. So...

Kate scrutinised the notice board and turned to her mother.

"Only sixteen time faults, Mum! That's practically the best of... I bet I know what happened!" She lowered her voice. "As I told you, we had this hold-up, which was a godsend, because he was so tired. Anyway, I think the fence judge didn't get the timing quite right. I think he made a mistake and did us a favour!"

Joan was still looking up at the board.

"You got 20 jumping penalties," she said.

There it was. To the left of the column for time-faults was the column for penalties picked up on the way round - for falls, refusals, wrong course, and such like. In this column, opposite Alcapony's name, was the figure 20. 20 penalty points meant he was right out of contention for honours.

"But we never did anything wrong!" Kate wailed.

*

Inside the Secretary's tent all was hustle and bustle. The officials were under pressure, so it took time to persuade one of them to look into the matter. A young man sifted through a mountain of fence-judges' reports and announced that Kate had had a stop at number 8, the double coffin.

"But I watched her jump that," Joan protested. "I had gone up to a spot from which one could see seven, eight and nine very clearly She did nothing wrong!"

The young man raised his hands helplessly and said, "I'm sorry, Mrs Ferris. The Judge at No. 8 reported a stop. If you wish to lodge a protest..."

Joan and Kate made their way to Fence Number 8. The late starters were still going round, and the judge was in position, in a chocolate four-wheel-drive.

They waited while a competitor negotiated the obstacle, and waited some more to give the judge time to make her notes. Only then did Joan approach the driver's window and smile.

The door opened, and there sat a lady in rather tight plum-coloured trousers and a yellow turtleneck sweater. In her thirties, blonde, plump and handsome.

"But I remember you well," she said to Kate, when they had explained their mission. "You were on a little horse, a little bay horse."

"That's right."

"You stopped at the first log," she said, pointing.

"No, I..."

"Indeed you did, young lady. Then you took a turn, and the second time you went through perfectly."

"One hates to make a fuss," Joan said, "but I watched Kate at this obstacle, and she went through without a hitch."

This time even Joan's smile was a failure.

"You were in red and black," the judge said to Kate.

"Yes I was. Red cap, black sweater."

"Number 6?"

"Yes, but..."

"There you are, then!"

"It's such a shame," said Kate, as they made their way back to the box. "But I can't think how it could have happened. Am I dreaming, Mum, or did we jump that one perfectly?"

"If you're dreaming, so am I," said Joan. "Still, never mind, he did really well. Maybe that judge is blind. Or her notes got muddled up. It doesn't matter. What happens today is of no importance in the long run."

"Yes, but..."

"I know, I know," said Joan. "But you've just got to forget it. Anyway, what about that hold-up? The time-faults you perhaps should have had? Swings and roundabouts, dear!"

CHAPTER THIRTY-EIGHT

On his way back to Hampshire after a visit to Windsor races, John Dunne called in at Glebe Farm Cottage and found Joan on her own. It was the first time they had met since the Triumph Hurdle. She knew all about Shen and had watched it on TV. She was lavish with her praise. Then the conversation turned to Al. She brought John up to date, up to and including the drama at Trensham.

"Poor Alcapony!" said John. "So he had a hard slog and then got cheated!"

"Might be the best thing that ever happened."

John looked at her and waited.

"Do you remember how old he is?"

John counted on his fingers. "Six,"

"Six is quite young to be showing promise in Novice events."

"You're telling me that he's bright for his age?"

"That's part of it."

"I still don't understand how a blind judge, who robs us of a good result, can be the best thing that ever happened." .

"Do you remember us explaining to you the way a horse progresses as a BE-registered Eventer?"

"The way he moves from Novice to…to..."

"Intermediate."

"To Intermediate, and then, if he's very good, to Advanced. You lectured me on the subject in the autumn, and Rosemary has lectured me since then, but I've forgotten most of it."

"Novice classes," Joan began. "Each time a horse finishes in the first six, he scores points. 6 for winning, 5 for second, and so on down to 1 point for sixth. Clear?"

"Clear."

"If he accumulates 21 points, he is thereafter excluded from Novice events, and moves up to Intermediate, where the courses are a bit more demanding, and the competition is stronger. Al got 2 points for fifth at Crookley."

"Really? I had no idea. Well done him! So, 2 points in the bag, 19 to go, before he stops being a Novice."

"Exactly right. Now can you understand, John," said Joan slowly, "that in some ways it is a bad thing to accumulate points too quickly."

"Let me think about it."

Silence reigned. Then he said, "If you're a horse, and you win three Novice events in a month, that's 18 points, and then you finish fourth in another, that's another 3, which makes 21 points. You are brilliant, but you are very young and inexperienced... and yet now – willy-nilly - you have to face better opponents and bigger courses, in Intermediate events. After only a very short time as a Novice. And you think, 'Oh, hell! I wish I hadn't accumulated points so quickly. I would have been much better off staying a Novice for a year or two, gaining experience, learning my job, finishing in the middle of the field rather than among the leaders, and growing bigger, stronger and wiser all the time. What a pity I was in such a hurry!'"

Joan clapped her hands. "Welcome to eventing! Now, the final question, John: can you think of another factor that is important in the same context?"

John knuckled his brow, scratched his head and eventually gave up.

"If you're selling a Novice," Joan said, "there's another reason why it's a disadvantage to have already earned too many points. They show that your horse is good, but they limit the opportunities the new owner will have of competing in Novice competitions on this horse. And that's particularly important when selling a horse to a young rider. If the rider is not yet experienced enough to go for Intermediates, he or she will not want to buy a horse that's accumulated too many points and is also comparatively inexperienced."

"Got it!" said John. "So that blind judge *was* the best thing that ever happened!"

He thought for a moment, then said, "A year ago, you would never have considered the notorious Al Capone as a ride for a young person. Now it sounds as if you've reconsidered. Does that mean you trust him?"

"He's gone the right way, and he's entitled to be given another chance. I think *he* has begun to trust *us*, at last. And I think it's Kate who has persuaded him to turn the corner. He loves her to bits. So long as we don't hurry, and avoid making mistakes, I think he will keep the faith. I also think that Trensham took a lot out of him – the heavy ground and the vile weather. And that was quite soon after Crookley. My plan is to give him an easy time and turn him out for several weeks as soon as the sun starts shining and things get a bit warmer. Then back to work, gently-gently!"

*

Saturday morning. Kate had just finished exercising Al. She came out of his box, where she had been dressing him over.

"Mum?"

Joan looked out of the next door box.

"Mum, shall I turn him out now, or wait till you've exercised Dalesman?"

"Turn him out. You can turn Dropshot out with him. Emerald's not here this weekend."

When Dropshot was loosed off, Al was over the far side of the field, with his head down. The bright chestnut trotted away from the gate, and Al cantered over. In the middle of the field they met, small bay horse, smaller chestnut pony. They halted, sniffed, whinnied and immediately reared up for a spar.

Joan was now standing in the yard, adjusting Dalesman's bridle. Horse and mistress stood and watched the performance.

"It's all your fault," said Joan, rubbing the guilty one's nose.

"Mum," said Kate, "do you think I've got too much on my plate?"

"How d'you mean?"

"With Prospero, and the Junior National Team … do you think I'll have time for Al?"

"Second best thing that ever happened," said Joan.

"What's the first best?" Kate asked, and Joan told her about her conversation with John. "Al's been working hard and doing well, so he can have a holiday. When the weather improves we'll turn him out for a month – maybe longer – so he can re-charge his batteries.... and we won't start serious business with him until you can give him your full attention. So the more time you spend on Prospero the better it is for Al. Anyway, the chance of getting into the National team is not to be sneezed at."

"It's great," Kate agreed. "I just don't want to let you down."

"Don't you worry about that," her mother assured her.

As if it had been listening to this conversation, next day the sun switched itself on, the temperature rose and Doctor Grassgrass did the needful for any horse that was lucky enough to be prescribed large doses of his medicinal compound. Al was just such a one and he revelled in the new regime, under the all-seeing eyes of Mrs Ferris and Emerald, now a valuable member of staff. Meanwhile Kate and Prospero concentrated on performing well enough to be selected for the national team – and this they duly achieved.

CHAPTER THIRTY-NINE

Annette Bridger turned the Bridger kitchen into a no-go area for her beloved and dished up slices of fish, the occasional egg and now and then a lettuce leaf. Their two boys were commanded not to upset their father because he was likely to bark at them. In the evenings Harry would swathe his body in long johns, long-sleeved vests, sweaters, gloves, woolly hats and a waterproof golf suit. Then he and John (more reasonably attired) would jog off towards the gallops and put in the miles required to make the victim sweat like a pig and come back smaller than when he went out. Then he would lie in a hot bath to keep the baking process going. Steadily a worthless outer layer vanished, and the essential Harry emerged, like a butterfly from a chrysalis.

A month after the Triumph Hurdle, Shen (ridden by Harry) appeared in a quite valuable mile and a quarter flat race at Salisbury, for horses that had not won on the flat. The generous prize money attracted what looked like quite a number of decent animals.

Shen went into the stalls with no fuss (good). He came out slowly (on purpose). Mile-and-a-quarter races are run pretty fast and this one was no exception, even though more rain meant that the ground was very soft. He was among the last three (of sixteen) for two furlongs. He then worked his way over to the inside rail and gradually improved his position – nothing fancy, weaving his way through gaps as and when they appeared; learning the business of flat racing. Finally he ran on up the straight, passing beaten horses as they fell away. He finished sixth and had a good blow. That was very satisfactory. If he was a two-mile-plus horse, this outing (over half that distance) required him to work plenty hard enough, and allowed Harry to ride him in a discreet manner, so as not to draw too much attention to his potential.

Of course there was plenty of interest in a dead-heater in the Triumph Hurdle competing at Royal Ascot. Two of them, in fact, as Diamond Crown was apparently keen to renew his argument with Shen. However the official Weyhill assessment for public consumption was low key. It suggested that the owner's wish to have a runner at the Royal meeting had played a significant part in the decision-making process. It mentioned that, apart from the Triumph, Shen's hurdles form had been fair, but at a comparatively humble level. At Cheltenham he had done really well, on very soft ground. If the ground was firm at Ascot, it might not suit him. In addition two miles, six furlongs was unknown territory. It was a cautious approach that reflected the realism of the horse's connections, rather than any wish to deceive.

*

On the day, Mr Fearnley was a picture of elegance from the top of his black top hat to the glittering toecaps of his equally black shoes. Homer Langhorne and three other American gents were equally well-turned-out. In fact, if there was a group prize for fine upstanding gentlemen in full regalia in the packed Ascot paddock prior to the final race of the meeting, they would have had every chance of winning it.

The centre of the group's attention, however, although just as elegant, was a somewhat smaller model. Lean and muscular, Harry was a fine example of his profession in Homer Langhorne's green, grey sleeves and cap. He carried a whip, with which from time to time he tapped his boots.

Beyond a forest of tall hats and gorgeous "creations" seventeen runners were parading round the paddock. Shenandoah's rich chestnut coat glittered in the bright sunshine and the grey Diamond Crown was jig-jogging happily. His ears were pricked and he was clearly enjoying every minute of the occasion.

"There's your friend," Fearnley said to his jockey, pointing to the Irish horse.

"Yes, I've had a chat with his jockey," said Harry. "Mr Cassidy's got an advantage," he added. "He's built like a whippet. He hasn't had to starve himself half to death like I have. And he thinks he's got us beat."

"What makes him so confident?" said Fearnley.

"Last spring they thought Diamond Crown was a Derby horse. But he got sore shins which took a while to clear up. Then the ground was too firm, and finally he got ringworm and that put the kybosh on his year. That's how come he went hurdling. This time he's a hundred percent, as we found out at Cheltenham. He's had two good runs on the flat since then, and they think he's a better horse on this good ground. So..."

"And what do you think, Harry?" Homer Langhorne enquired, and three fellow-Americans in penguin uniform craned their necks and pinned back their ears.

"The draw is a bugger, sir," said Harry. "17 out of 17. Up against the rails on the left-hand side of the track. Trouble is, all the bends are right-handed. The right-hand rail is the shortest way round, and we've drawn the exact opposite."

"So we've got no chance?" Langhorne suggested.

"I'll just have to work a miracle, that's all." Harry sighed.

"Could you not be a little more positive, Harry?" complained Fearnley. There was a murmur of support for this suggestion.

Harry glanced from face to face. Could he find words of encouragement? That was the trainer's job! Harry decided to go to the opposite extreme - realism.

"Just you look at the course when you get back to Mr Fearnley's box, gents. The first mile is on the climb all the way. Then a right-hand bend followed by two, three furlongs on the slope down to Swinley Bottom. Then another right-hander . From Swinley Bottom to the winning post is uphill all the way including another right-hand bend – thank you very much! He who presses the button too soon falls in a heap too soon. After losing ground at all those right-hand bends – it could be us!"

The silence that followed was shattered by Mr Fearnley. "So you don't think we'll win?"

. "I didn't say that," said Harry. "We will give it our best shot, sir. Hello! There's the bell! Action stations! Where's my 'oss?"

*

The racing world will never forget Frankie Dettori's ride on Golden Horn to win the Prix de l'Arc de Triomphe at Longchamp, arguably the most prestigious race in the world, in the autumn of 2015. Drawn 14 of 14, on the far left of the field, on a course with two right-handed bends, some good judges said that he had no chance.

As the horses stood in the stalls that day, Dettori looked ahead at four furlongs of straight before the course curved out of sight - to the right.

When the gates opened, the majority scrambled for the right-hand rails. But not Dettori and Golden Horn. They came out on the left of the line, and appeared to be maintaining a straight-ahead course. But they weren't. The wily Italian knew that he had four furlongs in which to manoeuvre across the course in order to take up a position close to, or in among, the massed ranks on his right. He also knew that if he used every yard of those four furlongs to move from the bad side to the good side very, very slowly, his straight line would be only a very few yards longer than that of the horses better drawn than he was.

His situation was not without at least one advantage. Being on his own, Golden Horn had nothing charging up his backside, no jockeys swearing in many languages, no cracking of whips to contend with. The benefit was not obvious from the stands but it was considerable: Golden Horn was positively sauntering as he made his way in solitary splendour up the course, all serene and saving energy with every stride.

As the runners reached the first right-hander, he was alongside the middle of the pack and reasonably close to it. By the end of that bend he was fourth and only two off the right-hand rail. There he stayed, and when the field straightened up for home a relatively fresh Golden Horn strode to the front and won with his head in his chest. That was then...

*

This was now... Down at the bottom of the Straight Mile, the starting stalls crashed open, seventeen runners burst out and Harry Bridger set out to "do a Dettori."

The first feature of the race was when the runners passed the stands, because the crowds greeted the field with a mighty roar, and the more impressionable of the runners grabbed hold of the bit and demanded to be allowed to go faster. This caused quite a bit of argument between horse and jockey, which is not ideal so early in a race of two and a half miles, plus a bit.

Shenandoah was unaffected by this exuberance. On his own, he was now in the middle of the track, halfway through his gradual lateral movement. Past the stands they went and on, until the field reached the first right-hand bend, then the mile-and-a-half start and the downhill stretch. Shen had almost, but not quite attached himself to the procession, as that procession started to quicken up, which it did because that's what running downhill does to horses.

If Shen had been seventh coming round the bend, he now found himself tenth or eleventh, because Harry hadn't allowed him to speed up and a few had passed him on his right. Why had Harry not gone with the flow? Because he knew that the ease with which the others seemed to be going was an illusion which had charmed them into burning more energy than was prudent; energy which should have been kept in reserve for the struggle that lay ahead.

When the field reached Swinley Bottom, the second right-hand bend brought them past the Round Mile start (on their left) to the beginning of the climb towards the distant winning post. The leaders slowed up a bit, and Shen finally joined the main group in seventh place and just two away from the inside rail, moving easily.

Now they were climbing the mountain, with the imposing architecture of the stands looming at its peak; looming over the wide strip of green which was about to put the runners to the sword.

Two of the leaders ran out of puff and drifted away from the rails on their right. Harry clicked with his tongue, and in two strides Shen was on those rails and through the gap. Fifth as they turned right-handed into the straight. Fourth a moment later, as another contender cried "Enough!" and Shen slid past him.

Now was the decisive moment. Harry wasn't worried about any of the four ahead of him. They had been there for too long, and the chance of power-failure had to be well on the cards for all four. In addition, the width of the track up the run-in meant that the chance of getting past them would be better than at any time in the race so far.

But... where was that bloody Irishman? Harry glanced left and right – no sign. He glanced between his legs, and there was the grey head – once again Diamond Crown was directly behind him. In Harry's mind there was just one thought. "If I let him sit on my tail, he might outspeed us at the death. He was a Derby horse. Time to go!"

A gap appeared between the pair just ahead and Shen went through it in three strides. Then the two leaders drifted away from the rails and gave him room to hit the front. Three furlongs from the finish Harry began to push, to click, to growl and to pray.

It was the pivotal moment. Making the opponent work a long way from home could be the answer, but not if your own horse capitulated first. Harry just hoped that both the gaps through which he had just sailed had slammed in the grey horse's face. He pressed on and Shen responded. But the strip of green ahead of them seemed never-ending.

Two furlongs out, and the sounds of hot pursuit grew louder. A movement caught the corner of Harry's left eye. There was the grey horse, less than a length behind. There was mister Cassidy, his bobbing head, his flashing whip, finely balanced, in perfect rhythm. Inch by inch the grey kept coming. When he was just a neck behind, Harry feared the worst...

And then the grey head checked and lifted, as Diamond Crown hung away under pressure. He had given his all, and had come up short. Shen ran on straight as an arrow, and passed the post three lengths ahead of his rival. Bottomless stamina, excellent strategy (and a couple of lucky breaks in running) had won the day.

When John added a further £180 to his sock, (£10 at 8 – 1 on Shen, plus another £100 from Mr Langhorne), he was sure that life could not get any better. But it did, when the word came from America that Skyline Drive had won the Arlington Million, at 20 -1. More joy for John, and more money. £5 at 20 – 1 meant a further £100, and Mr Langhorne remembered John's early work on Skyline to the tune of another £100. The sock now held £530 and the envelope was beginning to split at the seams.

CHAPTER FORTY

It was in the second week of August that a letter arrived. This time he recognised the handwriting.

"Dear John,

Mum suggested I bring you up to date.

I'm back from Oslo and the Junior Europeans. You may have seen that we finished third in the team event, and I was 4th individually on Prospero. The dressage judging was very fierce. A bit better dressage and I might have got a medal!

We brought Al in from the field when the grass lost its zing – is there such a word? I think he's grown an inch since last year. He's been doing a lot of roadwork to reduce his waistline and Emerald has joined mum and me in riding him. She has improved out of all recognition. The first time she got on him, Mum gave her "the look" and said, "You can bully Dropshot, because he sometimes deserves it and he's a toughie - so it's OK. Al is different. You love him, you pet him, you may even scold him a little bit, but you never get into a battle. If you sense trouble ahead, you just sit there and show how disappointed you are, and you sing out for me or Kate to come and help. Sing loudly, make him feel guilty." So far they have got on fine. They've even done some dressage together, with no problems. Al has been invited to turn out at Everdon at the beginning of October. A class for potential Junior horses for next year. A bit of a compliment – he's beginning to be noticed!

I should have congratulated you on your Ascot winner. We were all thrilled! Dad keeps buying the Racing Post, which is not like him at all!

See you soon. Much love, Kate."

*

Three weeks later, Joan rang John and announced that on the following day, which was a Sunday, she would be at Hurstbourne Tarrant, which was fairly close to Weyhill. She suggested a rendez-vous, so that they could have a chat.

When he arrived, he found himself in the midst of a Pony Club event – something called Combined Training – a bit of everything. He rather thought that Al had outgrown this level of competition.

This was his first experience of the Pony Club at play and he was quite astonished. Never had he been exposed to so many teenage females (most of the participants seemed to be female), who were clearly determined to outgrow their clothes before his very eyes. Rather pale, he navigated towards one of two dressage arenas and identified Joan by her floppy brown cap, her tan corduroy trousers, and a quilted green waistcoat over her shirt. She was a splendid example of the mature woman, standing some way back from the arena and watching intently.

Greetings and compliments having been exchanged, there followed a short silence. John eyed Joan keenly, for he suspected that a Sunday morning chat was probably a serious matter.

"Is he here?"

"Who?"

"Al."

"Good heavens, no!"

"I see," said John, which was far from the truth.

"Just hold on a minute," she added.

She had one eye on the dressage ring, so John paid attention. A chestnut pony, ridden by a girl, was doing its test.

"Should she be familiar?"

"Emerald Perry... on Dropshot... I can't remember if you met..."

"The little jogger," said John, "in the tracksuit... fitness fanatic. She's grown, hasn't she?"

"That's her, and you're quite right, she has."

Emerald Perry completed her test. John and Joan accompanied her back to the horse-box. There he stood and listened while coach and pupil dissected the performance. Not for the first time he noticed how clear Joan made everything she said. If it was something important, she would pause and think, and then the words that followed would be impossible to misinterpret. No wonder she's such a good teacher, he reflected.

In due course Emerald went off to prepare Dropshot for his next class, and Joan led John to the mobile canteen and bought them both coffee, and a bacon sandwich for John, who hadn't had any breakfast. After silence while he wolfed his rations, and then a few minutes of chat, John began to wonder when she was going to broach the subject which was the object of the exercise, whatever it might be. Not yet, apparently, because she glanced at her watch, finished her coffee, made him bring his sandwich and led him to the vicinity of a show-jumping class.

More chat, more silence, and John felt it appropriate to say, "Right, Mrs Ferris, what did you...?"

"Oh, bother," said Joan, looking over his shoulder. "Here she comes already."

John looked round and there was the little chestnut. Into the ring he trotted, elegant, well-balanced, ears pricked. The bell rang and away he went. Emerald seemed nice and relaxed, but as she went past on the way to the first obstacle John caught the look in her eye: she was concentrating one hundred percent – and she did a clear round.

"Wasn't that good?" said Joan, and John agreed, after which he was allowed to take Dropshot for a walk while Joan and Emerald walked the cross-country course. When they came back, all three had a sandwich and a cup of tea beside the horsebox, before Emerald mounted Dropshot and they left for their next appointment.

"Come on," Joan said. "We'll have to hurry."

She led him at a brisk pace between the two dressage arenas, and over a post and rail fence; then across a grass field, and through a belt of fir trees. As they started across the next grass field, a grey pony popped over a hedge on their right, cantered past and jumped a rail in the fence line towards which they were heading.

"Hello!" said John. The grey had leapt the rail, and then disappeared completely. When they reached the obstacle all was revealed: on the far side the ground fell away steeply, and then less steeply. The grey pony was negotiating a log at the bottom. The next obstacle involved jumping another log and landing in a stream about twenty feet wide.

The grey pony arrived at the second log, rose high into the air, landed with an enormous splash, and continued on its way.

Joan led John to an oak tree on the near side of the stream, quite near the water. Providence had seen fit to position three straw bales at the base of the trunk. Seating themselves, they had a fine view of proceedings.

Joan pointed back to the rail at the top of the slope.

"Keep your eye on..."

As she spoke, a black and white check cap and a chestnut head appeared simultaneously, and Dropshot floated out over the rail and landed neatly. He and Emerald completed the descent, and hopped over the log at the bottom. As she rode past the tree, oblivious to the presence of two interested parties, John heard her growl. It was a most extraordinary sound. A bulldog guarding his stricken master from the attentions of a wounded buffalo could not have been more emphatic. Dropshot's ears flickered back and forth. He bounded across the grass, popped over the second log, landed in the stream under a torrent of spray and hurried on. Last seen, he had reached dry land, with Emerald patting a wet chestnut neck.

"What do you think?" Joan asked.

"I wasn't expecting that growl from your jockey."

"Riders are allowed to encourage their mounts," Joan said. "Better to growl than to beat."

She paused, then said, "So... what did you think of Emerald's performance?"

"Ten-out-of-ten?" John suggested. "Pony did everything right, and jockey seemed determined that he should. Did I miss something?"

"No, no," Joan reassured him. "That's exactly how I saw it. Straight in, straight out, no problem, really well done."

She laughed, and added, "It's probably absolutely meaningless, but I did rather want to see what would happen. And I wanted you to see it, too. I was looking for an omen."

John raised a pair of puzzled eyebrows.

"Dropshot loathes water," Joan explained.

"Good heavens!"

"And this is a particularly unhelpful water-jump, because you can see it right from the moment you jump the rail at the top of the bank. The horse knows there's water ahead. You can't surprise him, or kid him. He's got all the time in the world to think of reasons for declining to cooperate."

"But he went ... sweet as a nut," said John. "Partly because of the growl?"

"Exactly."

"How do you account for it?"

Joan said, "Emerald Perry is a most improved young rider, and I give her much of the credit for transforming Dropshot from a bit of a pig – a cheeky pig, nothing sinful - into what he is now – pretty useful. Kate helped a lot, but her idea was to let Emerald do the business, while she merely advised - and so far it has worked. And when she is not growling, she can be extremely sensitive and diplomatic towards whatever she's riding."

"So the omen was... a good one? For what?"

Joan said, "She'll soon be too big for that pony, and she'll want to move up a class in a year or so... and I'm her coach, which fits in well... I'm thinking we might sell Al to her!"

"Is that where we're at?" John exclaimed. "Already?"

"Not absolutely this minute."

"When do you think…?"

"Next year… in the Spring."

"I see," said John. "What does Kate say?"

"If Al has to change hands, Kate would like Emerald to have him."

"How much would Al make?"

"I don't think we could ask less than £10,000."

"Cripes! Really?"

"A young horse, which has been second in a BE 80 and 90 and third in a BE 100, and finished 5th in his first Novice class? That's the kind of money one should be asking."

"Would that be a problem for the Perrys?"

"Not at all. They're very well off."

"What does Emerald think?"

"She doesn't know anything about it. Nor do her parents."

"I'm bowled over," said John.

Joan smiled. "We have time to mull it over. But if, in due course, the opportunity to sell materialised, would you be in favour?"

"For that kind of money… I'd certainly be in favour. What about you, Mrs Ferris?"

"Windfalls don't come along all that often. One really should strike while the iron is hot. How else will one keep the wolf from the door?" She paused, then added, "One thing at a time. Let's see how Al gets on at Everdon."

CHAPTER FORTY-ONE

In the middle of September Joan decided that Roscoe (her tall and rather narrow ex-racehorse) was ready for a preliminary examination - in the form of a very humble competition designed for beginners. During the summer he had done a number of Pony Club events, ridden by Emerald, so he was not unfamiliar with the various disciplines. This time Joan would ride him herself, and she found just such a beginners' class early in the day at the Everdon meeting.

"We're going to Everdon with Al," she said to Kate. "We'll take Roscoe as well."

Al had been invited to take part in the Junior Autumn Plate. As Kate had said in her letter, this was for horses and riders aspiring towards junior international honours the following year. It would attract many of the best young riders, and many of the best young horses. As it was limited to junior riders, it was not classed as an "open" competition; so there were no points to be earned. This made it ideal for Al. It was good experience against high-class opposition. He was unlikely to finish "in the money" in such company, but if he did it wouldn't affect his status as a Novice. No valuable points would be squandered.

So it was that, at 6.30 a.m., mother and daughter thrust two mildly disconcerted quadrupeds into the horsebox and set out on the journey to Northamptonshire. Father and dog were absent: he was at work (this was a midweek occasion) and Brownie was deemed too precious to take without her personal minder.

Emerald heard the box set off, then snuggled down for another thirty minutes. She was in charge of the home front with Belinda, a Scottish girl who had recently joined the team in response to overspill: all five boxes at home were now occupied, and there were four more horses living at Glebe Farm, across the road, where Belinda lodged. So there were boxes to muck out and set fair; horses to exercise, groom, feed and water; and a repeat performance, apart from the exercise, at teatime.

Heading north, Joan made good time, taking advantage of the precious minutes before the traffic became the rush hour. Beside her, Kate thought about the day ahead. The fact that both she and her mother were competing bothered her a little bit, especially as Dad wasn't with them. It meant that the valet-groom-maid-service to which she was accustomed would be much reduced, and she, Kate, would be expected to provide all those services for Mum! Not to worry. Roscoe's class started at 10.30 and would be over before Al's got under way. Everything would be all right. Then she remembered that Al's mane still had to be plaited. No peace for the wicked!

Everdon greeted the new arrivals with sunshine, autumn leaves in several interesting shades of brown and a gentle breeze. Once they had settled in and dispatched a leisurely picnic breakfast, Kate's first duty was to unite a neat and tidy Joan with a neat and tidy Roscoe, and dispatch them to warm up for their dressage and then do their test.

As things turned out, all her misgivings about the pressure under which she would be working were needless. Al's mane was tamed without too much trouble, and Roscoe came back having done a good dressage and consequently carrying a rider who was full of the joys. Carried along by Mum's euphoria, Kate threw herself into the turn-around necessary to prepare Roscoe for his show-jumping, while Joan dashed off to walk the cross-country course. Meanwhile Alcapony stood quietly in his stall in the horsebox. Only one thing bothered him: no haynet at this stage of a working day.

Joan returned, flushed and breathing hard. She glanced at her watch and mounted Roscoe.

"What's the course like?" Kate asked, hoping to get the full benefit of her mother's inspection.

"Watch out for the farmyard complex," responded Joan darkly. "It's not as easy as it looks!" And off she rode, leaving her daughter only a little the wiser.

Roscoe rattled three of the show-jumps, but only one pole actually hit the ground. This created even more euphoria, and also a little bit of extra tension. Two good performances and just one more test to face – would the partnership be capable of finishing the job in style? It has to be said that Roscoe seemed quite indifferent to the moment of destiny that awaited him – his brief experience of racing had clearly endowed him with nerves of steel.

His rider was less self-assured. As she rode off towards the cross-country start, Joan looked rather more than normally serious: a first cross-country outing on an ex-racehorse is no laughing matter for anybody, and is particularly testing for a lady at an age when the boldness of youth has been replaced by the more circumspect attitudes appropriate to a wife and mother.

However the Fates were in a good mood. When the partnership came back, Joan was smiling, Roscoe was clearly elated, and both were blowing like steam-engines.

"He went really well!" Joan gasped, as she fell out of the saddle. "And didn't he pull! My arms are two inches longer than they were! Jump? He jumped like a stag!"

They went off for a cool-down walk which the rider needed as much as the horse, and Kate set off to walk the cross-country course. The first field was a fine example of ridge and furrow. Thousands of years previously agricultural practice had created a surface not unlike a sheet of corrugated iron. Not the most comfortable for a horse and rider to negotiate. Thereafter the ground rose and fell in long, smooth stretches of springy downland turf which had probably never done anything apart from energising sheep, who repaid the favour generously in the only ways they know how – by cropping and fertilising.

Kate walked and trotted along, and the first seven obstacles seemed harmless enough. Then there was quite a steep hill which made her puff a bit, but the fence at the top was the smallest so far. Next, the farmyard complex: a gate in, a right turn, jump a low trailer, a left turn and jump out over a water-trough. Quite tricky (as Mum had warned): but the actual obstacles weren't too formidable.

After that, level ground and several downhill slopes. Kate was well aware that downhill may make life a bit easier, but downhill fences require full measure of eternal vigilance, and then some. Eventually the course levelled out again, and there, on the other side of an inviting log, were the red and white flags of the finish.

Kate hurried back to base, in need of a rest, she reckoned. Instead of which it was all systems go. Joan had put Roscoe back in the box, and brought out Al. Together mother and daughter brushed him over, tacked him up, checked all the moving parts and oiled his hooves.

"Riding in" proved problem-free. Both horse and rider behaved themselves. Physically and mentally they seemed in good order and in harmony. Kate looked at her watch. Just right. Let's go...

The dressage test went well. Al made no mistakes, and his heart was in the right place throughout. Like a guardsman on parade, he was comfortable, confident, competent, conscientious and serious without being dull. Eventually closure was achieved: halt, stand still, stand straight, bow to the judge, walk out of the arena, trot back to the box.

Where was Mum? Nowhere to be seen. Kate put Al back in the box and treated herself to coffee and a sandwich.

Still no sign of Mum. Kate got Al out again, tacked him up and rode away to prepare for show-jumping. She had a little trot round the practice area, then cantered in towards one of the two jumps. "Steady! Steady! Steady!" Al flew the obstacle, but there was precious little "steady-steady" about it; in fact he was unusually keen and Kate had some difficulty pulling him up. Has the guardsman gone mad? Then all was revealed: Kate had forgotten to put on his martingale! Al always wore it for show-jumping and cross-country. It encouraged him to bend his neck, which gave Kate that little bit of extra control, and helped the partnership to be accurate at the obstacles.

Mum, where are you in our hour of need? Suddenly Kate discovered that she had been quite right to worry about the difficulties that might occur with two horses, two jockeys, no James and no Emerald. But there was nothing she could do about it, because Al's time had come.

Kate trotted him into the ring, praying that a strange set of obstacles in a strange arena would imbue him with a sense of responsibility, and it helped. He started off a bit fast, but relaxed as he warmed to his task. The further he went, the better he went, and he had no trouble in doing the clear round, within the time limit, which was all that was required.

Joan was waiting for them as they came out of the ring.

"You went walkabout!"

Mum was full of apologies "Colonel Bailey turned up and we had to go and have a drink. And I couldn't stop telling him about Roscoe! So sorry! But you managed - that's the main thing. Well done."

As she took charge of Al she said, "You were equal first after the dressage. Equal with Ginny Hayter. You both had 21 penalties. Then she went clear at the show-jumping."

"So did I," said Kate. "Al was brilliant."

Ginny Hayter was a friend of hers since way back. They had been team mates in Oslo.

When the time came to prepare Al for his cross-country, mother scored heavily by remembering the martingale, which Kate had once again forgotten. As they set off for a little walk and a trot in the practice area, Kate was particularly grateful, because she found Al still a bit too revved up. He was like a spring, coiled perhaps too tightly for his own good. Perhaps he had spent too long in the horsebox.

They made their way slowly towards the start. The starter called them into the pen. Al felt very strong.

"Five... four.... three...." He tried to charge off. Kate turned him away from the start-line, then back again – just in time.

"...two, one, go!"

At least we're facing the right way, Kate thought, as she felt Al surge forward. The timing was right, the direction was right, but the speed was too fast.

The ridge and furrow lived up to its dubious reputation. Al's stride-length contrived to make him land in the bottom of alternate furrows and on the top of alternate ridges. This produced anything but a steady rhythm and didn't help Kate to persuade him to slow down. They came to the first fence, which he jumped well. He was good at the second and at the third – but much of the credit belonged to Lady Luck. In spite of the martingale, Al wouldn't relax.

Now the course curved to the right before the fourth, which was a low wall supporting a very solid timber rail. Al met it wrong and hit the rail hard with his front legs. In a split second his propulsion slowed dramatically, but Kate's didn't. As they landed, she found herself falling, falling, falling over his left shoulder, with the green grass grinning up at her.

"I can't fall off! We've only just started!"

In desperate endeavour she hung on to Al's neck and the right rein, which was all that was keeping her aloft. Her partner, in spite of a body hanging round his neck and a lot of very uncomfortable pressure on his mouth, kept going straight. Somehow Kate wriggled back into the saddle - just in time for the next fence, which Al cleared by a foot. He jumped the next line of fences as clever as a cat. But this cat was still galloping too fast for his own good.

"Steady! Steady!" Kate begged, as they faced a long stretch of level turf before the next three fences, but Al was not in the mood for half measures. Only when those fences had been safely negotiated did his ears twitch and his stride shorten, as he responded to her pleadings.

Had the damage already been done, Kate asked herself? How much petrol remained in the tank, after such profligacy of effort? She was about to find out, because the hill was still to come.

When they met the rising ground and faced the three obstacles that had to be negotiated, Kate determined to nurse Al slowly and patiently to the summit. This she managed to achieve, and as they reached the crest she felt a mixture of emotions: guilt for having so nearly fallen off, and relief that Al had apparently got this far without suffering the exhaustion he had experienced in the mud at Frensham.

Down the far side of the hill they went, and neatly through the farmyard. One by one she nursed him into and over the remaining jumps. Speed was not an issue; all that mattered was a safe closure to a round that had not gone according to plan. It seemed to take forever, but at long last they came to the inviting log and the beckoning flags. A click of the tongue, a pat on the neck. Good little man. Done it!

"You set off much too fast," Joan said, as they made their way back to the horsebox, Kate on her feet and leading Al.   .

Kate said nothing for a moment, and then told her the rest of the story.

"What a nightmare!" said Joan.

"All my fault, mum."

Joan took a turn round Al as he walked along.

"No damage, as far as I can see. We may have got away with it."

Al was washed down, then "scraped" to get rid of surplus water, and then taken for a walk while he cooled down and dried off. Finally he was put away in the box, where Roscoe and a haynet awaited him. He took no notice of the former, and got stuck into the latter – another indication that perhaps the day's exertions had not done him any real harm.

At last, horse-work done, pressure off, mother and daughter realised how hungry they were. Sandwiches and the thermos were dug out, and that gave them the strength, eventually, to go over to the Secretary's tent to wait for the results. It was a beautiful afternoon, and in the west preparations for a flaming sunset were well in hand.

In the tent, messengers kept appearing from all over the course, bringing in the scores from the fence-judges. On a large blackboard numbers were constantly being updated; in fact the scores for most of the contestants had been fully filled in. Ginny Hayter was well clear of the field. Her penalties read:

Dressage: 21

Show-jumping: 0

Jumping penalties cross-country: 0

Time-faults cross-country: 6

TOTAL: 27

Only six time faults; she must have gone jolly fast, Kate reflected. Al's cross-country marks weren't up yet. It was only partly his fault that he had been too keen; only partly his fault that she had tried to throw herself to the ground at the fourth fence. Wherever he finished, he had done well. He had done well to finish at all.

They went back to the box; stuck a hand under each horse's rug to make sure they hadn't started sweating again. Both were dry, warm, and comfortable. They offered them water, and both horses said "Thank you very much!" Then they made sure that all the tack had been packed and loaded, and that nothing had been left underneath the horsebox.

Everything shipshape, they went back to the tent and checked the board. All the results were in.

Alcapony's penalties were:
Dressage: 21
Show jumping: 0
Jumping faults cross-country: 0
Time faults cross-country : 4
TOTAL: 25

It took a moment before the penny dropped. Alcapony had won the Junior Autumn Plate - by two points. Not some tinpot little contest for run-of-the-mill performers, but the Junior Autumn Plate, no less – against some of the *crème de la crème* of the nation's junior horses and riders!

*

Apart from the roar of the engine and the hum of the rush-hour traffic, the journey home was comparatively quiet. This was because mother and daughter were blissfully happy. They smiled a lot.

Behind them the achiever-in-chief was continuing to feed his face. Beside him the lanky Roscoe was similarly employed, but with better table manners. Apart from pulling Joan's arms out, he had never put a foot wrong and had finished fifth in his class – a debut of considerable promise.

That evening, Joan rang John Dunne. Before breaking the news, she warned him against getting over-excited, but it did no good.

"What?" he yelped. "He beat the best?"

"They were all there!"

"And he could have done even better... a faster time?"

"Kate thinks so - if she had anchored him early on."

"Well, I'm.... I don't know what to say! I really don't!"

"Don't have a fit, John! But it is exciting. Before today one could hope that he was worth £10,000. Now we know for a fact that he's worth *at least* that amount!"

CHAPTER FORTY-TWO

"Ten thousand pounds," said John. "What do you think?"

"Are you short of money?" Bod asked.

"Not really. I've won a few pounds recently, thanks to Harry and one of the owners," John revealed. "But we've got to sell, don't you think?"

Bod glared at his glass, then pushed it aside and glared at John.

"I think that's rubbish!"

"But I can't ignore the money..."

"Stuff the money! You buggered up that pony and then you got lucky. If I remember correctly, Paddy O'Malley pointed you in the right direction and your Mrs Whats-her-name..."

"Ferris."

"Your Mrs Ferris and her daughter, they did the business. They turned a load of rubbish (created by you) into something that sounds like a very useful animal. And now you can't wait to cash him in!"

"It's not like that at all," protested John. "If the Perry family buys him for Emerald, he'll still be under the management of ..."

"Didn't you tell me once upon a time that the little girl's mother was a temperamental cow?"

"Yes, but..."

"Yes, but nothing!" Bod snorted. "If you've learnt nowt about horses, learn this: an animal that's been through what this one's been through (thanks to you) is always going to be just a little bit more..." (he searched for a word) "more fragile in his head than the normal horse. He's been lucky enough to find surroundings in which he is comfortable, and people who understand him. He's come back from a bad situation, a very bad situation."

Bod looked at John as if a nasty smell had invaded the air-space under

his nose. "He could have done you a serious injury, that time...
Remember?"

John nodded.

"And now he's a different horse and he's performing very well – and
the last thing he needs is for you to change his situation in any way."

John opened his mouth, but Bod was off again. "It's not just the horse
I'm thinking of. All the good work that other people have done could go
out the window, too."

Having neglected his glass for a most unusual length of time, he
emptied it and replaced it on the table.

He got to his feet. "He's landed in a good place, and now you're
planning to throw him back to the sharks! For money! No amount of
money entitles you to do that! I'd better go now - before you make me
angry."

*

John sought comfort in the company of Rosemary. She listened to his
account of the interview with Bod and squeezed his hand
sympathetically. She could see that he was suffering.

"Oh dear. That's terrible," she said. "And I'm not going to be much
help, I'm afraid."

"Not?"

She shook her head.

"You don't agree with him, do you?"

"I'm afraid I do. I agree with everything he said. You made this mess.
And you've cleared it up really well, up to now. But you've got to keep
going, and if you take the money and run you won't be the adorable
creature whose hand I have been squeezing."

Saying which, she withdrew her paw.

John sighed. "Go on," he said dolefully.

"D'you remember Noel Murless? Champion Trainer in the distant
past. You told me about him. We were driving back from somewhere.
He learnt more about horses from his first pony... Mary Jane, wasn't that
her name? He learnt more about horses from Mary Jane than from any
one else in all his life."

She looked him in the eye. "And you said 'One day I might be saying,
'I learned more about horses from my first pony than I did from anyone
else - but I did it the hard way!' But I don't remember you saying that Mr
Murless got a good offer for Mary Jane and sold her."

CHAPTER FORTY-THREE

It was Sunday teatime at the Ferris home. Sitting on the sofa beside John, Rosemary studied the ornaments on the mantelpiece.

John cleared his throat. "We mustn't sell!" he announced.

"I beg your pardon?" said Joan.

"Likewise," said James. At his feet Brownie rolled her eyes to show that she too was amazed.

John set off at a gallop. "Alcapony was my first solo effort in the horse world and I really messed up... really messed up. The only thing I did right was to keep trying, which led to him coming here. Then you and Kate.... and Mr Ferris..."

"And me! That's good to hear," James murmured.

"The Ferris family performed a miracle, and created something out of nothing, something wonderful, out of worse than nothing, and I really don't want to do anything that might undo all your good work – just for money."

He paused, and Joan said, "But, John..."

"Let me finish... You've also turned him into something quite valuable. We were talking the other day about ten thousand pounds, half of which would be yours if we sold, and you deserve every penny. So I would like to buy your half for £5,000, which may take me a bit of time to pay, and I want to start paying for half his keep. In a nutshell I want him to stay with you for ever."

Silence greeted this bold aspiration. John reached into his inside pocket and produced a bulging and crumpled envelope which he put on the coffee table. The very faint aroma of vintage unwashed winter sock drifted upwards. Only Rosemary's nose was sensitive enough to quiver in response.

"There you are - £530. A deposit. I've got a bit more in the bank, and I'm going to speak to Mr Fearnley... and I'm going to do whatever it takes..."

He stopped, and glanced at Rosemary. She gave his arm a squeeze.

"Well," said Joan, "that was quite a mouthful, John. What made you change your mind?"

"It was something old Bod said... You've heard me talk about Mr Boddy?"

"The ex-head lad," said James, "with the livery yard?"

John nodded. "I told him I was about to make a fortune, and he was disgusted. He said I owed it to the pony to make sure he stays where he is. Not because Al's done me any favours, but because I did him so much harm. Up to now I've paid off a bit of that debt, by getting you involved. But *you* know, I'm sure, (and even I know, now that Bod's pointed it out), that if he got into the wrong hands he could easily return to a bad, bad place. I want to do whatever I can to see that that doesn't happen - ever."

Silence reigned, but not for long.

"Oh, I forgot to mention – Rosemary – she agrees with Bod. She's given me hell."

Rosemary confirmed same with a nod, a grin and a gentle elbow.

"Well, well, well," said Joan. "Only one small mistake on your part, and thank God you spoke out. We... we, the Ferris family, have no wish to sell our share in the little man."

"But you said..."

"I know what I said."

"About the money?"

"Windfalls don't come along all that often?" she said. "Something like that? Strike while the iron is hot."

"Yes... Didn't you mean it?"

"I meant it. But it wasn't for our sake. We may not be very, very rich, but we don't have any worries in that department. James has slaved all his life to keep the wolf from the door."

. "A truer word was never spoken," said James. "I've worked my fingers to the bone." He extended a hand: the digits were in fact very adequately covered. "The financial pressure to which we responded was yours. How could we not notice that we were dealing with a pauper? You couldn't afford this, you couldn't afford that, you had to give away half of your only asset, the mighty Alcapony, in order to keep yourself afloat. Our hearts bled for you, and that's why my saintly wife pretended to be a ruthless money-grubber. Now you say you don't want our help! Are you ever going to make up your mind?"

"I wanted the money, I can't deny that," said John. "But I was also concerned that Mrs Ferris should get a fair reward for what she has done. And I still am concerned. But once Bod said what he said, and once Rosemary agreed with him, I saw the light."

"Well, your second thoughts," said James, "are music to our ears. Kate has two more years as a junior, and after that Emerald Perry could well take over, but only if our little friend takes a liking to her. If not, she gets the chop, and we find someone else. Ruthless, I know, but that's the way we Ferrises are! All in all, that gives us three or four years to play with, during which who knows what might happen? Think about it."

"I will. I am. I have. It sounds like the answer to everything," said John. He turned to Rosemary. "What do you think?"

"The best news in the world. Better than you deserve."

.Joan rose to her feet. "Let's go for a walk, before it gets dark."

She and Brownie led the way outside, through the gate, across the track, and along the passage between the blocks of wooden boxes. The nearest of the three that faced the house was still the tack room; next door was Dropshot's friendly chestnut head, and the third box was occupied by Prospero. At the other side, the three boxes facing out towards the field were also occupied.

John and Rosemary joined their hosts beside the rails of the manège. Far away across the field Alcapony and Dalesman raised their heads for a moment, then went back to their grazing.

"You see that?" said Joan pointing towards what looked like a building site to their left. "That used to be a row of pigsties. We're building ten loose boxes there. We've now got six horses across at the farm waiting to come over. Kate, Emerald and Belinda (you haven't met her) are over there now, doing evening stables."

"When they finish there," said James. "They will return to HQ and do the same over here. When all is shipshape my wife will inspect the cavalry and supervise the feeding."

"What you are seeing," said Joan, "is the evidence that the Ferris establishment is on the up-and-up. Most of this is due to Kate and Prospero; but quite a lot is the response to Al's performances. That's another reason why it makes sense for us to keep our share in him."

. "And there's something in it for you, John," James added. "If we have a yard full of horses, all paying customers, the expense of half one animal which doesn't bring in a monthly income can be absorbed. Especially if its performances are helping the business to prosper. You may therefore continue your no-expense regime for your half of my little friend Alcapony until further notice. Mind you, I'll have to clear that spontaneous and perhaps rather irresponsible extravagance with the boss."

"The boss is content," said Joan, straight-faced.

"Well, I just don't know what to say," said John, and he sniffed twice. Rosemary glanced at him and decided another nudge was in order. Whereupon John sniffed again, cleared his throat emphatically, and frowned in a manly and threatening manner.

"Thank you," he said.

"Are you in a hurry to go?" Joan asked Rosemary as they headed back to the house.

"I don't think so. John, are we in a hurry?"

"Not at all."

"Stay for supper. Kate and Emerald will be back soon."

*

Wined and dined, three hours later they gathered round the flames and crackle of the hearth in the withdrawing room: two guitars (father and daughter Ferris), three sopranos (Emerald, Rosemary, Kate), Joan's rich contralto, John's unruly tenor, with James' magnificent baritone keeping the "toute ensemble" timely and tuneful.

As on so many occasions in the past, James gazed at his wife and daughter and thanked his lucky stars. And what about the guest under their roof, sitting there singing like an angel? A year ago Emerald was a bit of a mess - look at her now! An excellent rider, an excellent worker, and altogether a wonderful young woman. All off her own bat and in spite of considerable obstacles.

"Will thou come with me, sweet Tibby Dunbar?
Will thou come with me, sweet Tibby Dunbar?
Will you ride on a horse or be drawn in a car
Or walk by my side, O sweet Tibby Dunbar?"

Rosemary had never seen John looking so completely goofy, so completely relaxed. She knew why. For the last four years he had carried a load of guilt on his shoulders because of Alcapony. Now he was off the hook and floating on a cloud of bliss. She caught his eye and winked. He started to laugh. It crossed her mind that she might just have to marry him one day. But not any time soon. Heaven forbid!

"Now some delight in haymakin', and some delight in mowin',
But of all the jobs as Oi loike best, gi' Oi the turnip hoein'.
The Fly! The Fly! The Fly be on the turnip!
And 'tis all my eye that I should try - to keep him off the turnip!"

*

The midnight darkness wasn't dark at all – a full moon took care of that. In the field shelter, Dalesman sniffed the straw, and pawed at it gently with a persistent hoof. Then he turned in a tight half-circle that was almost a pirouette. His front legs buckled. With a grunt he sank gracefully (for a large horse) into his bed.

At the other end of the shelter Alcapony left his haynet, picked his way to the rails, and looked out across the field. His ears twitched as he listened to the music from the house.

The trees beyond the distant fence whispered as a light breeze tickled their ribs, the stars glittered merrily and the moon presided like a benevolent nanny. A shadow emerged through the fence at the far corner: a fox trotted lightly across the grass and disappeared back into the woods.

Now all was silent. Alcapony sighed. He turned and made his way to his end of the shelter. There he too inspected the bedding with nose and hoof, and circled, and buckled and sank. For a while he stared through the rails, out across the field, head erect and ears alert. Then he sighed once more; his head sank by stages on to his knees. His eyelids began to close, but not for long. More singing...

"Where do yon blackbird be?

I know where 'ee be!

'Ee be up yon sycamore tree and I be after 'ee.

'Ee sees I, I sees 'ee, buggered if I don't 'ave 'ee!

Wi' a girt big stick I'll knock 'ee down.

Blackbird, I'll 'ave 'ee!"

Finally the concert ended. Silence reigned. Then, from the direction of the house, voices... chattering... laughing. A car door slammed - once... twice. An engine barked, growled, faded and was gone.

Alcapony sniffed the air. Ruminant, he flexed his jaw and crunched a stray oat which had surfaced in the back of his mouth. Then he sighed again, a good long sigh this time, as eyes closed and head sank once more. A sigh can convey any one of a multitude of messages. But in this case we have the sigh of one who has been tested in the crucible of life, in company with many of his nearest and dearest. All have passed the test, and none better than Alcapony himself. That being so, there is reason to believe that such a long sigh could only have been an expression of perfect contentment.

THE END

33762141R00123

Printed in Great Britain
by Amazon

Come On Up

A One Act Comedy/Drama by Sylvia Walker
(Running time 50 mins)

Scene 1
Rosie's sitting room *(Throughout Play)*

LIGHTING
Warm & Bright *(throughout)*
(Fade to Black noted on script)

MUSIC
Harp Music

CHARACTERS

KATH 40/60
ROSIE 40/60
VICTOR 40/70
MS GOOD . . . . Any Age

birthday next week, we'll have a party at my house, so don't go sulking. I've bought you a box of your favourite cigars. *(Pause)* Yes dear, of course we can play some war games if it makes you happy. Now I really have to go. *(Pause)* Yes I'll be in touch. Let me know how you go on with the little boats. Goodbye. *(Replaces receiver & returns to table, picks up knitting & sits in arm chair)*

(TELEPHONE RINGS)

ROSIE: *(rises taking knitting)* Tut tut... *(picks up telephone)* Oh hello Peter. *(Pause)* Just a moment.

(Shouts to KATH who is off stage)

Kath - Victor's arrived and he's waiting at Security.

KATH: Ask Peter to send him up and we'll have a drink before we go.

ROSIE: *(to Kath)* That will be nice. *(on phone)* Tell Mr Sylvester to come on up please Peter.

(Replaces receiver)

(ROSIE quicksteps humming Victor Sylvester's signature tune over to side table, deposits the knitting and collects the tray with a bottle of wine and three glasses and places it on the coffee table. Pours drinks & sits in armchair)

ROSIE: Slow- slow- quick- quick-slow.

(Enter KATH dramatically. She has put on diamante necklace, tiara and ear-rings. She gives a twirl and strikes a pose)

KATH: How do I look?

ROSIE: You look lovely. George was right, it does suit you.

(KATH perches on the sofa)

KATH: There. - Do you think Victor will approve?

ROSIE: He's sure to. You'll be the belle of the ball - all eyes will be watching you as you glide round the floor.

(ROSIE gives a glass of wine to kath.)

(DOOR BELL RINGS)

(KATH arranges herself on the sofa)

KATH: That will be him now. Let him in please, will you?

ROSIE: Yes.

(ROSIE exits SL. She returns and stands to rear of armchair. VICTOR follows. He is dressed in full evening dress. He has a numbered card secured to his back. He strikes a dancing pose, then dances round the room)

VICTOR: Slow - slow - quick - quick- slow. Slow slow quick quick slow. - Oh ladies how nice to see you. Strict tempo - you just can't beat it.

(He goes over to kath and sweeps her in his arms, they dance a few steps then leans her over in tango bend and kisses her five times to the rhythm of "slow slow quick quick slow".)

ROSIE: *(as they kiss)* Slow slow - quick quick slow.

VICTOR: Oh Kath - you dance like an angel.

KATH: *(coyly)* I *am* an angel Victor - Well nearly.

ROSIE: *(laughing)* We're all angels, but don't mind me.

(KATH & VICTOR break & sit on sofa)

VICTOR: Sorry, but we just got carried away.

KATH: I always forget my troubles when I'm dancing.

ROSIE: I prefer something more modern myself, like Elvis Presley, he's so very sexy. *(Swings hips)*

KATH: Yes, but he can't dance as well as Victor.

(ROSIE hands wine to VICTOR)

ROSIE: There you go Victor - down the hatch.

(ROSIE gets her own glass & sits in armchair)

VICTOR: Thank you - bottoms up.

(He sips his wine)

KATH: Who was that on the phone just now?

ROSIE: Winston.

KATH: What did *he* want again?

ROSIE: He wanted me to help him with his war manoeuvres, but I don't feel like taxing my brain tonight.

KATH: Was he cross?

ROSIE: He sulked a bit, but he cheered up when I told him I'd arrange a birthday party specially for him.

VICTOR: That's extremely kind of you.

ROSIE: It will be a good excuse for a bit of a knees up.

KATH: Oh good - I love a party. - Who shall we invite?

ROSIE: The usual crowd, and I think we should ask Mr Van Gogh, he needs cheering up.

KATH: Good idea, although he can be a wet blanket.

ROSIE: He needs to get that ear fixed. I asked Winston if he could use his influence with J.C., but he said he would go straight to *HER* - the top - you know - *(reverent tones)* - She who must be kneeled to.

KATH: Will she give him an audience do you think?

ROSIE: She might for Winston - he's quite a powerful man, although at times he does some very silly things.

VICTOR: She's great, when you get to know her - very approachable. Why don't you ask her round for a drink, she enjoys a good natter with the girls.

KATH: *(impressed)* Do you know her that well Victor?

VICTOR: Yes I've taken her dancing a few times. Quite a nice pair of pins has Ms Good.

(Both women gasp)

ROSIE: Really!

KATH: Goodness!

VICTOR: I've lived up here a bit longer than you have - she and I have become firm friends. She does a fair quick-step.

ROSIE: Well I never!

KATH: One doesn't think of *HER* dancing a quick-step, does one?

ROSIE: No. I've only seen her at the Annual Generals and she's always so business-like, she won't stand any nonsense. She gives those disciples one hell of a time if they step out of line. Peter was quaking in his sandals last meeting, because he hadn't answered the phone after three rings.

VICTOR: Oh yes that's company policy. She can be very firm, but she's always fair, she puts a lot of thought into her decisions.

ROSIE: You can't argue with that.

VICTOR: And she's done so much for the economy - Nobody can say they're poor. Look how she gave free butter to the pensioners last week.

KATH: I was disgusted with the way they all rushed - it was like the Charge of the Light Brigade.

ROSIE: And there's no need to rush here - I think it was only the new arrivals. - they aren't used to the routine yet - there's plenty for everyone, isn't there Victor?

VICTOR: Of course. They'll soon learn. She's the soul of patience with the OAP'S.

KATH: That's nice.

VICTOR: And she's very fond children - they have a wonderful time. She runs the Ovaltineys, the Tufty Club, and the Brownies and Cubs. She puts a lot of effort into the children's activities, she's even organising a trip to Disneyland

KATH: *(surprised)* But that's down there.

VICTOR: We have one here as well, and Walt meets all the children personally and arranges to have their photograph taken with Mickey Mouse.

KATH: How lovely.

ROSIE: I'm getting a very different picture of her from you Victor, I've always felt slightly in awe of her.

VICTOR: That's because you've only seen her in a business environment with her managerial team and she can be a tough cookie with them, even though she adores them. She insists they do everything to her high standards, but you get her at a party and she's the life and soul. She has a great sense of humour.

ROSIE: Has she? Not many people realise that.

VICTOR: Oh yes. She gave Peter on the Gate a CD of the Supremes singing

"I Can't Deny you Baby."

(Both women laugh)

ROSIE: She sounds good fun, I think I will invite her to Winston's birthday party. What do you think Kath?

KATH: I think it's an excellent idea. I've only met her at my initial interview when I first came into the light. I'm due for another quite soon. I'm waiting to be summoned, but I must admit I'm a little apprehensive.

VICTOR: You've nothing to worry about but it might be a good idea to invite her round socially. Ask her round for a drink.

(All sip wine)

ROSIE: More wine Victor?

VICTOR: Thank you. *(ROSIE re-fills glass)*

KATH: *(pause)* Rosie?

ROSIE: Yes.

KATH: Do you think she'd mind if I asked her advice. You know about George coming up.

ROSIE: I don't think she would mind at all. I asked her about John and she advised me to leave him down there a bit longer. She looked down her Earthascope and told me he was fine and I would enjoy myself better without him for the moment, and I must say she was right.

VICTOR: She always is. Yes Kath, I would certainly see what she has to say. She will help you with any problem at all - you just have to have faith in her.

KATH: But I don't want to rush him, if he's not quite sure.

ROSIE: No of course not.

KATH: Right that's settled - let's ask her round then.

(TELEPHONE RINGS)

(ROSIE answers)

ROSIE: Hello Peter, *(Pause)* Yes please, put him through. *(Hand over mouthpiece)* It's George *again.*

KATH: *(to Victor)* Excuse me.

(Takes receiver from ROSIE. ROSIE sits in armchair)

(Impatiently) Hello George. What's the matter now? *(Pause)* Of course I'm going dancing, Victor is here now.*(Pause)* I'm sorry you're worse - take some vitamin pills. *(Pause)* Of course I love you. *(Pause)* That's not the point. The

point is - do you love *me* enough to come up here? *(Pause)* Well in the meantime I'm getting on with things. To be honest George I'm having doubts about you coming at all. *(Pause)* We've decided to invite Ms Good for a drink, so I'll ask her opinion. *(Pause)* She's er... er... like an agony aunt. Now don't ring again tonight I'm off out and Rosie is busy too. *(Pause)* I'll speak to you sometime next week - Goodbye.

(She replaces receiver &turns to face front.)

ROSIE: Still not made his mind up.

KATH: No - but I think he's getting closer...

ROSIE: You never asked him about the bleeping noise. Was it still there?

KATH: Yes.

ROSIE: I really must ask Peter to fix our line.

(VICTOR stands, puts glass on table & collects KATH's evening bag off sofa & passes it to her)

VICTOR: Come along Kath. Are you ready for the Cha Cha Cha? *(He takes her in his arms)* Let's go to the ball!

(They exit SL dancing a Cha Cha together)

NB. **Quick change for KATH from her evening dress into a day dress for next scene.**

(ROSIE follows to wave them off.)

ROSIE: *(stands smiling to herself)* What a lovely couple, I'm quite envious. *(ROSIE goes to telephone and dials)* Peter put me through to Ms Good please. *(Pause)* Good evening ma'am, Rosie Lawton of Hope Cottage, sorry to disturb you but Kath would like a word about her little problem. She isn't actually one of us yet, but she is thinking of staying permanently and she'd like some advice about her husband. I wondered if you would like to come to tea tomorrow. *(Pause) (delightedly)* You would! That's most kind ma'am. We'll look forward to seeing you. *(Pause)* Three o'clock would be splendid. Thanks again - goodbye.

(ROSIE replaces the receiver and crosses for the knitting (SR) then sits in the

armchair).

ROSIE: Knit one - purl one - pass stitch over - wrap wool round needle. Blast I've dropped a stitch. Oh dear it'll never be finished in time...

(FADE TO BLACK)

MUSIC: - Harp through to Scene 2

Strike tray of glasses & wine

NB: Quick change of outfit for ROSIE.

Scene 2: The following day

(KATH is on the telephone.)

LIGHTING: Fade in to daylight - fade music

KATH: I'm sorry George but you've rung at a very bad time, we're expecting an important visitor any moment. *(Pause)* No George, - a lady visitor - Ms Good - and I am extremely nervous - we want to make the right impression. *(Pause)* Of course it's important - you'll soon find out just how important her visit is - it could have quite a bearing on you, as a matter of fact. *(Pause)* No I don't want to say anything more until I've spoken to her. I'll speak to you again but I don't know when because we're busy arranging a birthday party for Winston Churchill. *(Pause)* I know it's your birthday soon, that's why I'm trying to finish your jumper. It might end up as a tank top if I can't finish the sleeves in time.*(Pause)* Yes I did have a lovely time with Victor - I always do, he's a wonderful dancer. Rudolph Valentino was there as well, I had a tango with him. He's a superb dancer but he's very vain, he's looking round all the time to see if the other women are watching him. I much prefer Victor - he's so attentive. *(Pause)* Me? I'm driving you to drink!! You can do that on your own without any help from me, It's a problem, particularly in your profession. *(Pause)* I know you don't normally drink on duty, but you shouldn't drink at all. You're walking on a knife's edge George. *(Pause)* No that wasn't meant as a pun. You'll never make it up here if you don't stop drinking.

(ROSIE enters & puts vase & daffodils on coffee table. Sits in armchair & arranges daffodils.)

(Pause) Cutting down isn't enough, you must stop completely. *(Pause)* I *am* holier than thou, - I'm nearly an angel. *(Pause)* Yes George, I do love you, but I really must go... and remember what I said about the drinking. Good bye for now.

(KATH replaces the receiver and looks worried)

ROSIE: George still having his little tipple then?

KATH: He says he's cut down, but I don't think he has. I told him he shouldn't drink at all in his profession.

ROSIE: Yes I would have thought a steady hand was the absolute minimum requirement for a surgeon.

KATH: His staff must be really worried.

(KATH Sits on the sofa. MS GOOD sits in the armchair)

ROSIE: Now, would you like a cup of tea or would you prefer a glass of wine?

MS GOOD: Wine would be lovely!

(ROSIE exits & returns with tray, bottle & three glasses)

(Over shoulder) I do hope you haven't gone to any expense, I can always change water into wine, you know. It helps the budget, especially since my Chancellor felt it necessary to add the extra tax. *(ROSIE pours wine and hands MS GOOD a glass.)*

MS GOOD: Thank you dear.

(Then pours two more, takes them to sofa & sits)

KATH: *(Taking glass)* Thanks.

MS GOOD: *(leans back and sighs)* It's so nice to relax. I feel like Barbara Cartland without her royal jelly today.

(They all sip their wine)

ROSIE: You've had a busy morning Ms Good?

MS GOOD: Absolute hell! - Tremendous agenda! I had to call a special managerial meeting. The multi- nationals, you know, I had to speak in many tongues - always exhausting. And then of course - the worst happened.

ROSIE: Oh dear.

MS GOOD: *(Conspiratorially)* It's Moses.

ROSIE: Has he been setting fire to bushes again?

MS GOOD: I'm afraid so. He's getting past it poor love, but a marvel in his heyday, Who do you know who could pull stunts er.. er... I mean perform miracles like he could? - The parting of the Red Sea was something else. - I don't think even Paul Daniels could have achieved that.

ROSIE: No.

MS GOOD: And he had such a poor start in life - to be abandoned in that way. Oh, I know he had rich foster parents but it's not like your own, is it?

ROSIE: So what's going to happen to him now?

MS GOOD: The management team are deciding, but I've advised them to put him in the retirement home. My house has many mansions, you know.

ROSIE: Of course.

MS GOOD: And then we had Judas, the trade union official in. He's after another pay rise. Offered him 25%, but he won't settle for less than thirty. - Judas has a thing about thirty. I told him he'd be lucky to get 5% on earth, but there was no convincing him, so it will have to go to arbitration.

ROSIE: Some people don't know when they're well off.

MS GOOD: I thought I'd convinced him after I delivered my sermon on the mount, but apparently not. Difficult nut to crack is Judas, I don't think he was hugged enough as a child. Anyway, that's enough of my problems, what can I do for you?

KATH: You do have your cross to bear, don't you Ms Good? I'm sure you have enough to worry about without me adding to your troubles.

MS GOOD: I have very broad shoulders. So how can I help?

KATH: Well if you're sure you've got time.

MS GOOD: I'll give you all the quality time it takes.

KATH: It's George, my husband. You see I had to leave him rather suddenly.

ROSIE: Kath had a stroke, she was in a coma for ages. She tried and tried to hold on. - it was such a shock for poor George. It's made him really ill.

MS GOOD: I know.

KATH: And now he's not sure if he wants to join me. He's drinking far too much and I'm so worried. But I don't want him to come if he isn't ready.

MS GOOD: And what exactly do you want me to do?

ROSIE: *(indicates telescope)* Victor said you could look through your Earthascope and see the truth.

MS GOOD: I already know the truth.

KATH: Do you?

MS GOOD: Oh yes. He is missing you very badly, but he is finding it very difficult to come to terms with being finite in an infinite world - that is holding up his decision, and his work is suffering as a consequence. I'm afraid dear, George is to surgery, what King Herod is to baby sitting. Before long he is going to cause an accident. I've been meaning to do something about it for ages, but I've been so distracted with these endless meetings.

KATH: What can we do?

MS GOOD: When I get back to headquarters I will look down my large Earthascope and let you know my decision. *(Picks up telescope)* This mobile is for short distances only, I need a stronger lens for detailed scanning. I'll be in contact when I've had time to assess the situation thoroughly. Try not to worry dear, I will give the matter my undivided attention.

KATH: Thank you very much Ms Good.

ROSIE: There is another thing we intended to talk to you about.

MS GOOD: Oh?

ROSIE: Winston's birthday. I'd like to hold a party for him, he enjoys a bit of fuss, and we would like you to come. Victor said you enjoy a party.

MS GOOD: Thank you, I'd love to. It's been nothing but business lately, it's about time I let my hair down.

ROSIE: Super. I thought we'd hold it here.

MS GOOD: I'll ask my son J.C. to help with the catering, he can make food go such a long way. Remember how he coped with the multitudes. But I'll see he comes up with something a little more exotic than fish paste and manna this time, we wouldn't want to disappoint Winston would we? Leave it with me.

ROSIE: You have enough to do - let me. I enjoy cooking.

MS GOOD: Well if you're sure - I do have a lot on at the moment.

KATH: Who shall we invite?

ROSIE: Tommy Cooper and Eric Morecambe - they'll make everybody laugh.

MS GOOD: Good thinking.

ROSIE: And possibly Tony Hancock - when he's on form there's nobody better.

KATH: He's always been a favourite of mine.

ROSIE: Right we'll invite Tony then.

MS GOOD: What about Judy and Sammy?

ROSIE: You don't mean...?

KATH: *(impressed)* Do you think they'd come?

MS GOOD: By my command! - of course they'll come. I'll even arrange they do a couple of numbers for you. How about "Somewhere Over the Rainbow" and "Mister Bojangles".

KATH: I don't believe this is happening. Oh I wish George could be here.

ROSIE: *(irritated)* Oh Kath!

KATH: He lovesSammy and Judy. What a treat. Can you really fix it?

MS GOOD: I'll see what I can do.

ROSIE: Then I thought Mr Wordsworth and Victor of course.

MS GOOD: How about King George? He knows Winston very well.

ROSIE: Goodness, do you think he would attend?

MS GOOD: He's a very private man, but I'm sure he'll drop by.

KATH: Gosh! - All these famous people - Is it really possible?

MS GOOD: Everything is possible here.

KATH: I'm beginning to realise that. - Who else?

ROSIE: Winston - the birthday boy.

MS GOOD: Of course Winston- There's no show without Punch. But I must have a serious word with him, he can bore everybody to death, so to speak, with his endless war tales.

ROSIE: Yes he does go on a bit. Would you like another drink Ms Good?

MS GOOD: No thank you dear, I must be going. *(Stands followed by ROSIE & KATH)* I have another meeting in half an hour on dysfunctional families.

KATH: Oh dear. Are there many dysfunctional families up here?

MS GOOD: Oh yes - amongst the new arrivals. Following that, I need to negotiate better conditions for one parent families, of which I am one.

(MS GOOD collects telescope, phone & brief case)

But tomorrow is Sunday and I can put my feet up. What a treat. Personally, I always make it a rule never to work on the seventh day. It makes one's mind so much sharper for the working week. I don't know how all those shop assistants at Sainsburys and Tescos go on - they must be shattered working Sundays. *(Sighs)* But alas, that's what they call progress.

ROSIE: Thank you for coming, we really do appreciate it. We'll go ahead with the party arrangements.

MS GOOD: Excellent.

(MS GOOD starts to exit. KATH & ROSIE follow)

KATH: Don't forget about George please.

MS GOOD: *(Turning at exit)* I most certainly won't. I'll be in touch.

KATH: Thank you. Good bye.

MS GOOD: Good bye.

ROSIE: I'll see you out.

(Exit MS GOOD & ROSIE SL and KATH returns & sits on sofa.)

ROSIE: *(entering)* Well what did you think about that? *(Stops rear of armchair)*

KATH: She's magnificent and I can't wait for the party.

ROSIE: What about George?

KATH: It would be nice if he came in time, especially if Judy and Sammy are singing, but I will abide with Ms Good's advice.

ROSIE: That's very wise, she knows best, she's all powerful.

KATH: I'll say. I think I'll just ring George to tell him.

ROSIE: *(irritated)* If you must.

(ROSIE clears the wine glasses & exits with tray SL KATH Crosses to phone picks up receiver)

KATH: Hello Peter, could I have a line to Earth please? *(Pause)* Thank you *(She dials the number)* Hello George - it's me. How are you? *(Pause)* Oh dear! For goodness sake buck up. I've just rung to tell you we're going ahead with the party for Winston and you are invited - we could make it a double - And guess what - Judy and Sammy are going to be performing. *(Pause)* Yes them! I thought you would be impressed.*(Pause)* No I'm not joking it's true, Ms Good is arranging it. - And something else George - she's going to look down her Earthascope to see what you are up to - So put that whisky down she certainly doesn't approve of a drunken surgeon in charge of a scalpel. *(Pause)* What news? *(Pause)* *(Surprised)* I don't believe it! *(Pause)* You George! Are you absolutely sure? *(Pause)* Oh well you certainly can't come up here then -

not until after. *(Pause)* When did you know? *(Pause)* They obviously don't know about your drinking. *(Pause)* Of course I congratulate you George - it's very good news.

(ROSIE enters & stands SL)

I'm only sorry I won't be there to wear a big hat.

ROSIE: *(stage whisper)* What's up? Is he getting married again?

KATH: Hold on George. *(Hand over mouthpiece)* No he isn't. I'll tell you in a minute. *(Hand off mouthpiece)* Rosie thought you were getting married again.

(ROSIE sits in armchair)

(laughing) Tell me what happened.*(Pause)* Huh huh *(Pause)* Huh huh. *(Pause)* Well that's absolutely wonderful. I'm very proud of you *(Pause)*

So you won't want to come here before that will you? *(Pause)* I quite understand, but don't spoil it by doing anything silly beforehand. There's all the time in the world afterwards. *(Pause)* We will be together someday. I'll be in touch. - Goodbye.

(Replaces receiver. She sits on sofa)

ROSIE: What's he up to? What did you mean about wearing a big hat?

KATH: He's had word from the palace.

ROSIE: From Ms Good's palace?

KATH: No, - Buckingham Palace!

ROSIE: Oh!

KATH: What do you think? George is to become a Sir - Sir George Patterson. He's on the New Year's Honours List - Imagine!

ROSIE: George is!

KATH: Yes for his services to medicine.

ROSIE: Goodness - I bet the Queen doesn't know about his whisky intake.

KATH: Only we know about that, and I did warn him to be careful. This will probably stop him, it's such a great honour. He sounded very pleased.

ROSIE: Just think - you would have been Lady Kathleen.

KATH: *(laughing)* I would, wouldn't I?

ROSIE: We must tell Ms Good.

KATH: I suspect she knows already. If truth was known, she's probably arranged

ROSIE: I never thought of that - of course - it's obvious - she's using delaying tactics - she mustn't want him up here yet. She is manipulating events.

KATH: She works in a mysterious way.

ROSIE: She does indeed. - Was that bleeping noise still on the line?

KATH: Yes I could hear it in the background but I was so excited about his knighthood I forgot to ask him about it.

ROSIE: It's most irritating. I heard it when I was speaking to John the other day.

KATH: Was it there when you were speaking to Winston?

ROSIE: No.

KATH: It must be only on the Earth line then.

ROSIE: Peter will have to get in touch with Mercury Telephone Company - it will be a fault on their line. I'll mention it.

KATH: Right.

(ROSIE stands)

ROSIE: Come on Kath we have a lot to do. The guest list and all the invitations.

KATH: *(rising)* And the food - with a little help from J.C. of course.

ROSIE: *(moving to SL)* It's wonderful to have professional help.

KATH: *(following to SL)* It's magic. It really is the good life here.

LIGHT - Fade to black *(Both exit)*

MUSIC: Harp through to Scene 3.

Scene 3: Next day
Fade up to daylight. Fade music out

(KATH is sitting on the sofa. MS GOOD Is sitting in the armchair. ROSIE enters SL holding a tray of tea & biscuits. She puts them on the coffee table.)

ROSIE: It's so kind of you to come round again Ms Good, we really do appreciate it.

MS GOOD: Think nothing of it dear.

(ROSIE is pouring the tea)

KATH: Only I know how busy you must be.

MS GOOD: It has been one of those weeks I must admit. A very time- sensitive period, what with the Annual General looming and the pay negotiations to deal with.

(ROSIE pours the tea and hands the cups to MS GOOD then KATH)

MS GOOD: Thank you. Is it Tetleys?

KATH: We wouldn't dream of using anything else.*(to ROSIE)* Thanks.

(ROSIE pours own cup, replenishes teapot with hot water and takes to sofa & sits)

MS GOOD: *(taking a drink)* Umm... that's wonderful. I do like a good strong cup of tea.

ROSIE: You should relax more - enlist more help, I'm sure there must be many men willing to help you.

MS GOOD: The world is full of willing men, a few willing to work and the rest willing to let them. No - it takes a woman to get things done. I always say, don't rest on your laurels, they make a poor mattress.

ROSIE: I think we all agree with that.

KATH: *(nodding)* But you made the world in six days. I'll never know how you managed that.

MS GOOD: Although I say it myself - that was pretty impressive - I mean, I just said "let there be light," and there was. I think even the Electricity Board would struggle to do that. I surprise myself sometimes. It's not the big miracles that tire me, it's all the petty, little squabbles that get me down. I really wish people would be more reasonable and listen to what I have to say. I only ever do things in their own interest, but they don't always realise it.

KATH: I don't know how you have the patience.

MS GOOD: *(sighing)* It can wear a little thin at times, but I do try. It's because they don't know me very well. I think they only realise what a difficult job I have when they get up here.

ROSIE: I think you're suffering from executive stress you should take more time off.

MS GOOD: I wish! I really will have to have a word with my Time Manager. - Good chappie is Solomon.

KATH: I don't think I've met Solomon.

MS GOOD: He's great - a bit flash of course, in all his glory. Those ties! Words fail me! He's always been overly concerned with his appearance, but he knows the ball game. I'll ask him to cast an eye over my schedule.

ROSIE: It might help to lighten the load.

MS GOOD: Yes indeed. He knows about time, he's been up here for ages.

KATH: He must be very old?

MS GOOD: Growing old is just a habit which really busy people have little time to form.

ROSIE: I hope I'll be around as long as Solomon.

MS GOOD: You will if you want to. It's all a matter of faith and hard work of course. The secret is participation. If you are involved with people, you forget your age, it's purely a state of mind. Time is irrelevant here, all the time channels merge into each other. You are able to communicate with anyone from any era. I have every generation data-based. But it takes a fair amount of organisation I can tell you. Hours of input.

ROSIE: But you make everything seem so simple.

MS GOOD: To be simple about anything dear, you have to know a great deal about it. See how simple Torville and Dean make ice-skating look, but they practise every hour I send.

KATH: Yes they're so graceful - just like Victor. He's always practising too.

MS GOOD: Exactly. Victor Sylvester is a prime example of excellence in his field. But your dancing is excellent too, I was watching you the other night on my Videoscope - doing all those twiddly steps.

KATH: Could you see me - Gosh!

MS GOOD: I see everything.

ROSIE: That's quite a thought.

KATH: *(modestly)* I can do some of the twiddly steps, but I'm not that good yet. Victor is so much better.

MS GOOD: Always remember Kath, when critics were comparing Fred Astaire to Ginger Rogers, they said he was the better dancer, but like Ginger and all women in fact - *you are doing it backwards and in high heels*. No easy task. Women always get the rough deal, they have to be twice as good as men to be considered average.

KATH: I never thought of it that way. Fancy you watching me.

MS GOOD: It's not that I'm spying - I would hate you to think that, I just like to make sure my people are experiencing maximum enjoyment.

KATH: Do you watch everybody all the time?

MS GOOD: Mostly.

KATH: What? Just in heaven?

MS GOOD: No on earth also. It's a time consuming task, but I do have a very efficient management team to help me. And of course there is my beloved son J.C. He's a little treasure. As a matter of fact between you and me, I'm considering sending him down to earth again - the second coming you know. I think they are about due for another visitation.

KATH: Goodness! When?

MS GOOD: Fairly soon. That's one of the reasons why I've been so busy, it entails a great deal of preparation, but we are quite geared up.

ROSIE: Is J.C. looking forward to going?

MS GOOD: I think so. He agrees with me, that the earth people need tremendous help, they seem to be turning into a money orientated society. A hedonistic life style is all very well, but they need to get back to basics.

ROSIE: Indeed. More tea anyone?

KATH: Yes please.

(Pass cup to ROSIE who fills it & returns it to KATH. ROSIE returns to table, checks teapot & picks up hot water jug & stands.)

MS GOOD: Anyway, as I was saying, I intend to send my beloved son J.C. down to Earth to sort matters out. But I don't want to say too much about that just now.

ROSIE: Is this hush hush information?

MS GOOD: For the moment.

KATH: We feel very privileged you have taken us into your confidence

MS GOOD: Keep the information on ice until his visit has been finalised.

ROSIE & KATH: *(together)* Of course.

MS GOOD: The only trouble with J.C., is that he wants to do everything at once - he's so impetuous - course he's only young, but he's a good boy - such a love. He said to me the other day, " why can't you just do another miracle mum?" But I don't work that way. Things have to take their course. There's a fine line between individual conscience and corporate intervention and one has to know when to stand back and allow the individual to reach the right decision.

KATH: You're so wise Ms Good.

MS GOOD: I try dear - I do try.

ROSIE: What form will J.C. appear as, on Earth.

MS GOOD: He has excellent woodworking skills, so he can go back as he came a joiner. He can mingle unobtrusively. He will need a little updating on methods of course, but he'll cope - after all a piece of wood is a piece of wood.

KATH: It's all done by machinery now, isn't it?

ROSIE: And computers.

MS GOOD: That's progress - and there's nothing wrong with that, just as long as it doesn't get out of hand.

ROSIE: Indeed I remember how things were deteriorating on earth and I must say I'm glad to be up here. I feel so contented.- I'll just get some more hot water.

(ROSIE exits with jug SL)

MS GOOD: *(after pause)* And how do you feel Kath?

KATH: Me? - Oh I love it here, although I still worry about George. It was all so quick. I didn't get chance to say goodbye to him I was in a coma for days, but I could hear him talking to me. He even kept me up to date with Coronation Street. He didn't know if I could hear him - but I could, I never got the chance to tell him how much I loved him.

MS GOOD: I'm sure he knew my dear.

KATH: Do you think so?

MS GOOD: I'm certain. As a matter of fact I looked at him through my Earthascope and tuned into his thought waves.

KATH: Did you know the queen is bestowing a knighthood on him?

MS GOOD: Yes dear I am aware of that fact. Are you pleased?

KATH: I'm delighted for him.

MS GOOD: You know what this means, of course.

KATH: Yes, he probably won't want to come up here until afterwards.

MS GOOD: And how do you feel about that?

KATH: I'm disappointed in a way, that I won't be seeing him, but I wouldn't dream of stealing his thunder.

MS GOOD: That's generous of you my dear.

KATH: Well I love him. I just hope he doesn't blot his copybook before the big event, - you know what I mean ma'am.

MS GOOD: I do indeed. Don't worry dear, George's future is in my hands - trust in me.

KATH: I will.

(TELEPHONE RINGS)

MS GOOD: That will be for me. *(Picks up her mobile phone)* Hello Peter, Ms Good here. *(Pause)* Not at the moment, I am not in the mood to discuss pay rises. Tell Judas if he insists on being shirty I will send Demetrious in with his gladiators. Also tell him I haven't forgotten the thirty pieces of silver. He can go down below and apply for a job as a stoker if he's not satisfied with his treatment here. I do my best. 25% is my final offer. He can take it or leave it. *(Pause)*

(ROSIE enters with jug. Pours tea & sits sofa)

I've heard it all before Peter. Oh sing unto the Lord a new song - that's Psalms 96, verse 1. tell him. *(Pause)* Now what is it? *(Pause)* No Peter I have far too much to attend to at the moment. I'm working every hour I send already. *(Pause)* Believe me, I know it's tough at the top I've been there. I am there. *(Pause)* Remember the bottom line Peter. The law and morality are not indivisible, we will have to seasonally adjust those figures.*(Pause)* Yes I'm coming back to the office shortly, we can look at it then and would you be so kind as to tell Martha to have a cup of strong black waiting for me, it's going to be one of those days. *(Pause)* I don't care how many are queuing, we are not letting any more in. So shut the gate and keep it shut. Put them in the Hospitality Room and get Martha to make them a cup of Tetleys. *(Pause)* Yes Peter I'm on my way. I'll see you later.

(She clicks off mobile and puts it on table)

This altruistic attitude they think I should adopt is all very well, but I need some quality space at the moment, I desperately need a window in my timetable. It's not always easy being a superior being.

ROSIE: You were very forceful Ms Good.

MS GOOD: You have to be when you are at the helm. I like to run a tight ship.

KATH: You look tired.

MS GOOD: I am, but matters will improve. When J.C.'s visit is finalised I can return to the more domestic issues. His visit has temporarily thrown us out of flunter, but don't worry, things will soon be back to normal. It just needs some disciples - no names - no pack drill, to get off their backsides. Less of the fishing and casting of nets, I say.

ROSIE: Of course.

(MS GOOD gathers her belongings and stands. ROSIE & KATH also stand)

MS GOOD: It's such a haven of peace here but I really must be going. *(Moves centre & turns)* May I come again?

ROSIE: *(Moves to side of sofa)* Certainly, we would be delighted.

KATH: *(Moves impulsively offering her hand to MS GOOD)* And thank you for all your help.

MS GOOD: *(Taking KATH'S hand)* Remember dear, you never leave people you really love - you take a small piece of them with you wherever you go.

KATH: What a lovely thought. It is heart rending to leave someone you have been with a long time, isn't it?

MS GOOD: Don't be saddened by partings, as partings are necessary before we can meet again and meetings - whether after moments or lifetimes are certain between those who are friends.

KATH: What beautiful sentiments- Oh, you are so clever with words Ms Good.

MS GOOD: Oh it wasn't me who said that. I can't take the credit. - It must have been some poet or other - I have a few up here, they come in very handy for supplying me with comforting words. *(Both laugh)* I can't be good at everything, can I? It's quite pointless keeping tame poets and making up your own rhymes, isn't it? Always try to delegate the mundane tasks to the professionals. It gives you more freedom to do the things you enjoy. Write that down Kathleen - the worst ink survives the best memory. That reminds me, I must get Martha to order me a Chinese take-away for supper tonight. They do it so much better than us, don't they? - the Chinese.

ROSIE: Kath would you mind if I had a private word with Ms Good before she leaves.

KATH: No of course not. I'll go and do some more knitting. I've left it in the bedroom. I must finish it in time... Good bye Ms Good and thank you. I hope to see you again very soon, possibly at my second interview.

MS GOOD: Yes Kath - that could be any time now. Be patient dear.

(KATH kneels and MS GOOD places her hands on KATH's head in a blessing gesture)

MS GOOD: Bless you my child.

KATH: *(rising)* Thank you Ms Good.

(KATH exits SL. ROSIE moves to MS GOOD.)

(ROSIE waits to make sure KATH has gone)

ROSIE: Sorry to keep you, but do you think Kath is ready to stay? *(Moves SFR)* It's been absolutely wonderful having her here to visit. I missed her so very much when I came up here, even more than I missed John in some ways. We were so close we even knew what each other was thinking - there was always this kind of telepathy between us.

MS GOOD: I know dear.

ROSIE: I loved John of course, and I miss him terribly, but he wasn't really my soul-mate. Kath and I could tell each other anything.

MS GOOD: It's often the case when you find a really true friend.

(Puts belongings back on table & sits armchair)

ROSIE: It was terribly kind of you to send her to me. She's such a darling, and I can't tell you how much I have enjoyed our time together and I think she has too. She's been thrilled with all that has happened to her, but I know she's still clinging on. She's still hearing the bleeping noise.

MS GOOD: Yes she is, and she cannot stay here until it stops. She's yet to realise - that death is part of life and you must understand its meaning. The end of life on Earth is not the end of forever.

ROSIE: *(Crosses to sofa)* It took me some time to realise that. That's why I wonder if Kath is ready. I would hate her to make the wrong decision and regret it. *(Sits)*

MS GOOD: George is in the same position. He desperately wants to be with Kath, so he's afraid to let her go. I think once George decides, it will be easier for Kath to settle. The bleeping noise is her life support machine - George is afraid to have it switched it off.

ROSIE: Will that decision be left to him?

MS GOOD: An extremely difficult choice.

ROSIE: Can't you intervene.

MS GOOD: I can, - but she must finish the jumper.

ROSIE: The jumper! Why is that so important?

MS GOOD: It's a sort of symbol - a link with George. Once she gets it finished - she'll have made her decision.

ROSIE: If she did stay down on Earth, how would she be? I mean would she ever get back to normality?

MS GOOD: No I'm afraid not. She'd be helpless. She's had a near death experience, she's only hanging by a thread.

ROSIE: Oh dear I wouldn't want her to live like that - not Kath - she is so full of life.

MS GOOD: I agree, she'd be better here with you, but give her a little more time. We want her to be absolutely sure, don't we?

ROSIE: I'll help her with that blessed jumper.

MS GOOD: Before you make that decision - remember the bleeping noise you heard when you last communicated with John. It wasn't a fault on the line, he's on his way up here too.

ROSIE: My God!

MS GOOD: And George won't be long - but I think we'll just let the queen bestow his knighthood first. *(Laughs)* George can operate on Vincent's ear.

ROSIE: Wonderful. It'll be like old times - the four of us together.

Fade in life support BLEEP

MS GOOD: *(smiling)* I thought you would approve. Three's a funny number.

ROSIE: We'll have to arrange another party.

MS GOOD: Good idea. *(Both laugh)*

BLEEP continues then goes into long tone

(ROSIE & MS GOOD listen and realize - then long tone stops.)

(KATH bursts in waving the jumper)

KATH: *(beaming)* Look girls - I've finished the blessed jumper for George.

ROSIE: Well thank Ms Good for that!

(ROSIE proffers hand to KATH who takes it, sits sofa with ROSIE and smiles.)

Black out

MUSIC: Harp

END

SET

Middle class sitting room

Armchair *(SL.)*

Sofa *(SR.) (placed at right angles to each other.)*

Long coffee table between sofa and armchair. *(FS)*

Table or drinks trolley right wall containing tray with three glasses and wine bottle.

Table or sideboard *(CB)* containing ornaments & telephone. Easel centre back. *(Forward of table/sideboard)*

NB: this play could also be set in a conservatory.

Rosie is dressed in smart day dress covered by a smock. She is holding a palette and is standing at the easel painting.

Kath, dressed in long evening dress is sitting in the arm chair. She is knitting a man's jumper. Knitting pattern is on the coffee table.

PROPERTIES

Telephone *(on Back Table)*

Drinks Tray *(on Table (SR) (on Tray - Wine Bottle 3 Wine Glasses)*

Easel,

Picture,

Paint Brush,

Palette,

Paint Rag,

Smock/Shirt *(for Rosie,)*

Knitting Pattern,

Partly done knitting.

Numbered card *(for Victor)*

Evening Dress,

Necklace,

Earrings,

Tiara,

Evening Bag *(for Kath.)*

Vase,

Daffodils.

Briefcase,

Mobile Phone,

Small Telescope or Opera Glasses *(for Ms Good)*

Tea Tray *(on 3 Cups, 3 Saucers, 3 Teaspoons, 1 Plate of Biscuits, Teapot, Milk Jug,*

Hot Water Jug.

1 Man's Jumper (Same colour as Knitting)

SOUND

Harp Music *(or other suitable)* for playing at opening and between scenes.
Telephone rings.

Doorbell rings.

Life support bleep going into long continuous sound